DEVELOPING A
DEFENSIVE GAME PLAN

Kenny Ratledge

ISBN: 978-1-58518-053-0
Library of Congress Control Number: 2007930496
Book layout: Deborah Oldenburg
Cover design: Cheery Sugabo
Front cover photo: Brian Bahr/Getty Images

Coaches Choice
P.O. Box 1828
Monterey, CA 93942
www.coacheschoice.com

Dedication

I would like to dedicate this book to my family.
Thanks to Debbie, Patrick, and Laura for all your support.

Acknowledgments

I would like to give a special thank you to Darlene Metcalf for typing the manuscript. Thanks also go to official Lee Hedrick for reviewing the rules included in the book.

Contents

Introduction

In the dictionary, game is defined as "sport or contest." Plan is described as "a method for accomplishing something." Game plan then, could be characterized as a "method for accomplishing a stated goal for a sporting event or contest." Obviously, the stated goal is to win the contest.

Football is the one team sport that, above all others, is conducive to in-depth game planning. A degree of planning is involved in other team sports, such as baseball, basketball, and soccer, but for the most part, these games are spaced over a shorter period of time. One reason for the allure of baseball is that it is played on a daily basis. Basketball on the high school and collegiate levels is played three to four times a week. Pro basketball is played nightly for what seems to be an eternity. The typical high school or college basketball team will play around 30 games a year, depending upon how far they advance in the post-season. NBA teams play 82 regular season games a year. Major League Baseball has a 162-game schedule. Compare these schedules to college football teams that normally play 12 to 13 games in a season. The NFL plays a 16-game regular season. Teams that play only one game per week have ample time to plan and prepare. As a matter of fact, more time is spent preparing for a football game than actually playing the game. High school teams prepare from Saturday to Friday to play 48 minutes, while college and professional teams work all week to play a 60-minute game. Teams that wisely and efficiently use the interval between games have a better chance of winning than a team that doesn't prepare as well. As the wise Solomon in Proverbs 25:8 succinctly stated, "Go not forth hastily to strive lest thou know not what to do."

Even though everyone realizes the importance of planning or preparing for an opponent, coaching resources that deal with defensive game planning are few and far between. Recently, I typed "football game planning" into my computer and got the following response: "Your search—defensive game planning—did not match any coaching sites in our database." A coach surfing the Internet can pull up a million things about offense or defense, but would have to search long and hard to find any defensive game-planning materials. For the most part, planning tips are tucked away in articles or books that focus on other matters. These planning tidbits, many times, seem to be an afterthought. A pronounced shortage of defensive game-planning materials defines the current market.

A profound need for a body of work on defensive game planning exists. After all, what part of game preparation is more important than game planning? As Sun Tzu opined in *The Art of War*, "If you know the enemy and know yourself, you need not fear the result of a hundred battles." A well-rounded game plan will give the defensive coordinator a menu or toolbox of calls to use for a variety of situations. A comprehensive defensive game plan should allow the defense to:

- Surmise an offense's capabilities.
- Minimize the offense's strengths through alignments or favorable match-ups.
- Maximize the offense's weaknesses. Attack the offense's weakest players.
- Predict tendencies in various situations.
- Take advantage of defensive players' individual abilities by placing them in situations to make a play.
- Minimize a defender's weakness and maximize his strengths.
- Be able to bring pressure inside or outside.
- Keep physical-type defenders close to the core of the formation, while placing finesse-types wide.
- Have an audible system to get into a particular front, coverage, or blitz, or to be able to check out of a front, coverage, or blitz.
- Afford smooth transition from defense to special teams.

This book contains ideas and procedures that have developed over a long period of time. A plethora of research has gone into the production of this book. Many of the ideas in the book are original, while others have been gleaned from in-depth film study, clinics, and perusing playbooks. An attempt has been made to cover as many contingency-based situations as we can. Down-and-distance, field zone, and hash variables are covered in detail. Time-related segments such as two- and four-minute defense, time-out procedures, fourth-quarter defense, quarter change, and clock strategies are examined. Reactive events, which are the most intense and pressure-packed aspects of the game—such as first down after an explosive play or sudden change scenario—are addressed.

This book is applicable to any defensive framework. 4-3, split-4, 50, even, odd, pressure, or conservative defenses can apply the information included in this book. No matter the philosophy or style of defense used, this book can be an aide in game planning.

1

Defensive Concepts

Before a defensive coach can begin to break down and game plan against an opponent's offense, he first should solidify his base. In *The Art of War*, Sun Tzu writes: "If you know the enemy and know yourself, you need not fear the result of a hundred battles." The first step in defeating an opponent's offense is to fully understand defensive concepts. This chapter will seek to define and explore principles of defense and present an overview of currently popular defensive schemes. The chapter will conclude with a discussion of pigeonholing players to defensive schemes and building schemes around available players.

Defenses will usually be comprised of three main units or groups: defensive linemen, linebackers, and the secondary (defensive backs). The defensive line is on the line of scrimmage, usually in three- or four-point stances. The line will be backed up by players in two-point stances. These players are referred to as linebackers. The secondary will consist of players who align deeper than the linebackers. As a basic rule, defensive linemen are charged with defeating the opponent's running game first and rushing the quarterback second. In some systems and packages, this statement may not always be true. Linemen may be pass rushers first. The linebacking corps is equally responsible for the opponent's running and passing game. Deep defenders usually play pass first and run second. Modern football sometimes blurs the distinction between these groups. In an effort to get more speed on the field, coaches are moving defensive backs to linebacker and linebackers to linemen. A linebacker may actually be a defensive back in a nickel or dime package. A defensive end in a four-down-lineman look may actually be an outside linebacker in a 3-4 scheme. Some of the old standard defensive fronts—such as the wide-tackle-6 or split-6 defenses—are still being used with coaches tweaking the package by inserting different types of players in certain positions.

Defensive Linemen

Spacing

No matter the structure used, a defense has either even or odd spacing. If a defensive man aligns over the center, the defense is odd. A defense is considered even if no defender is on the line of scrimmage over the center.

Alignments

Defenders can align in one of three places on offensive linemen. Those include head-up when he is directly over the offensive man, shaded when the defender aligns on the offensive man's inside or outside, and gap when the defender aligns in the gap adjacent to the blocker. Illustrated is a commonly used alignment system that designates shades. Diagram 1-1 shows even alignments, while Diagram 1-2 illustrates shaded alignments.

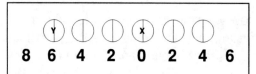

Diagram 1-1. Even alignments

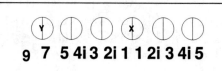

Diagram 1-2. Shaded alignments

Linebackers

Linebackers will either align over offensive blockers or they will stack with a defensive lineman. When linebackers play unprotected over an offensive lineman, they are given a number to distinguish their alignment. For example, if the linebacker aligns over the outside shoulder of the guard, he is said to be in a 30 alignment. This linebacker-alignment system simply uses the set-up illustrated in Diagrams 1-1 and 1-2 and adds a 0 to the shade to denote a linebacker's alignment. Thus, a 30 alignment means the linebacker is in a 3 alignment off the ball. A linebacker on the outside shoulder of the offensive tackle would be considered to be in a 50 alignment. A linebacker who lines up behind a defensive lineman is referred to as a stack linebacker. Should he stack with a 3-technique lineman, he is tagged as a 30-stack linebacker. A linebacker aligned behind a 2 technique is a 20-stack linebacker. The spacing of linebackers is usually reflected by the number of linebackers. Should the defense have an even number of linebackers (two or four), half the linebackers will be on either side of the ball. When the defense has an odd number of linebackers (three or five), one linebacker will usually be directly over the center who, in turn, will be flanked right and left by one or more of the other linebackers. If only one linebacker is used, he will usually be placed over the center.

Secondary

Most defensive secondaries will present one of the following alignments/shells:

- Two-deep box
- Three-deep diamond with either a three-spoke or five-spoke secondary
- Four-deep umbrella
- Four across

    From these alignments, defenses can play man, zone, or combination coverages.

Defensive Style

Regardless of the defensive configuration used, defenses use one of three approaches to a particular down:

- Read and react: players diagnose the play and then react.
- Attack and read: players attack while diagnosing the play.
- Combination of read and attack: some players read and react, while others attack while reading the play.

Read-and-React

Defenses in the read-and-react style usually play horizontally along the line of scrimmage. Upfield charges, which press the line of scrimmage, are limited in favor of looking for certain keys or reads before players act. Defenders only react when they process the offense's intentions. The defense has a "bend-but-don't-break" philosophy, which involves giving up bits of ground while bleeding slowly. This type of defense seeks to play field position and make the offense go the long way, while counting on the offense to eventually make a mistake. Defenses try to match up with offensive personnel packages as well as offensive formations. Defenses seek to cheat their alignment to play off offensive tendencies. Defenses may have to substitute a heavy lineman or a defensive back package to offset offensive intentions. Simply stated, read-and-react defenses allow offenses to dictate.

Attack and Read

An aggressive style of play results in the defense dictating to the offense. Attack-and-read defenses want to turn the tables on the offense and force them to react to the defense. Aggressive defensive play results in defenders pressing the line of scrimmage to force the issue. Defenses attack points on the field, personnel, or formations in an attempt to disrupt the flow of the play, and as a result create big plays for the defense (i.e., fumbles, interceptions, sacks, minus yardage plays, etc.). A drawback to the use of this aggressive mindset is that defenses leave themselves open to giving up big plays to the offense because of the need to use man coverage in many pressure schemes. Many teams are finding that to offset this liability they can zone blitz. Some 3-4 teams are very adept at applying pressure, while backing it up with zone.

Combination

Effective defenses have the capability to combine aggressive and read/react techniques within individual defensive calls. Within a particular defensive call, some defenders may be reading and reacting, while others are executing an aggressive maneuver.

Even though basically three styles of defense exist, not many teams subscribe to a particular style 100 percent of the time. Teams that primarily use the read-and-react approach are usually more talented than their opponents and can buy time until the offense makes a mistake (i.e., turnover, penalty, or missed assignments). Physically overmatched teams can't use this philosophy, so as a result they turn to an aggressive and pressing style of play, which gives them a chance to be successful. Even then, stunting should be used judiciously to avoid giving up explosive-type plays. Most effective defenses use all three styles or philosophies: read and react, attack and read, and combination.

Execution

Within the three defensive styles previously outlined, six theories or subsets of execution exist. These following six theories illustrate how a defense executes or seeks to reach the goal of stopping the offense. Included will be advantages and disadvantages of each.

Base

In a base look defensive linemen are not slanting, linebackers are not stunting, and the secondary plays pass first with force rules well defined.

Advantages

- Simple
- Defensive mistakes held to a minimum
- Fosters excellent team pursuit

Disadvantages

- Defense can be overmatched personnel-wise.
- Offensive blocking assignments will be well defined.
- The offense dictates to the defense.

Stunt

Stunting involves linemen moving from one position to another on the snap with linebackers and/or defensive backs crossing the line of scrimmage on the snap.

Advantages

- Covers up mismatches
- Element of surprise; defenders show up in unexpected areas.
- Confuses pass- and run-blocking schemes
- Minus yardage plays—tackles for loss/sacks
- Free runners at the quarterback
- Turnovers—fumbles and interceptions
- Defense dictates to the offense

Disadvantages

- Defenders can stunt themselves out of a play.
- Lost gap integrity on missed assignments
- Pursuit can suffer.
- Offense has the potential for a big play.

Angling

Angling or slanting occurs when defensive linemen move from one position or alignment to another alignment on the snap. Defenders will key the lineman they are slanting to and will feel the offensive lineman they originally aligned on, or they will simply explode into the assigned gap. Once the slant is executed, the defender will diagnose ball direction and get in a good pursuit angle.

Advantages

- Element of surprise
- Moves inferior players—makes them a moving target
- Confuses pass and run blocking schemes
- What the offense sees pre-snap is not what they will get post-snap.
- Takes advantage of smaller more agile players

Disadvantages

- Pass rush can suffer with defenders working parallel instead of vertical.
- May slant away from the play
- Effective zone blocking can pick up the slant.

Pre-Snap Defensive Movement

Defenses will present one look to the offense and will shift into another configuration just prior to the snap. This pre-snap movement can be done a number of ways. One way is the "move to," which is triggered on command. For example, on the move command, the defense can move as one from a 4-3 shell to a Bears (or 46) look. This defense is called a "move-to" defense. The same objective can be realized with a stem concept, where defenders move on their own from the 4-3 look to the 46 defense. With this look, players move individually so a steady stream of players is moving in and out (or up and back) and isn't synchronized like the move-to call. Another simple pre-snap movement that could cause offensive problems is a simple individual move on the part of only one or two defenders. This "prowl," which a player can be coached to do on his own, could necessitate an at-the-line-of-scrimmage blocking adjustment. For example, a defensive tackle in a 4-3 defense moving from a 3 technique to a 4i alignment has presented the offense with a completely different defense.

Advantages

- Surprise tactic
- May force the offense to alter their cadence

- Forces the offense to go on quick counts, which may eliminate checkoffs
- May force the offense to run a lot of check-with-me calls, which could result in missed assignments
- Confuses pass- and run-blocking schemes

Disadvantages

- The defense may be caught moving on a quick count.
- A defensive misalignment may result in an unmanned gap.
- Approach makes it harder for defenders to read pre-snap cues, such as offensive-line stances.

Base-Stunt Combination

A defense that combines base and stunt techniques on a particular play reaps the advantages and disadvantages of both styles.

Angling-Stunt Combination

This concept has linemen slanting while a linebacker or linebackers execute a stunt with or opposite the line charge. This concept has all the inherent advantages and disadvantages of both angling and stunting strategies.

Now that the groundwork of defensive concepts has been laid, an overview of popular defensive schemes will be presented. This section offers a basic look at defensive structures. Both even and odd defenses will be explored. Strengths and vulnerabilities of each system will be revealed.

3-4-4 Defense

Strengths

- Defense can be a bend-but-don't-break defense, or an attacking-upfield defense—depending upon the desires of the defensive coordinator. This mix in philosophy can change from play to play.
- Defenders can be schemed to use a two-gap technique, or can be placed on the edge of offensive players and defend one gap.
- Flexible enough to adjust to pro-type offenses with their attendant motions, multiple formations, and balanced run/pass game.

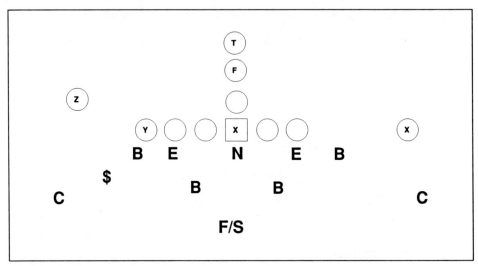

Diagram 1-3. 3-4-4 defense

- Since most teams use the popular 4-3 defense, the 3-4 defense is hard to prepare for. Its unfamiliarity is an asset.
- This defense mentally stretches offenses with alignments and the different combinations of pass rushers. Combinations of rushers include:
  - ✓ Two inside linebackers
  - ✓ Two outside linebackers
  - ✓ One inside linebacker plus one outside linebacker
  - ✓ One inside linebacker and drop a lineman
  - ✓ One outside linebacker and drop a lineman
  - ✓ One secondary player plus an inside linebacker
  - ✓ One secondary player plus an outside linebacker
- Defenses put more speed on the field with a plethora of linebackers.
- Eight men in two-point stances enhances the coverage package.
- Easy to incorporate nickel, dime, and quarter packages.
- Easy to get eighth man in the box.
- Defense covers a center who is used to playing against an even front. The 3-4 forces the center to be a player.
- A linebacker placed over the tight end can impede his release.
- An added advantage of the 3-4 defense is the availability of more linebackers (who can run and tackle) to play special teams. As a result, special-teams play is enhanced.

Weaknesses

- Wide line splits can cause problems and isolate the nose tackle.
- Ends are in position to be double-teamed.
- Ends aligned primarily over the tackles can be outsized.
- An extra tight end adds an eighth gap to a seven-man front.
- Two bubbles exist over the guard areas.
- If the defense flip-flops with a strongside and weakside, problems can occur if the offense trades the tight end. The weak or quick side then has to play to the strong side of the offense and the strong side of the defense must play to the quick side of the offense. Mismatches may occur.

3-3-5 Defense

This defensive concept can either be a 3-3-5 with three linemen, three linebackers, and five defensive backs, or a 3-5-3 configuration with three linemen, five linebackers, and three defensive backs. The decision will be made depending upon the type of competition to be faced and the personnel available.

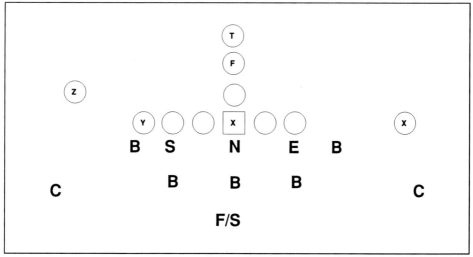

Diagram 1-4. 3-3-5 defense

Strengths

- This defense has many of the same benefits found in a 3-4 defense. As a matter of fact, the 3-4 and 3-3 can be interchangeable.

- Speed is placed on the field with three linemen and eight defenders in a two-point stance.
- The defense can be designed as a two-gap scheme or one-gap defense.
- The base front is an eight-man look.
- A 3-on-2 ratio is employed off tackle.
- The tight end can be covered to impede his pass release.
- This defense allows a multitude of rushers in different combinations. Some possibilities include:
  - ✓ Rush three, drop eight.
  - ✓ Rush four, drop seven.
  - ✓ Rush five, drop six
  - ✓ Rush six, drop five
  - ✓ Rush seven, drop four
  - ✓ Rush eight, drop three
- It includes the availability of line slants with possible linebacker fires.
- Uniqueness of the defense fosters offensive unfamiliarity.

Weaknesses

- Many of the deficiencies found in the 3-4 are also found in the 3-3.
- Offenses will pass against a 3-5 (five linebackers).
- Offenses will run against a 3-3 (five defensive backs).
- Effective zone-blocking teams can pick up line slants.
- In a base 3-3 look, no defender exists on the tight end.
- Nose can be isolated with aggressive line splits.
- Tight end trades are effective versus flip flopping personnel.

46 Bears Defense

This defense was popularized by the great Chicago Bears teams of the 1980s. Many teams currently use a 46 (or Bears) package in their total defensive scheme.

Strengths

- Offers a great change up or change of pace to an even-front defense.

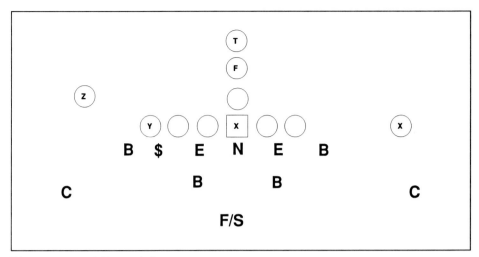

Diagram 1-5. 46 Bears defense

- Adaptable to any defensive system, 5-2, 3-4, 3-3, 4-3, pro 3-4, 6-1, and split-4 systems are all receptive to the Bears' look.
- Limits an offense's game plan so that offensive coordinators can't use all of their playbook.
- Forces major adjustments in run/pass-blocking schemes.
- Can be used versus a wide variety of offensive philosophies (power I, wing-T, run-and-shoot, pro I, etc).
- Can be used in any field zone.
- Applicable for any down-and-distance situation.
- Placement of the nose can result in a five-man overload or a balanced 4-4 ratio.
- Eight potential rushers within five yards of the ball presents an eight-man look.
- Pressure can be applied without stunting.
- Pressures quarterbacks by alignment.
- Wide and varied stunt package.
- Wide and varied coverage package.
- Second-level defenders free to run to the ball because it is difficult for blockers to get to the second level.
- Great way to get pressure on first and second down without stunting.
- Defense outnumbers the offense from tackle to tackle.
- Beneficial for teams not blessed with great team speed.
- Speeds up fast players.

- Two outside-edge rushers.
- Three-on-three match-up in the middle.
- Offense can't double-team the best pass rusher.
- All runs are funneled to the middle of the defense.

Weaknesses

- Effective dive-option games can exploit this scheme.
- Off-tackle power plays with angle blocks can hurt.
- Must be able to cover the tight end with a linebacker unless the defense subs a nickelback.
- The defense is predictable coverage-wise if (as many Bears teams do) it predominantly uses man-free coverage.

College 4-3-4

This defense is used most often today on all levels. Many high school, college, and professional teams use the 4-3 as its base.

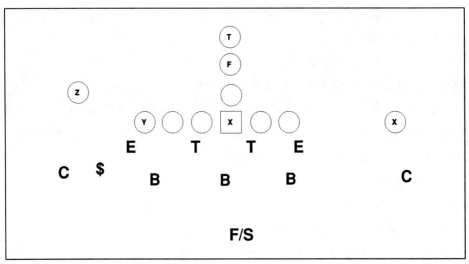

Diagram 1-6. College 4-3-4 defense

Strengths

- Allows a wide and varied assortment of coverage packages. Man, zone, and combination coverages are used.

- A flexible and effective stunt package is available.
- A small and quick team can be effective with an aggressive attacking mindset since this defense allows more speed on the field.
- Nine men in the box is possible.
- In many instances, defensive tackles will be larger than the offensive guards.
- The offense's biggest players, the tackles, must be able to operate in space.
- The offensive tackles also must be able to block quick and agile ends in space.
- Strong end is placed on the tight end. The end can harass the tight end's pass release.
- Since no defender is in the C gap, the tight end and tackle cannot double-team.
- Defenders are usually aligned on the edge of blockers. They are assigned one gap, which allows smaller quicker defenders to be successful.

Weaknesses

- Offenses will trap and draw if the defense is pressing the line of scrimmage with a vertical mindset.
- The addition of a second tight end adds an eighth gap to be defended by seven defenders.
- Three bubbles exist. Two bubbles are in the off-tackle areas with the third over the center.
- Wide line splits between the guards widens the defensive tackles.
- If the defense is built on speed, offenses with a power running game can be successful.
- Because of its popularity, offenses see it several times a year, which breeds familiarity.

Pro 4-3-4

Before the advent of the upfield-penetrating college 4-3 defense, the pro 4-3 was the staple of NFL defenses.

Strengths

- Multiple coverages are readily available. Cover 2, cover 3, man-free, and combination coverages are adaptable to this scheme.
- Multiple looks available with over, under, and stunt 4-3 configurations.

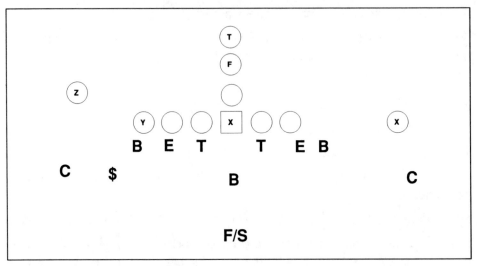

Diagram 1-7. Pro 4-3-4 defense

- Various force calls possible. Corner, backer, end, and safety forces are possible.
- Weakside outside linebacker is in a prime position to force the run or drop under the number-one receiver to the weakside.
- Highly effective stunt game.
- Effective two- or three-man line games.

Weaknesses

- Dive option could cause problems.
- Off tackle is vulnerable with a double-team in the C gap and a kick-out on the outside linebacker.
- Three-on-three ratio in the center area favors the offense.

4-2-5 Nickel or Dime Defense

Some teams use the 4-2 as their base, while others use it in long-yardage situations.

Strengths

- Can use six or seven defensive backs.
- Field speed is enhanced with all these defensive backs on the team.
- Defenses can use outside linebackers at the end position.
- Inside linebackers can be used at the tackle positions.

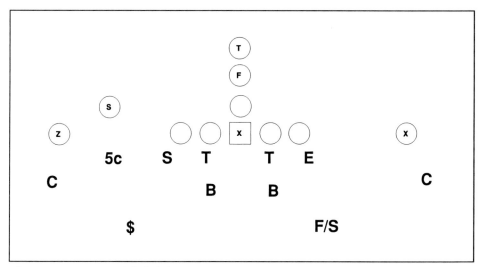

Diagram 1-8. 4-2-5 nickel defense

Weaknesses

- The defense is not as effective against the run with the plethora of defensive backs.
- Only six defenders are in the box.

Nickel or Dime 3-3 Defense

Many even front teams use the 3-3 scheme as their nickel package. This odd look is a more effective change-up than the even spacing of the 4-2 package. Many of the same advantages and weaknesses are inherent in the 3-3 package as the 4-2 look.

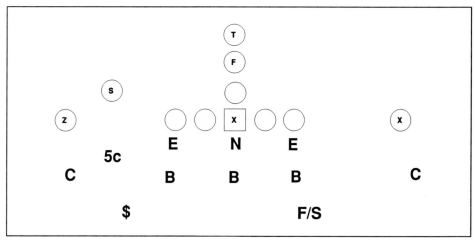

Diagram 1-9. Nickel or dime 3-3 defense

The following four defensive systems represent football in a bygone era. Not many teams currently use these defenses in their pristine form. However, many coaches tweak these oldies but goodies and use them with great effect. For discussion purposes the strengths and weaknesses of the defenses will be explored in their archetypal form. Allowances should be made for any personnel deviation.

Wide-Tackle 6 Defense

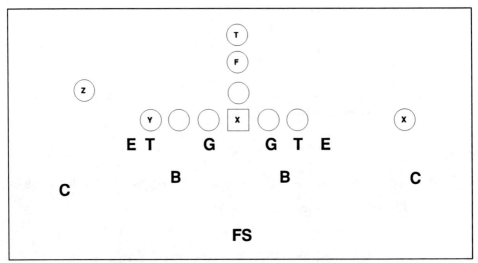

Diagram 1-10. Wide-tackle-6 defense

Strengths

- Base is an eight-man front.
- Guards can shade the offensive guard inside, outside, or head up.
- Tackles can shade the offensive end inside, outside, or head up.
- Ends are in great position to contain wide runs or sprint passes.
- Ends are in great position to play bootlegs, counters, and reverses.
- Defense is flexible enough to adjust to offensive sets.
- A multitude of stunts are available.
- Defense can easily shift to a 7-1 look with a linebacker on the line over the center.
- Tackle can hold up the tight end's release.
- Defense is very strong in the C gap with a 3-1 ratio.
- Position of the tackle eliminates the double-team in the off-tackle area.

Weaknesses

- Attack the guards by running outside if the guards align in A gap.
- Attack the guards by running inside if the guards align in B gap.
- Attack the tackles by running outside if they align inside the blocker.
- Attack the tackles by running inside if they align outside the blocker.
- Offensive-guard splits can weaken the middle.
- Offense has a 3-2 ratio in the middle.
- Quick hitters, sneaks, and wedges are effective in A gaps.
- Short trap game is effective, especially with good line splits.
- Tackles should have the speed and agility to contain the quarterback.
- If the end is a true end, he may have to play in space.
- Inside-outside fold blocks are effective.

Split-6 Defense

In many respects, this defense is similar to the wide-tackle-6 package.

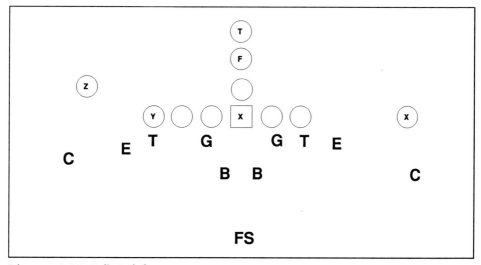

Diagram 1-11. Split-6 defense

Strengths

- Inside linebackers are protected.
- 4-3 ratio favors the defense in the middle.

- Very effective stunt game.
- Easy to get a wide-tackle-6 look by reducing the guards and widening the linebackers.
- Provides good contain versus wide runs or sprint passes.
- An eight-man front.

Weaknesses

- Attack the middle area with the addition of an extra blocker (isolation).
- Sneak and wedge plays are effective, especially on short-yardage and goal-line plays.
- Inside-outside fold blocks are effective.
- If the guards are outside, run inside.
- If the guards are inside, run outside.
- Guards can be double-teamed.
- Tackles may have to contain on level-three passes.
- Flat areas are weak.

Stack 4-4 Defense

The stack 4-4 can be used as a change-up from the split-6 and wide-tackle-6 packages. A 4-3 defense can easily present a stack 4 with an eight-men-in-the-box look by sliding the linebackers to the tight end and inserting the free safety as a linebacker to the weakside, or shading the linebackers weak and walking down the strong safety to linebacker depth.

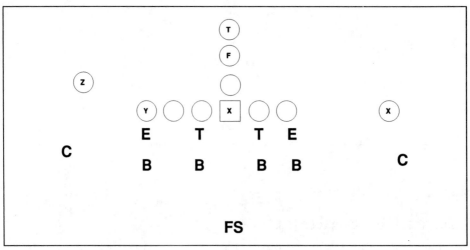

Diagram 1-12. Stack 4-4 defense

Strengths

- Eight-man front.
- Hard to block stacked linebackers.
- Easy to get into a wide-tackle-6, split-6, or a gap-8 configuration.
- Each gap is threatened.
- Line slants are good, especially from head-up alignments.
- Good package for smaller quicker players.
- Linebacker positions can be interchangeable with other linebackers or defensive backs inserted.
- Forces offenses to block area instead of man to man.
- Difficult to prepare for.

Weaknesses

- Flat areas are weak.
- Must play a lot of man coverage unless defensive coordinators dilute the core of the defense.
- Effective zone blocking can nullify parts of the stunt package.

Gap-8 Defense

A gap-8 look is effective in short-yardage or goal-line situations.

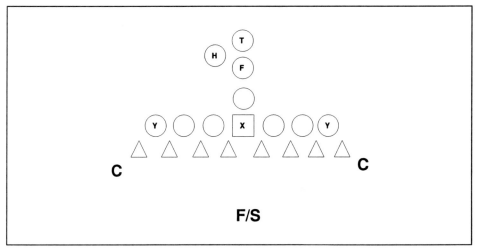

Diagram 1-13. Gap-8 defense

Strengths

- Each gap is filled.
- Penetration is a high priority.
- Forces minimum offensive-line splits.

Weaknesses

- Plays that break the line of scrimmage are usually unmolested.
- Pursuit is poor.
- With all-out penetration, trap plays are effective. Quick-hitting traps with the center turning back are highly effective, especially with no middle linebacker.
- Susceptible to a down block and kick-out in C gap.

Pigeonholing Players

Two basic methods are used in deciding which defensive style and structure coaches implement for their team. Coaches can either fit the scheme to the players, or fit players to the scheme. The "fit the scheme to players" method is the standard operating procedure for high schools and youth leagues. Recruiting is either nonexistent or minimal at best. Coaches on this level must make do with what they have. College and professional teams have the means and resources to go get the type of players they covet. Hence, they are able to fit players to the scheme. A major part of a college coach's job description is recruiting. NFL teams spend millions of dollars yearly to stock their teams. The pros draft and trade to meet their needs. If the organization wants to run a 4-3 defense, they draft and trade to get the type of player to fit into that system.

Other factors exist that enter into the decision on what type of defense to use. For example, a major determinant about a proposed defensive philosophy is the schedule of the team in question. What type of offenses will the proposed defense face in a given year? The designed defensive package should be flexible enough to operate against a wide variety of offensive philosophies. High school defenses especially have to contend with a diverse collection of offensive thought. In a given year, high school defenses may have to contend with pro I, power I, wing-T, option, and/or run-and-shoot styles of offense. Defenses should be able to compete without radical changes from week to week. College and professional defenses, for the most part, are going to get the same basic offensive thought almost every week.

Teams that one platoon (when players are asked to play offense and defense) should make a philosophical decision on which side of the ball to focus their best players. Does the coach place his best players on defense first and try to win with defense and special teams and merely survive on offense, or does he focus his best players on offense and try to outscore other teams? Teams that two platoon should also make the same fundamental decision. What priorities do they use? Do they use an offense/defense/special-teams track, or do they choose to follow the defense/offense/special-teams blueprint. The most important factor in designing a defense is what the defensive coach (or coaches) knows best. In order to implement and teach a particular style of defense, the teacher should possess the technical knowledge to get the job done. However, that doesn't mean that a defensive coach should stay married to a defensive scheme that is outdated or ineffective. With effort, perseverance, and research, any coach can change his spots.

One consideration when choosing a particular style of defense is: how will the proposed defense affect other aspects of the team? For example, if the coach chooses to take his lumps on defense, he may need to implement a ball-control offense to keep the defense off the field. If the coach chooses to stock the defense with solid players, it could result in the offense taking more shots down the field because the defense will get the ball back quickly.

Cataloging Players

The last section of this chapter will involve personnel decisions for stocking a proposed defense. For illustrative purposes, the two most common defenses in use today—the college 4-3 and 3-4—will be used. These two different schemes will be discussed position by position, and also the general or generic responsibilities of each position.

College 4-3 Defensive Personnel (Refer to Diagram 1-6)

Tackle

Tackles will usually be assigned one gap or shade in a base 4-3. These shades are usually on the guards. Some systems will place one tackle on a guard and the other tackle on the center. Most 4-3 schemes use an attack step where the tackles attack first and read second. Different shades can be explored with tackles aligning at various spots in the tackle box. Some 4-3 philosophies choose to use 300-pound tackles whose only job is to eat up space and blocks on early downs, and then replace them with more mobile defenders on passing downs.

Ends

Ends in a 4-3 are asked to supply the bulk of a defense's pass rush. Ends should be strong enough to hold the point on running plays by taking on 300-pound offensive tackles, and beat the massive offensive tackle on pass rushes. Vision is a must to play end. Most blocks will come inside-out from the pull lane.

Strong Outside Linebacker

The outside linebacker should be solid in run defense because most offensive teams will naturally run to their strongside. He should be stronger and possess more bulk than the weakside linebacker. He will be attacked by a wide and varied assortment of blockers. The strong linebacker may have to contend with tight ends, fullbacks, or guards. He may be assigned man coverage on tight ends or fullbacks.

Weak Outside Linebacker

Most running plays will be directed to the strongside away from the weak linebacker. As a result, he will need speed to chase down the ball. He may be the main adjuster versus one-back sets.

Middle Linebacker

Middle linebackers should be able to run down-running plays inside-out from sideline to sideline. The leading tackler on many teams is the middle linebacker. Most 4-3 defensive schemes are designed to funnel plays to the middle of the field. Effective middle linebackers possess great peripheral vision. Unlike outside linebackers where most blocks come from one side, the middle linebacker must defeat blocks from all angles.

Cornerbacks

The corner position requirements don't change much from one defense to the other. Corners should be able to function in zone, man, or combination coverages. The following two deviations are philosophical differences. How much bump-and-run is to be employed, and how prevalent is the use of cover 2? These concerns may change depending upon the coach's philosophy.

Strong Safety

Strong safeties should lead defensive secondaries in tackles. Many safeties are former outside linebackers who weren't big enough to play linebacker. Many defenses play the safety near the line of scrimmage as the eighth man in the box. Strong safeties should supply aggressive run support for a defense to be effective. In man-coverage schemes, safeties are usually assigned the tight end.

Free Safety

Most schemes require the free safety to be the defensive quarterback. He is usually held responsible to get the secondary lined up properly. A prototypical free safety is intelligent and possesses good speed. He has the responsibility of backing up everyone and is expected to keep everything in front. Some schemes require him to be physical enough to supply run support to the weak side.

3-4 Defensive Personnel (Refer to Diagram 1-3)

Ends

3-4 ends are the antithesis of 4-3 ends, who require speed and quickness. 3-4 ends require size and strength to occupy space and tie up blockers. These defenders are "space eaters." 3-4 ends should hold the point versus double-team blocks. They should tie up as many blockers as they can so the inside linebackers can run and make plays. Ends are not usually asked to contain the quarterback, since that job usually falls to the outside linebacker.

Nose Tackle

The 3-4 nose tackle is asked to align head up on the center or shade one side or the other on the center. Rarely, he may align on the inside shoulder of the guard. The 3-4 scheme demands that the nose be double-teamed. The integrity of the defense will be compromised if the center can handle the nose one-on-one. Obviously, the defender who plays this position should possess girth and leverage to be successful.

Inside Linebackers

The 3-4 scheme will require two inside linebackers. Some teams place the larger and more physical player to the tight-end side and the more mobile linebacker to the weak or open side. Some teams, however, merely designate right and left linebackers. One of the strengths of the 3-4 is that all four linebackers are blitz threats. Part of the job description for inside linebackers is that they should be effective stunters.

Secondary

The same basic requirements for defensive backs exist from the 3-4 scheme to the 4-3 structure. Both systems require comparable talent.

2

Fingerprinting the Offense

This chapter will establish a uniform nomenclature to describe an opponent's personnel, personnel groupings, formations, shifts, and motions. It is imperative that coaches be able to communicate with each other and with players in a clinical setting or on the sideline during the game when bullets are flying. Terminology can be of any style and it really doesn't matter what naming system is used. The names need only be consistent and understandable. Obviously, the more concise and succinct the terminology, the better. The ideal situation would be to use as much terminology as possible from the team's offensive system. This would allow carryover from one side of the ball to the other. This chapter contains one naming system. Coaches can use the whole system or only those parts that fit their needs or situation. In addition to establishing a working language, this chapter will illustrate various formations and describe the strengths and weaknesses of each.

Formation recognition and study of tendencies are paramount in game planning. Formations dictate the extent and types of defensive adjustments that should be considered. Players should be made to understand formational tendencies. Each defender should understand how the offense will attack him. To help transfer what players learn in film sessions, chalk talks, and scouting reports, they should be required to identify formations each time the scout team lines up to run a play. For example, cornerbacks should call the number of receivers to their side of the formation. Safeties will communicate the name of the formation as the offense lines up. While this is going on, linebackers should identify the backfield set. Effective defenses do a lot of pre-snap communicating to be on the same page. Once the formation is identified and players understand the game situation, they should be able to transfer all the information from films, skull sessions, and practice sessions to the play at hand.

Offensive Player Identification

The first step in the identification of offensive personnel is to label positions. A 21 (or regular) personnel grouping in a base set is shown in Diagram 2-1.

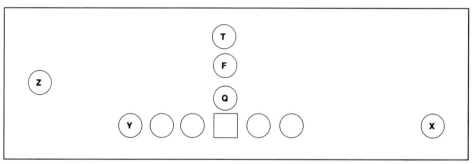

Diagram 2-1. 21 (regular) personnel

Regular Personnel

F: Fullback

Q: Quarterback

T: Tailback

X: Split end

Y: Tight end

Z: Off-the-line receiver

Substitute Back and Receiver Designations

Listed are possible substitutions for regular personnel.

H: Third back in a three-back set

R: Fourth receiver

S: Third receiver

U: Second tight end

V: Third tight end

W: Replaces Y in 00, 10, 20, 30 personnel groups

Personnel Groupings

It is imperative that the defensive coach knows who is in the game offensively. The defensive game plan's success hinges on how well the coach prepares for the opponent's personnel. Minimizing an opponent's strengths and maximizing their weaknesses is the cornerstone of a successful game plan. In many cases, offensive personnel will determine how and where the offense will attack. Knowing who is in the game will allow the defense to make substitutions to get desired match-ups and avoid mismatches. Offenses have become so specialized with various personnel groups that defensive coordinators are forced to match up or be overwhelmed. Modern offenses have backs who specialize in blocking, running, pass catching, or short-yardage situations. In today's game, offensive personnel identification is a must.

A simple and effective way to identify and communicate offensive personnel in the game is through the use of a two-digit number. The first number denotes the number of running backs in the game. The second number tags the number of tight ends. The number of wideouts can be determined by adding the first and second numbers and

Group	Name	Backs	Tight Ends	Receivers
00	Queens	0	0	5
01	Jacks	0	1	4
10	Flush	1	0	4
11	Tiger	1	1	3
12	Ace	1	2	2
13	Diamond	1	3	1
20	Opal	2	0	3
21	Regular	2	1	2
22	Deuce	2	2	1
23	Jumbo	2	3	0
30	Joker	3	0	2
31	Clubs	3	1	1
32	Kings	3	2	0

Table 2-1. Personnel groupings

subtracting from five. For example, 21 personnel means that two backs, one tight end, and two receivers are in the game. A 22 grouping reveals a two-back, two-tight-end, and one-receiver formation. Table 2-1 shows examples of various personnel groupings.

Possible Formations by Personnel Groupings

This section illustrates possible formations by personnel groupings. Illustrated are receiver alignments only. Back alignments will be listed separately. Formations are tagged using base designation terms.

00 Queens (Diagram 2-2 through 2-5)

- Zero backs
- Zero tight ends
- Five receivers (R, S, W, X, Z)

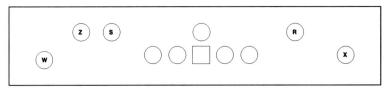

Diagram 2-2. Empty left

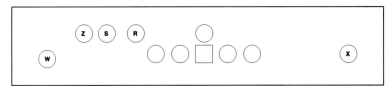

Diagram 2-3. Quads left

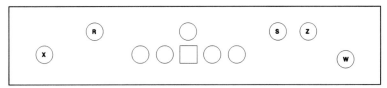

Diagram 2-4. Empty right

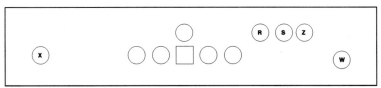

Diagram 2-5. Quads right

01 Jacks (Diagrams 2-6 through 2-9)

- Zero backs
- One tight end (Y)
- Four receivers (R, S, X, Z)

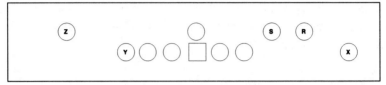

Diagram 2-6. Spread right

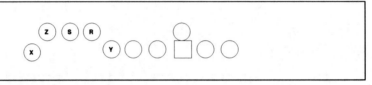

Diagram 2-7. Quads left over

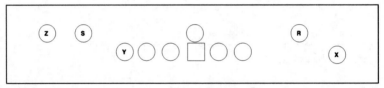

Diagram 2-8. Trey left

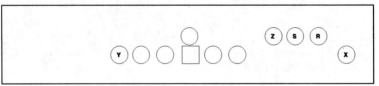

Diagram 2-9. Quads right

10 Flush (Diagrams 2-10 and 2-11)

- One back (F/T)
- Zero tight ends
- Four receivers (S, W, X, Z)

11 Tiger (Diagrams 2-12 through 2-16)

- One back (F/T)
- One tight end (Y)
- Three receivers (S, X, Z)

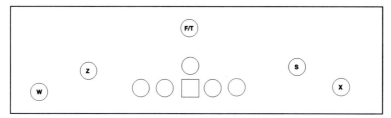

Diagram 2-10. Doubles left

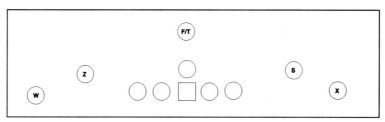

Diagram 2-11. Trips left open

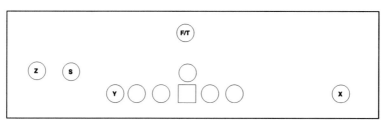

Diagram 2-12. Trey left

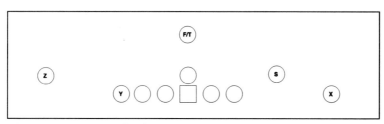

Diagram 2-13. Spread right

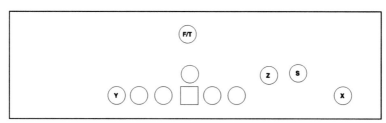

Diagram 2-14. Trips right

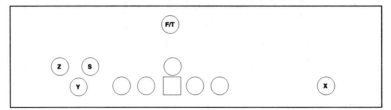

Diagram 2-15. Bunch left trey

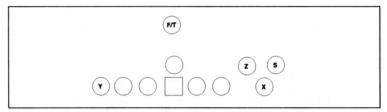

Diagram 2-16. Bunch right spread

12 Ace (Diagrams 2-17 through 2-20)

- One back (F/T)
- Two tight ends (Y/U)
- Two receivers (X/Z)

13 Diamond (Diagrams 2-21 through 2-23)

- One back (F/T)
- Three tight ends (U, V, Y)
- One receiver (Z)

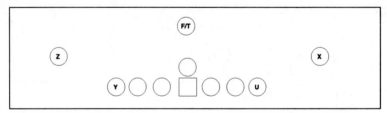

Diagram 2-17. Tech left

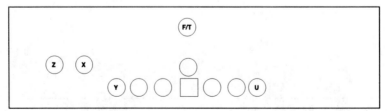

Diagram 2-18. Tech left over

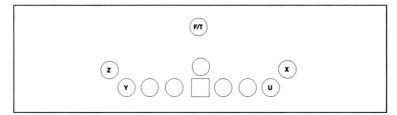
Diagram 2-19. Double wing

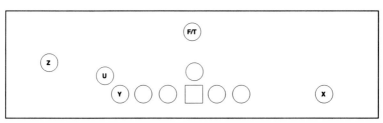
Diagram 2-20. Unicorn trey left

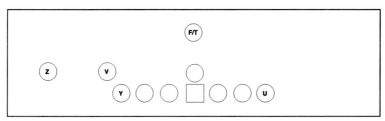
Diagram 2-21. Trey left wing

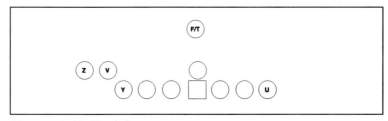
Diagram 2-22. Tag left

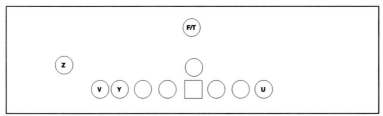
Diagram 2-23. Heavy left

20 Opal (Diagrams 2-24 and 2-25)

- Two backs (F and T)
- Zero tight ends
- Three receivers (W, X, Z)

21 Regular (Diagrams 2-26 through 2-30)

- Two backs (F and T)
- One tight end (Y)
- Two receivers (X and Z)

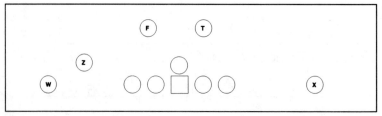

Diagram 2-24. Open left

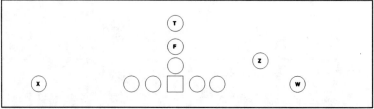

Diagram 2-25. Open right

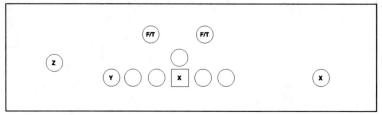

Diagram 2-26. Pro left

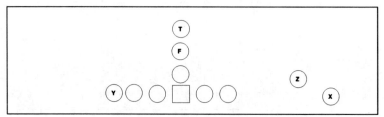

Diagram 2-27. Twins right

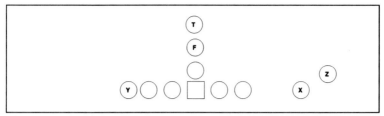

Diagram 2-28. Invert right

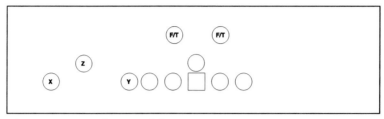

Diagram 2-29. Twins over left

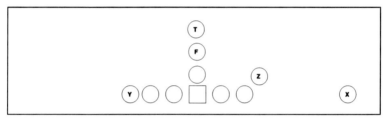

Diagram 2-30. Slot right

22 Deuce (Diagrams 2-31 through 2-34)

- Two backs (F and T)
- Two tight ends (U and Y)
- One receiver (Z)

*23 Jumbo (*Diagrams 2-35 through 2-37)

- Two backs (F and T)
- Three tight ends (U, V, Y)
- Zero receivers

30 Joker (Diagrams 2-38 and 2-39)

- Three backs (F, H, T)
- Zero tight ends
- Two receivers (W and X)

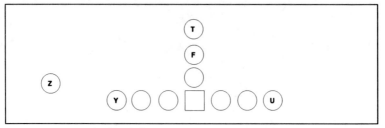

Diagram 2-31. Flanker left

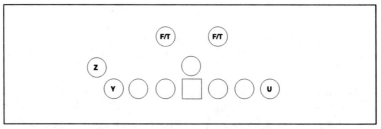

Diagram 2-32. Flanker left wing

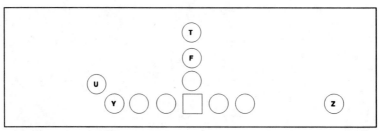

Diagram 2-33. Unicorn left wing

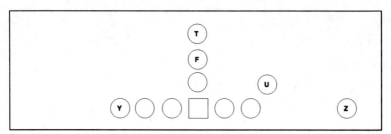

Diagram 2-34. Unicorn slot right

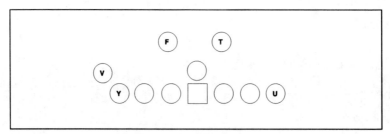

Diagram 2-35. Wing left

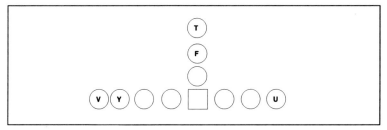

Diagram 2-36. Heavy left

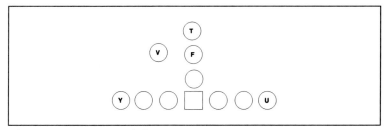

Diagram 2-37. Power I left

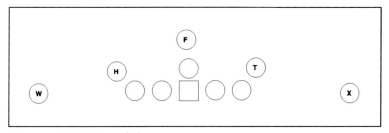

Diagram 2-38. Mirror left

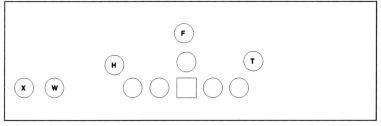

Diagram 2-39. Mirror over left

31 Clubs (Diagrams 2-40 and 2-41)

- Three backs (F, H, T)
- One tight end (Y)
- One receiver (Z)

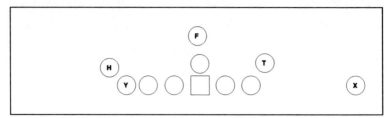

Diagram 2-40. Tight left

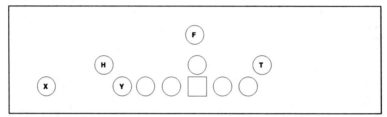

Diagram 2-41. Tight left over

32 Kings (Diagrams 2-42 and 2-43)

- Three backs (F, H, T)
- Two tight ends (U, Y)
- Zero receivers

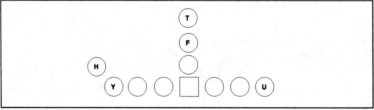

Diagram 2-42. I left

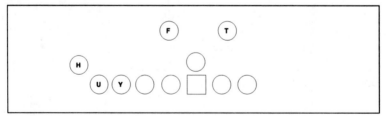

Diagram 2-43. Heavy left

Once the grouping has been deciphered, the reasons for the grouping have to be analyzed. A defensive coach should ask the following pertinent questions:

- Why is a particular group being used?

- Is the offense trying to force the defense into a predictable adjustment?
- Is the offense trying to manipulate frontal-gap responsibility or secondary run force?
- Where on the field does the offense use a particular package?
- What down-and-distance tendencies does the offense have for a particular grouping?
- Is the offense able to run its base offense with a particular group, or do they use a specialized set of plays?

Clues as to offensive intentions can be attained when such variables as down-and-distance and field position are factored in with personnel. Obviously, a 23 or 32 grouping would be most efficient in short-yardage, goal-line, or coming-out situations. These packages would present mostly a run scenario for the defense. Passes would undoubtedly be play-action in nature. Conversely, a wide-receiver-loaded package on a short-yardage play might indicate a spread-type formation with a sneak or middle run should the defense dilute the front. The defense should not allow the offense to know in advance its adjustments, or the offense will take the advantage unless the defense has vastly superior personnel. Following are abbreviations for formations, which can be used for brevity sake in film breakdown.

Formation Abbreviations

Bu: Bunch

Ch: Cheat

Do: Doubles

Dbl: Double

E: Empty

Fl: Flanker

He: Heavy

In: Invent

Lt: Left

Mi: Mirror

Ov: Over

Op: Open

Pi: Power I

Pr: Pro

Q: Quads

Rt: Right

Sl: Slot

Sp: Spread

Ta: Tag

Te: Tech

Th: Thunder

Ti: Tight

Tre: Trey

Tri: Trips

Tw: Twins

Un: Unicorn

Wi: Wing

Wk: Weak

Wd: Wide

Formations: Strengths and Weaknesses

All offensive formations have positive and negative aspects. This section explores the strengths and weaknesses of common offensive formations.

Pro (Diagram 2-44)

The pro formation is a balanced set with a double-width configuration. It horizontally stretches defenses. It has a basic three-strong and two-weak pass game.

Twins (Diagram 2-45)

Twins formation is conducive to combination routes between Z and X, and good for pick-type plays. The offense can easily get three weak. This formation lacks a double-width configuration. Defenses by game plan can overload or gang up on the two-receiver side.

Slot (Diagram 2-46)

Slot has the same advantages as twins with the added possibility of three-back types of run plays. Counters and reverses are available to Z.

Trey (Diagram 2-47)

This formation seeks to stretch the defense horizontally with the possibility of an overload to the three-receiver side. This formation features a three-strong pass-route

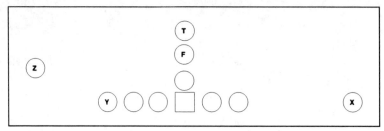

Diagram 2-44. Pro formation

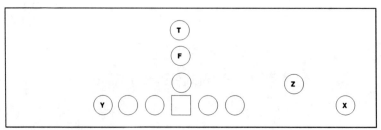

Diagram 2-45. Twins formation

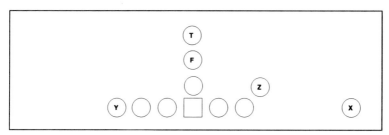

Diagram 2-46. Slot formation

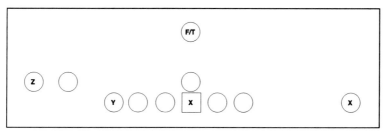

Diagram 2-47. Trey formation

concept with a possible fourth receiver should the F/T release strong. One aim of this set is to force the defense to remove a linebacker from the box, especially against defenses that use a 4-3 structure.

Trey Wing (Diagram 2-48)

Flood routes are possible. Depending upon the width of Z, bunch routes are possible. The close proximity of F/T adds an eighth gap to the defensive front. The strongside run game is enhanced.

Spread (Diagram 2-49)

The spread is a balanced set with a two-and-two ratio on alignment. This formation stretches the defense sideline to sideline. F/T becomes the #3 receiver to either side, depending upon which way he steps or releases.

Cheat Spread (Diagram 2-50)

The cheat spread is a good formation to get F or T into the route. It has all the advantages of the spread set, and also places F or T in a better position to be a ballcarrier than when he was aligned wider in a spread set.

Trips (Diagram 2-51)

The trips is an overloaded formation. Pick-type routes are easily run. Three-receiver combination routes, with F/T as a possible fourth receiver, are to be expected. Depending on the width of the receivers, bunch-type routes are a distinct possibility.

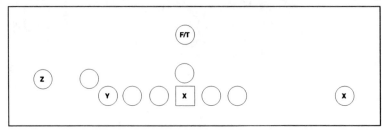

Diagram 2-48. Trey wing formation

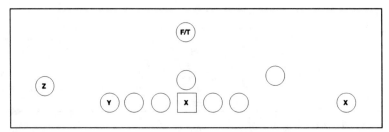

Diagram 2-49. Spread formation

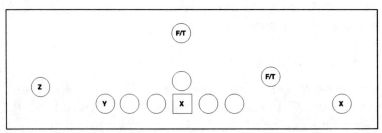

Diagram 2-50. Cheat spread formation

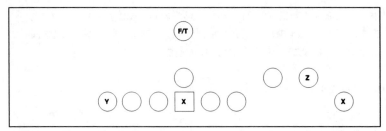

Diagram 2-51. Trips formation

Tech (Diagram 2-52)

The tech is a balanced formation with a two-to-two ratio, which stretches the defense horizontally. This two-tight-end formation helps the run game. This formation forces defenses to balance up, plus it adds an eighth gap.

Mirror (Diagram 2-53)

This run-and-shoot formation is great for a wide-open pass game or the option game. Short motion forces quick defensive adjustments. A drawback to this formation is the absence of a tight end. The absence of a tight end limits the power running game, especially in short-yardage or goal-line situations.

3 Wides (Diagram 2-54)

This particular formation is good for the pass game with all the advantages of twins to the two-receiver side. Quarters-coverage defenses must remove a linebacker from the box or check to a cover 3. Many teams, depending upon the situation, may elect to keep seven in the box and check to a cover-3 or man-free concept. Clearly the lack of a tight end affects the run game; however, should the defense decide to drop a defender and play with six in the box, the run game can be effective.

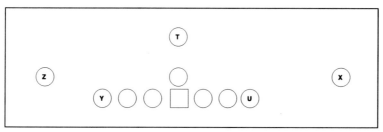

Diagram 2-52. Tech formation

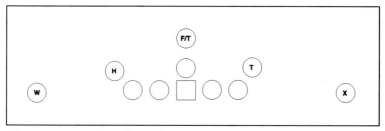

Diagram 2-53. Mirror formation

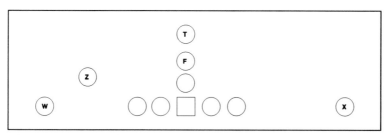

Diagram 2-54. 3-wides formation

Y Off (Diagram 2-55)

With the Y off the line of scrimmage, he can easily change formation strength with motion. Y finds it easier to release on pass plays. It is hard to hold up his release, especially should he motion. Y also can be used as a ballcarrier on misdirection-type plays. A definite drawback to this formation is the reduced effectiveness of Y as a blocker due to his off-the-line alignment.

Shotgun (Diagram 2-56)

The shotgun is a great set for passes. It is also a good set to move the pocket. Many teams are also effective running the ball from this pass-oriented configuration. Back options and tosses are effective. Quarterback keepers away from a play fake to the back are good if the quarterback is mobile. Away from the back, the run options would include handoffs to the back- or shovel-type passes.

One Back (Diagram 2-57)

One-back offenses usually tip their hand by the personnel used at the position. Depth and lateral alignments of the back offer clues as to offensive intentions. Should the back be a fullback (F) type, expect dives, traps, and cutbacks—especially if he aligns in the three position. If the back is a tailback (T), anticipate zone-type plays—especially if he aligns deeper. Pass plays also may be tipped off by personnel and alignment. In most cases, T or F will snug up to the line of scrimmage to better facilitate pass-blocking assignments or release on pass plays.

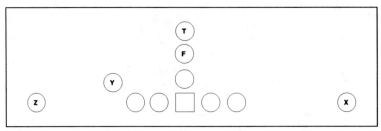

Diagram 2-55. Y-off formation

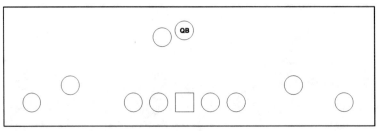

Diagram 2-56. Shotgun

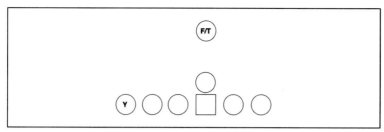

Diagram 2-57. One Back

Back Designations

Numbers can be used to show back alignments. A single number is used for one-back sets. A double digit is used for two-back sets. Three-back sets are described using three digits.

- One number = one back
- Two numbers = two backs
- Three numbers = three backs

The quarterback is referred to as Q. One-back sets use only one number. With two-back sets, the first number denotes the F while the second number tags the T. Three-back sets necessitate the use of three numbers. The third back (H) is listed first followed by the F and T.

Back Alignments

Following are possible running back alignments (shown in Diagram 2-58):

1: Wing (to strength)

2: Near (to strength). The back can be a wide 2 or a tight 2, depending upon width.

3: F home

4: T home

5: Far (away from strength). The back can be a wide 5 or a tight 5, depending upon width.

6: Cheat (away from strength)

7: U (backside tight end)

8: The back aligns in a receiver position to the strength.

9: The back aligns in a receiver position away from the strength.

Wide: Back aligns as the widest man. If to the strength, he is referred to as a wide 8. If he aligns weak, he is referred to as a wide 9.

If the quarterback is in the gun, label the backfield as "gun" followed by the back's position. Diagram 2-59 illustrates a gun-2 configuration.

If the backfield consists of one back, use a single digit for alignment. Diagrams 2-60 through 2-68 illustrate possible one-back alignments.

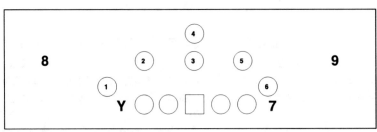

Diagram 2-58. Back Alignments

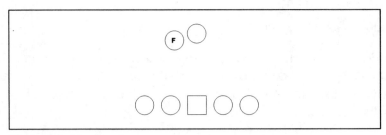

Diagram 2-59. Gun 2

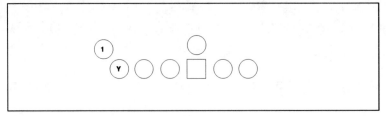

Diagram 2-60. 1 (wing, to strength)

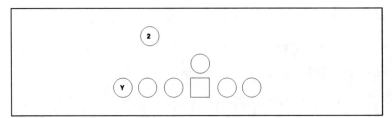

Diagram 2-61. 2 (near, to strength)

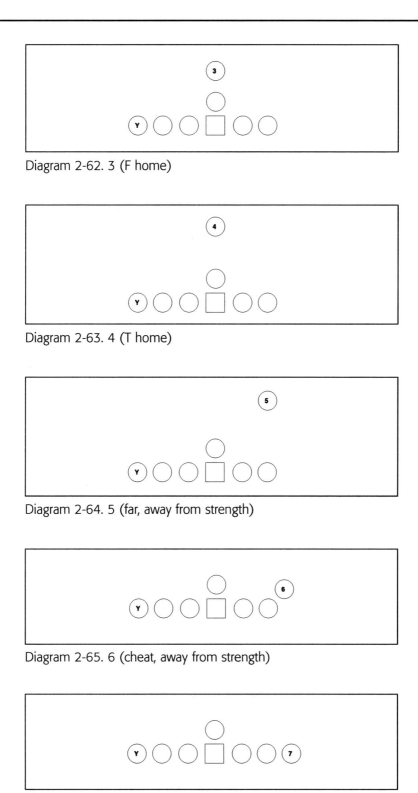

Diagram 2-62. 3 (F home)

Diagram 2-63. 4 (T home)

Diagram 2-64. 5 (far, away from strength)

Diagram 2-65. 6 (cheat, away from strength)

Diagram 2-66. 7 (U, backside tight end)

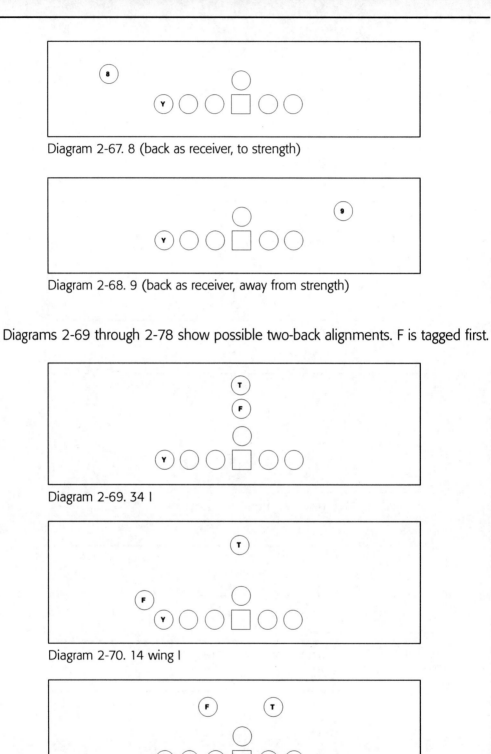

Diagram 2-67. 8 (back as receiver, to strength)

Diagram 2-68. 9 (back as receiver, away from strength)

Diagrams 2-69 through 2-78 show possible two-back alignments. F is tagged first.

Diagram 2-69. 34 I

Diagram 2-70. 14 wing I

Diagram 2-71. 25 split

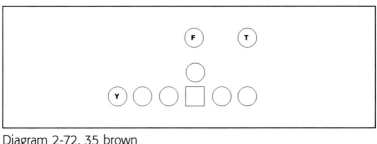

Diagram 2-72. 35 brown

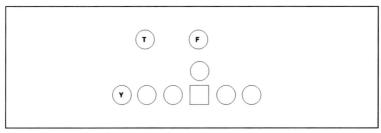

Diagram 2-73. 32 blue

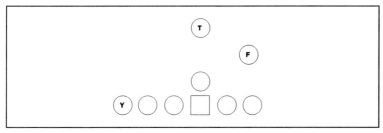

Diagram 2-74. 54 weak I

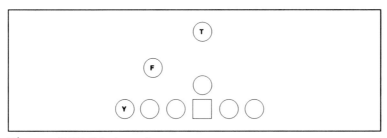

Diagram 2-75. 24 strong I

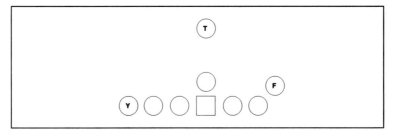

Diagram 2-76. 64 cheat I

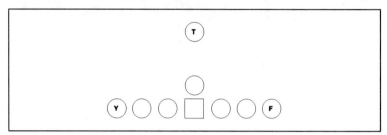

Diagram 2-77. 74 two tight

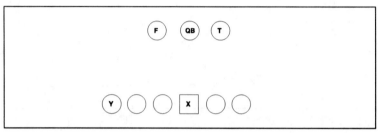

Diagram 2-78. 25 gun

Diagrams 2-79 through 2-90 illustrate three-back configurations. The third back (H) is listed first, followed by F and then T.

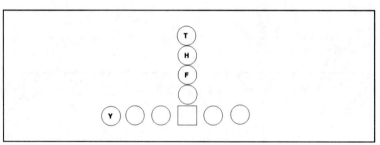

Diagram 2-79. 334 stack I

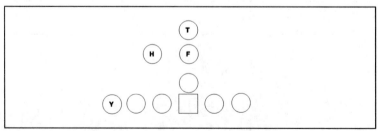

Diagram 2-80. 234 power I

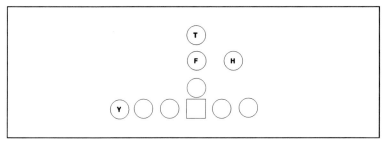

Diagram 2-81. 534 weak power I

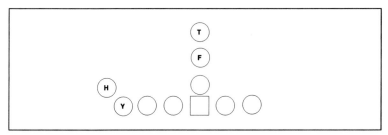

Diagram 2-82. 134 wing I

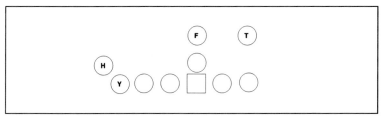

Diagram 2-83. 135 wing-T

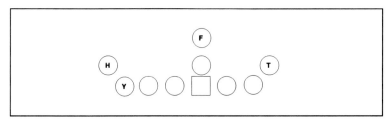

Diagram 2-84. 136 tight mirror

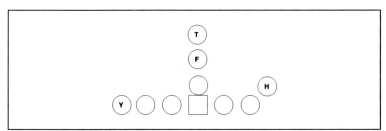

Diagram 2-85. 634 slot I

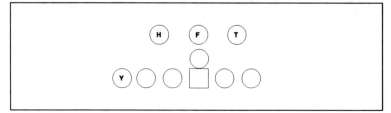

Diagram 2-86. 235 dead T

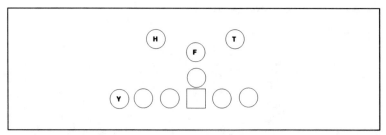

Diagram 2-87. 235 bone

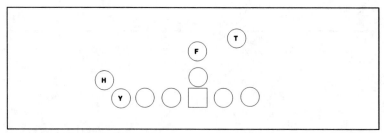

Diagram 2-88. 135 strong bone

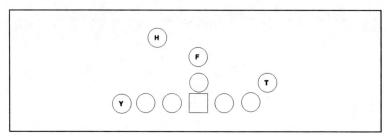

Diagram 2-89. 236 weak bone

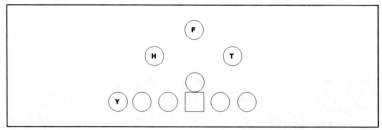

Diagram 2-90. 245 diamond

Backfield Sets: Strengths and Weaknesses

This section will illustrate some of the most commonly used backfield sets and illuminate their strengths and weaknesses. An integral part of game planning is understanding the strengths and weaknesses of the opponent's formations. Defenses have to find a way to compensate or cheat the defense to nullify the offensive sets to be defended.

I (34) (Diagram 2-91)

The I formation is a great running formation. It is highly effective for lead-type plays or counters. This backfield set is poor for pass releases by the backs. However, it is a good formation for play-action or flow-type passes.

Red (25) (Diagram 2-92)

A split (or red) backfield set is advantageous for slants, dives, or an outside running game. This set is conducive to pass releases by backs, especially if they cheat wide on alignment. On the other hand, it makes it easier for the defense to identify the numerical value of each receiver. T will usually be the #2 receiver weak with the F becoming the #2 or #3 strong receiver, depending upon the Y's release. F is rarely a threat to be the #3 receiver weak from this set.

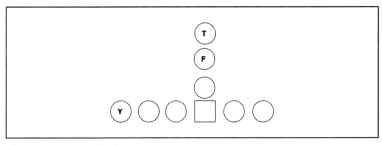

Diagram 2-91. I (34)

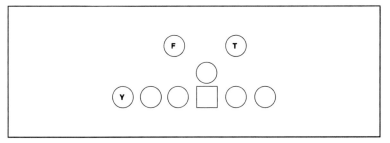

Diagram 2-92. Red (25)

Brown (35) (Diagram 2-93)

This set is very beneficial to the weakside run game. However, it weakens the strongside run game to some extent. This set allows both backs to get into the route to the weakside. F can easily be the #3 receiver weak or #3 strong.

Blue (32) (Diagram 2-94)

This overloaded set is great for the strongside run game, especially with power-type plays in short-yardage or goal-line situations. Offenses can easily run play-action flow-type routes to the Y side. It also can be used to get four receivers strong on dropback passes. A drawback in the pass game is that the #2 receiver weak is usually not a threat.

Weak I (54) (Diagram 2-95)

This set is beneficial for the weakside run game or strongside counters. A weakside counter game is hampered, however, by the F's weakside alignment. F is in great shape for pass weakside pass releases This set is also conducive to bootlegs or waggles.

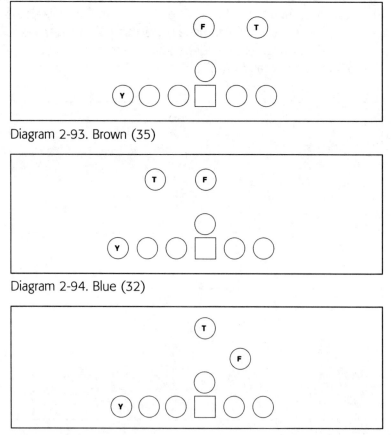

Diagram 2-93. Brown (35)

Diagram 2-94. Blue (32)

Diagram 2-95. Weak I (54)

Strong I (24) (Diagram 2-96)

F's offset to the tight-end side strengthens the run game to the strongside. It is a good set for the weakside counter game. Flow routes to Y's side are a distinct possibility. A counter running game to the strongside is at a disadvantage, as is a weakside pass game.

Power I (234) (Diagram 2-97)

This backfield set is great for the run game. It is used primarily for goal-line or short-yardage situations. Two back leads are a distinct possibility. The counter game is good. Passes will usually be play-action in nature. However, should X be an outstanding athlete, the defense could be in a quandary. If the defense single covers him, it takes a chance on giving up a big pass play. Conversely, should the defense decide to give help to the corner, it takes a chance of giving up yards to the three-back running game.

Wishbone (235) (Diagram 2-98)

The wishbone has many of the same characteristics of the power I. The major difference is that the bone presents a more balanced look than does the power I.

Stack I (334) (Diagram 2-99)

The stack I is another formation from the three-back family. It has the same inherent advantages as other three-back sets, plus the ability to present a balanced look right up to the snap of the football. The ability of the H to motion quickly presents the defense with an overloaded power-I philosophy with a minimum of time to compensate.

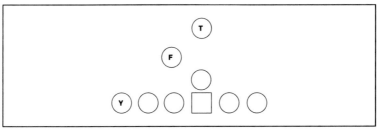

Diagram 2-96. Strong I (24)

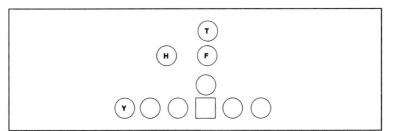

Diagram 2-97. Power I (234)

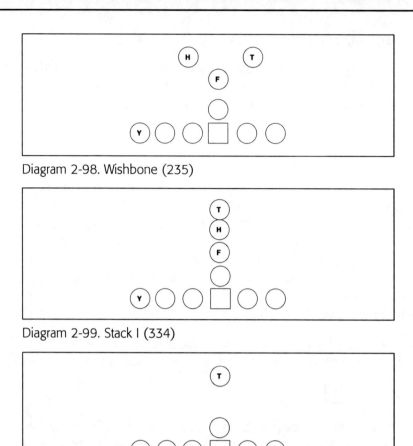

Diagram 2-98. Wishbone (235)

Diagram 2-99. Stack I (334)

Diagram 2-100. Single back

Single Back (Diagram 2-100)

Many teams feature a one-back set as their main backfield set, or have a single-back package in their offense. Common running plays include inside- and outside-zone plays, stretch, traps, options, toss plays, counters, and bounce-type plays. It is readily evident that one-back passing games are highly sophisticated and effective. The use of four quick receivers places stress on the defense.

Various Single-Back Alignments:

Wing (1): This alignment strengthens the edge of the formation. Wings strengthen the edge for running plays. Pass releases are highly effective. The only running threat to the offside would be a counter.

Near (2): Limits back's effectiveness to the weakside of the formation. Trap plays or counters are two ways to get the back to the weakside of the formation. The back is not much of a pass threat to the weakside.

Home (3): The running back is a legitimate run threat to either side of the set. He can pass release easily to either side, but he has farther to go at the 3 position than he would at a 2 or 5.

Home (4): A back in the 4 is a run threat to either side. However, running plays will be more of the slow developing type, such as the zone or stretch variety. Involvement in the pass game is somewhat hindered because of the depth of the alignment. Flares, checkdowns, and screens are possible.

Far (5): The same advantages and disadvantages of the near or 2 position are in effect.

Cheat (6): The same advantages and disadvantages of the wing or 1 position are applicable.

No Backs (Diagram 2-101)

Obviously a no-back set greatly limits an offense's run options. However, a no-back running game can be highly effective if used correctly. For example, as the defense expands to cover five eligible receivers in a short-yardage play, quarterback sneaks are highly successful. As the defense expands, natural seams are created. The same philosophy applies when offenses go empty in the red zone. Natural run lanes are created as defenders leave the box to cover receivers. Quarterback draws are staples in this situation for teams with quarterbacks that can run. Additionally, potential ballcarriers can be motioned into position to take a handoff. For example, the speed or jet sweep can be run with motion.

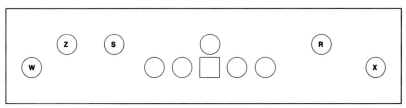

Diagram 2-101. No backs

Game Planning for One-Back Sets

Many offenses have one-back packages in their offense. Some offenses operate primarily from a one-back structure, while other offenses function primarily with two backs and use the one-back set as a change-up or as a situational formation. This section serves as an evaluation tool to break down and game plan for one-back offenses. Before getting into the nuts and bolts of evaluation of one-back sets, the coach first needs to know the offensive philosophy of the opponent. What are the base reasons for one-back sets?

The most basic question to be answered is does the offense use one back as a change-up and situational scheme, or is this their base look? Other philosophical questions to ask include:

- Is the offense trying to spread the field with multiple receivers?
- Is the offense spreading the field in an attempt to create vertical run lanes?
- Is the offense trying to limit or deter defensive blitz packages?
- Does the offense seek to create specific coverage packages?

Chances are great that they are seeking to create all the above.

One-Back Checklist

The following checklist serves as a guide for analyzing one-back philosophies and should be used as an integral part in game planning for one-back offenses.

- What personnel package does the offense use?
- One-back disguisement is effective if the offense uses 21 personnel. However, doing so may entail playing a back out of position. The use of 10 or 11 personnel, for example, would be more effective.
- Does the offense shift or motion to one back, especially if they are in a 21 personnel grouping?
- What formations, shifts, and motions does the offense use?
- Does the offense use a tight end? If so, what are his alignments? How effective is he as a blocker or receiver?
- Does the offense shift or motion the Y into the backfield to form a two-back set?
- Is the single back a receiving threat? How effective is he as a blocker?
- What is their base running scheme with the quarterback under center? Does the offense incorporate option plays?
- What is their base running scheme with the quarterback in the gun? Does the offense incorporate option plays?
- What is their base protection package? Does the offense use sprint protection?
- What is their screen package?
- Does the offense go no huddle, and if so, at what tempo?

Receiver Deviations

Receivers don't always align in "normal" positions. They will vary their alignments for a wide variety of reasons. They may adjust their positioning to gain an advantage on a pass release or blocking assignment. Adroit game planning should take these aberrations into account. Following is the system to use in tagging various receiver alignments:

X Variations (Diagrams 2-102 through 2-105)

- Over: Aligns on the same side as Y
- Tight: One yard or less split from the offensive tackle
- Nasty: One to six yards split from the offensive tackle
- Normal: Seven yards or more split from offensive tackle

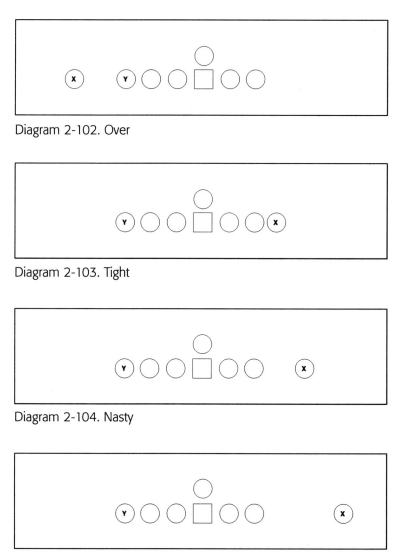

Diagram 2-102. Over

Diagram 2-103. Tight

Diagram 2-104. Nasty

Diagram 2-105. Normal

Z Variations (Diagrams 2-106 through 2-109)

- Wing: One to two yards from Y
- Close: Three to six yards from Y
- Normal: Seven or more yards from Y
- Numbers: Alignment in backfield using same number scheme used for running backs.

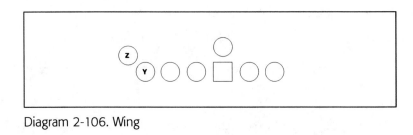

Diagram 2-106. Wing

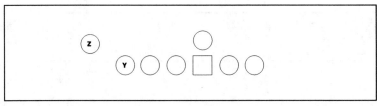

Diagram 2-107. Close

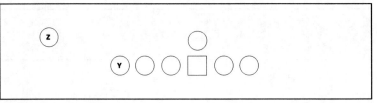

Diagram 2-108. Normal

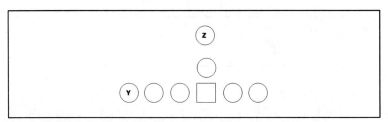

Diagram 2-109. Numbers

Y Variations (Diagram 2-110 through 2-114)

- Off: Y aligned outside the offensive tackle, but off the line of scrimmage
- Nasty: One to five yards from offensive tackle
- Flex: Six or more yards from offensive tackle
- YOZ: Y aligns outside Z
- Numbers: Alignment in backfield using the same number scheme used for running back.

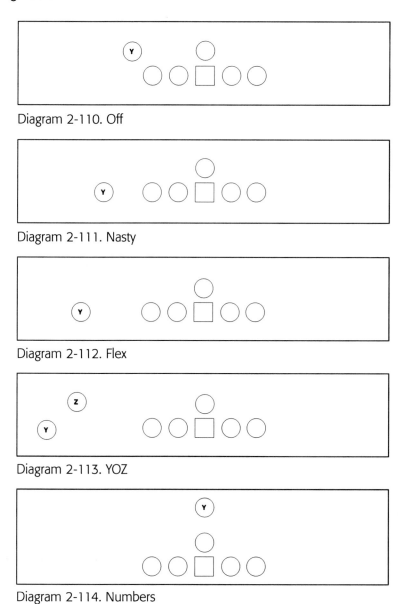

Diagram 2-110. Off

Diagram 2-111. Nasty

Diagram 2-112. Flex

Diagram 2-113. YOZ

Diagram 2-114. Numbers

Motion

Offenses use motion for a variety of reasons. It is imperative the defensive game plan deciphers why a particular type of motion is used. What is the offense trying to accomplish? Defensive coordinators should discover the reasons for motion and plan how to handle it. Adjustments to motion should take into consideration such variables as down-and-distance, field position, personnel groupings, and formations. A defensive call should be adjustable to any pre-snap movement. Movement and motion adjustments should be presented early in the defensive game plan. Doing so will result in the players thinking the adjustment is basic and not something new to be learned. The game plan should seek to match offensive movement with defensive modifications involving defensive linebackers and backs. The defensive line should be left unaffected if possible. Avoid checking out of a stunt or blitz if faced with motion. The defensive scheme should be flexible enough to handle any shifts or motion. Without this flexibility, the defense will have to check out of calls and, as a result, allow the offense to dictate to the defense. The defense should not allow offenses to force it to play a vanilla look.

Reasons for Motion

- Motion can place a back closer to the point of attack to be a blocking threat or ballcarrier.

- Motion can place a receiver closer to the core of the formation to be a blocker or ballcarrier.

- Motion can position a receiver to participate in a flow type route (bunch formation).

- Movement can be used to force defensive adjustments, which in turn allows the offense to manipulate defensive movement. Motion can remove defenders from the point of attack.

- Motion can be used to determine coverage. Movement may offer a tip-off as to whether the defense is in man or zone.

- Motion can be used versus tight man coverage to free up receivers, to foster a better pass release, or create mismatches.

- Motion can change formation strength. Offenses can maneuver into change-of-strength movements, which create areas of defensive weakness.

- Motion can endanger the force man, or it may cause the defense to change force or foster indecision.

- Motion can cause confusion or mismatches if the defense isn't properly prepared. Defensive mental error may result.

- Motion used to change strength forces defensive reaction. Busted coverages and mismatches are offensive goals.

- Motion can simply be superfluous or just window dressing.

Without a doubt, motion can cause defensive headaches. However, motions have some inherent disadvantages that well-prepared defenses can exploit.

- The defense can get a feel for the snap count.

- Motion may reveal some offensive tendencies.

- Offensive linemen, many times, can be "beaten to the punch" because they need to remain stationary for an extended period of time before the snap.

- Motion men should be moving parallel to the line of scrimmage on the snap. Doing so may hinder their move upfield.

The defense shouldn't give the offense a steady dose of base adjustments and should make the offense unsure of the adjustments made. In other words, don't give the offense the response they expected or planned for. Defensive adjustments should vary when confronted with motion. The offense can gain the upper hand should the defense adjust to motion the same way every time. Defensive predictability is hazardous. A wise defensive coordinator will game plan different adjustments to motion. Some options might include a check stunt to or away from the motion. Coordinators may decide to chase motion or may choose to bump the coverage. Motion may necessitate a check coverage. The main consideration on what type of adjustment to use is based upon offensive intentions. Scouting reports should discern what the offense is trying to accomplish with motion so the defense can adjust accordingly. Following are various types of receiver motions.

Receiver Motions

X-Motions (Diagrams 2-115 through 2-122)

- Jac: X across ball

- Jap: X-motion past offensive tackle with the intent to block a defender in the box

- Jarc: Jac with depth

- Jig: X-motion in-and-out and then back across

- Jing: X-motion to fringe of tackle box usually to block the end-of-line defender, crack the second-level defender, or run a crossing route (used in many cases on zone-type plays to the opposite side)

- Joom: X-motion from backfield

- X Orbit: X-motion in and back out

- Jout: X-motion away from core the formation

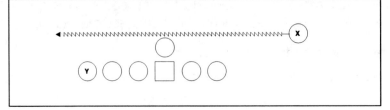

Diagram 2-115. Jac

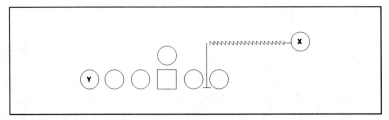

Diagram 2-116. Jap

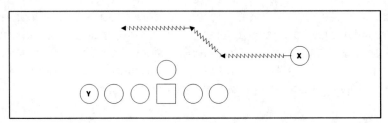

Diagram 2-117. Jarc

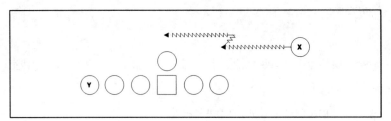

Diagram 2-118. Jig

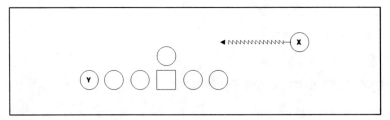

Diagram 2-119. Jing

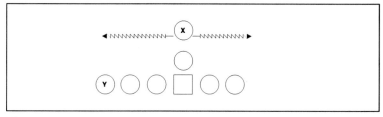

Diagram 2-120. Joom

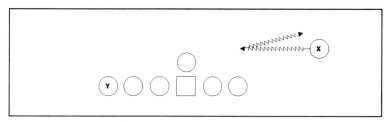

Diagram 2-121. X orbit

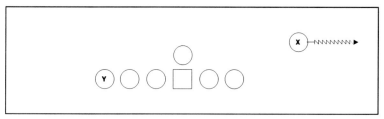

Diagram 2-122. Jout

Z-Motions (Diagrams 2-123 through 2-131)

- Red: Z deep motion away from the line of scrimmage
- Zac: Z across ball
- Zap: Z-motion past the offensive tackle with the intent to block a defender in the box
- Zarc: Zac with depth
- Zig: Z-motion in-and-out and then back across
- Zing: Z-motion to fringe of tackle box usually to block the end-of-line defender, crack the second-level defender, or run a crossing route (used in many cases on zone-type plays to the opposite side)
- Zoom: Z-motion from backfield
- Z Orbit: Z-motion in and back out
- Zout: Z-motion away from core of the formation

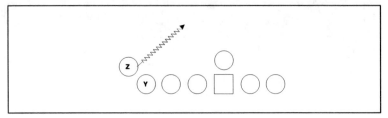

Diagram 2-123. Red

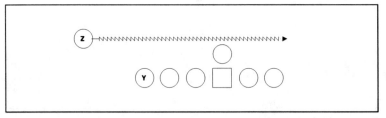

Diagram 2-124. Zac

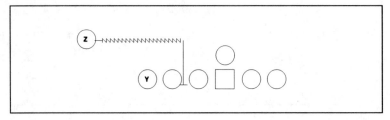

Diagram 2-125. Zap

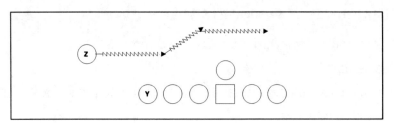

Diagram 2-126. Zarc

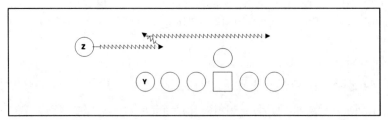

Diagram 2-127. Zig

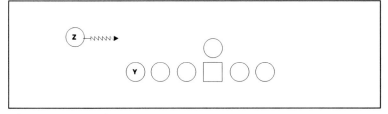

Diagram 2-128. Zing

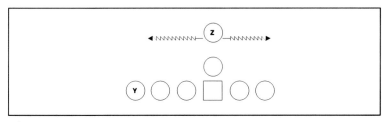

Diagram 2-129. Zoom

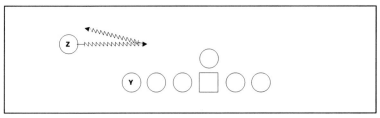

Diagram 2-130. Z orbit

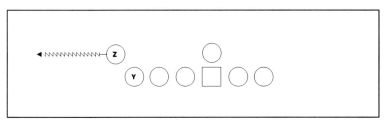

Diagram 2-131. Zout

Y-Motion (Diagrams 2-132 through 2-139)

- Yac: Y across ball
- Yap: Y-motion past the offensive tackle with the intent to block a defender in the box
- Yarc: Yac with depth
- Yig: Y-motion in-and-out and then back across

- Ying: Y-motion to fringe of tackle box usually to block the end-of-line defender, crack the second-level defender, or run a crossing route (used in many cases on zone-type plays to the opposite side)
- Yoom: Y-motion from backfield
- Y Orbit: Y-motion in and back out
- Yout: Y-motion away from core of the formation

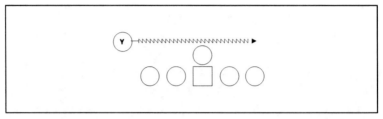

Diagram 2-132. Yac

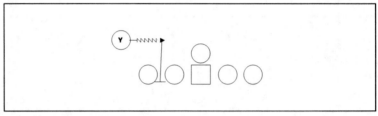

Diagram 2-133. Yap

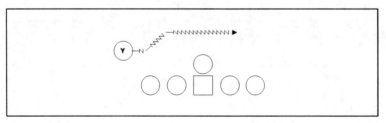

Diagram 2-134. Yarc

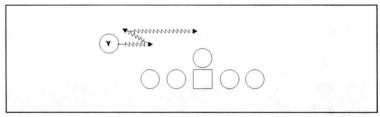

Diagram 2-135. Yig

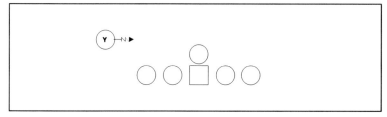

Diagram 2-136. Ying

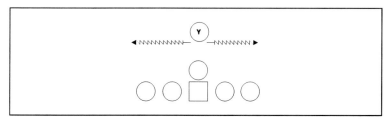

Diagram 2-137. Yoom

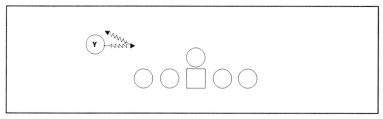

Diagram 2-138. Y orbit

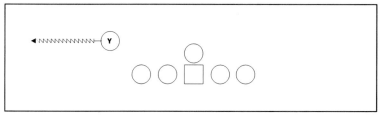

Diagram 2-139. Yout

U-Motion (Diagrams 2-140 through 2-147)

- Pac: U across ball
- Pap: U-motion past the offensive tackle with the intent to block a defender in the box
- Parc: Pac with depth
- Pig: U-motion in-and-out and then back across

- Ping: U-motion to fringe of tackle box, usually to block the end-of-line defender, crack the second-level defender, or run a crossing route (used in many cases on zone-type plays to the opposite side)
- Poom: U-motion from backfield
- U Orbit: U-motion in and back out
- Pout: U-motion away from core of the formation

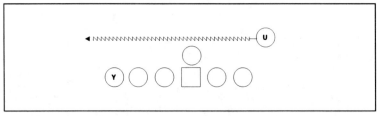

Diagram 2-140. Pac

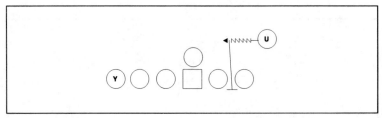

Diagram 2-141. Pap

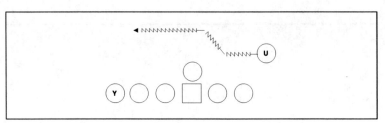

Diagram 2-142. Parc

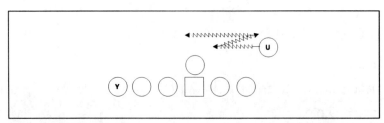

Diagram 2-143. Pig

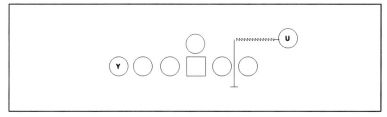

Diagram 2-144. Ping

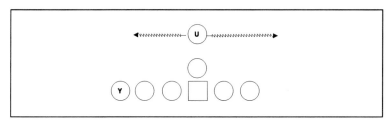

Diagram 2-145. Poom

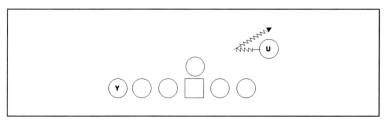

Diagram 2-146. U orbit

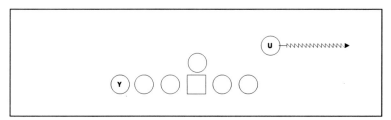

Diagram 2-147. Pout

V Motion (Diagrams 2-148 through 2-155)

- Vac: V across ball
- Vap: V-motion past the offensive tackle with the intent to block a defender in the box
- Varc: Vac with depth
- Vig: V-motion in-and-out and then back across

- Ving: V-motion to fringe of tackle box, usually to block the end-of-line defenders, crack the second-level defender, or run a crossing route (used in many cases on zone-type plays to the opposite side)
- Voom: V-motion from backfield
- V Orbit: V-motion in and back out
- Vout: V-motion away from core of the formation

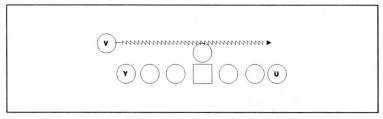

Diagram 2-148. Vac

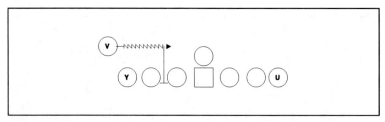

Diagram 2-149. Vap

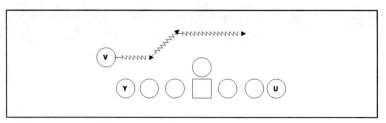

Diagram 2-150. Varc

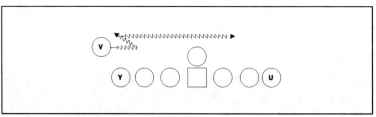

Diagram 2-151. Vig

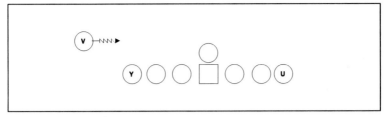

Diagram 2-152. Ving

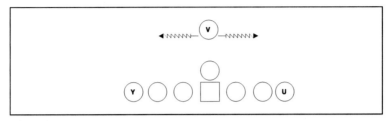

Diagram 2-153. Voom

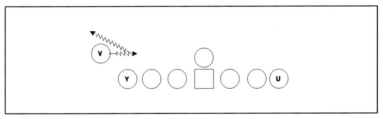

Diagram 2-154. V orbit

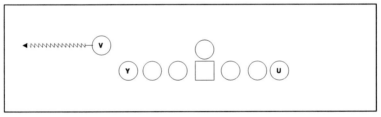

Diagram 2-155. Vout

R-Motion (Diagrams 2-156 through 2-163)

- Rac: R across ball
- Rap: R-motion past the offensive tackle with the intent to block a defender in the box
- Rarc: Rac with depth
- Rig: R-motion in-and-out and then back across

- Ring: R-motion to fringe of tackle box usually to block the end-of-line defender, crack the second-level defender, or run a crossing route (used in many cases on zone-type plays to other side)
- Room: R-motion from backfield
- R Orbit: R-motion in and back out
- Rout: R-motion away from core of the formation

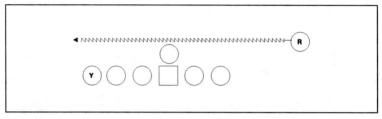

Diagram 2-156. Rac

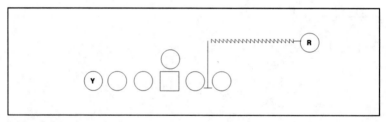

Diagram 2-157. Rap

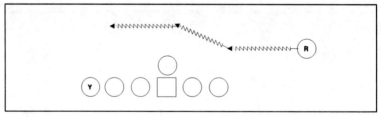

Diagram 2-158. Rarc

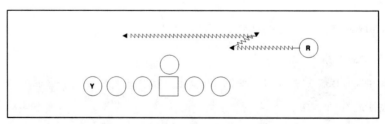

Diagram 2-159. Rig

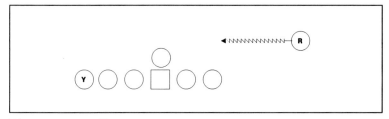

Diagram 2-160. Ring

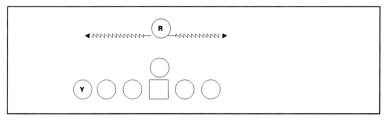

Diagram 2-161. Room

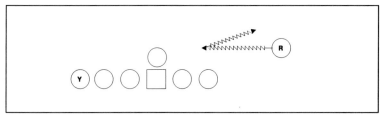

Diagram 2-162. R orbit

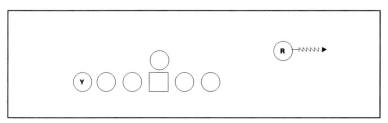

Diagram 2-163. Rout

S-Motion (Diagrams 2-164 through 2-171)

- Sac: S across ball
- Sap: S-motion past offensive tackle with the intent to block a defender in the box
- Sarc: Sac with depth
- Sig: S-motion in-out and then back across

- Sing: S-motion to fringe of tackle box usually to block the end-of-line defender, crack the second-level defender, or run a crossing route (used in many cases on zone-type plays to other side)
- Soom: S-motion from backfield
- S Orbit: S-motion in and back out
- Sout: S-motion away from core of the formation

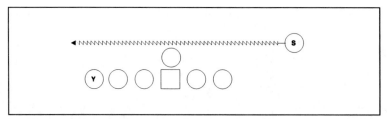

Diagram 2-164. Sac

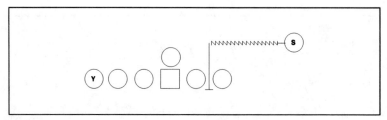

Diagram 2-165. Sap

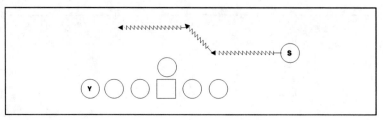

Diagram 2-166. Sarc

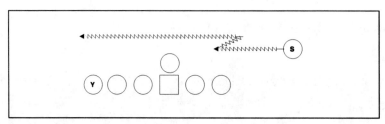

Diagram 2-167. Sig

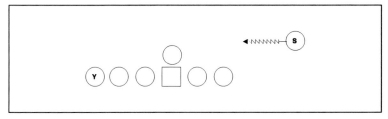

Diagram 2-168. Sing

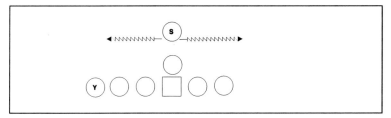

Diagram 2-169. Soom

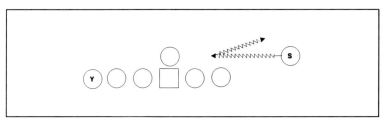

Diagram 2-170. S orbit

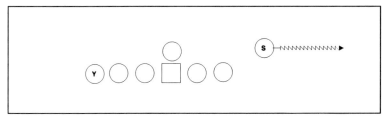

Diagram 2-171. Sout

Running Back Motions

Back motion is followed by tagging the snap formation. For example, Diagram 2-172 shows ton motion to a trey-left formation.

T-Motion (Diagrams 2-172 through 2-180)

- Ton: T-motion followed by snap formation
- Tac: T across ball

- Tap: T-motion past the offensive tackle with the intent to block a defender in the box

- Tarc: Tac with depth

- Tig: T-motion in-and-out and then back across

- Ting: T-motion to fringe of tackle box, usually to block the end-of-line defender, crack the second-level defender, or run a crossing route (used in many cases on zone-type plays to other side)

- T Orbit: T-motion in and back out

- Tout: T-motion away from core of the formation

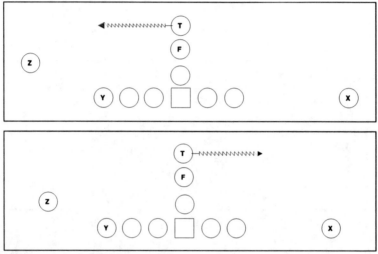

Diagrams 2-172 and 2-173. Ton

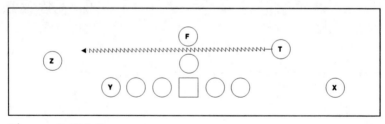

Diagram 2-174. Tac

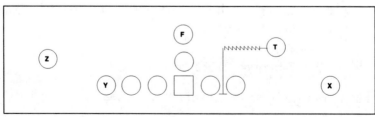

Diagram 2-175. Tap

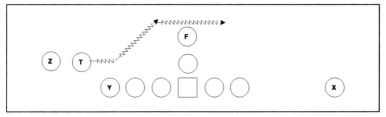

Diagram 2-176. Tarc

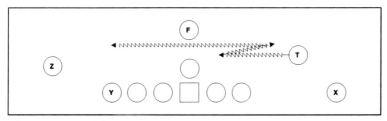

Diagram 2-177. Tig

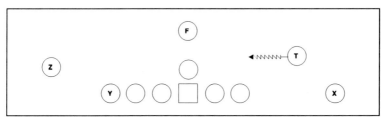

Diagram 2-178. Ting

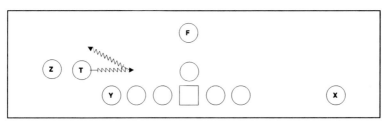

Diagram 2-179. T orbit

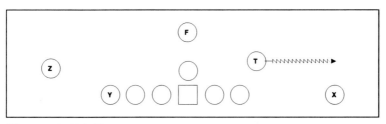

Diagram 2-180. Tout

F-Motion (Diagrams 2-181 through 2-189)

- F Shuffle: In the box, shoulders square to line-of-scrimmage motion (Receiver tags with the number he was on when the ball was snapped.)
- Fon: F-motion followed by snap formation
- Fac: F across ball
- Fap: F-motion past offensive tackle with the intent to block a defender in the box
- Farc: Fac with depth
- Fig: F-motion in-and-out and then back across
- Fing: F-motion to fringe of tackle box, usually to block the end-of-line defender, crack the second-level defender, or running a crossing route (used in many cases on zone-type plays to other side)
- F Orbit: F-motion in and back out
- Fout: F-motion away from core of the formation

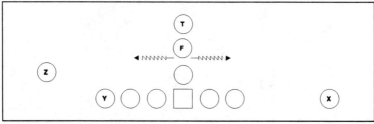

Diagram 2-181. F shuffle

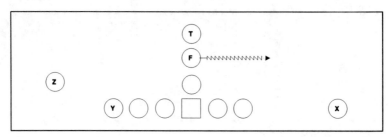

Diagram 2-182. Fon

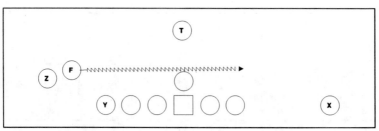

Diagram 2-183. Fac

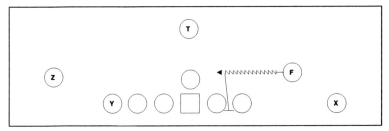

Diagram 2-184. Fap

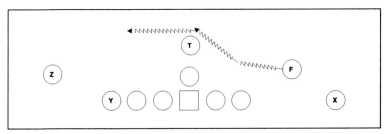

Diagram 2-185. Farc

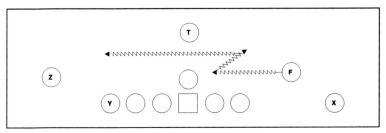

Diagram 2-186. Fig

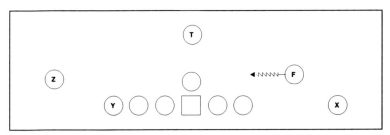

Diagram 2-187. Fing

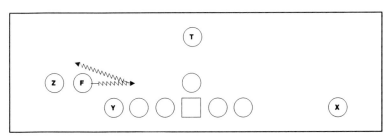

Diagram 2-188. F orbit

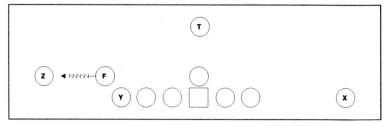

Diagram 2-189. Fout

H-Motion (Diagrams 2-190 through 2-194)

- H Shuffle: In the box, shoulders square to line-of-scrimmage motion (tag with number he was on when the ball was snapped).
- Hon: H-motion followed by snap formation
- Hac: H across the ball followed by snap formation
- Harc: Hac with depth
- Hout: H-motion away from core of the formation

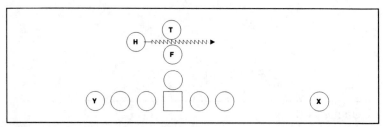

Diagram 2-190. H shuffle

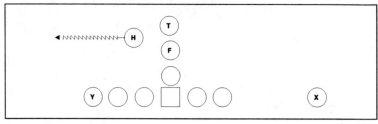

Diagram 2-191. Hon

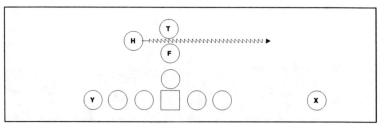

Diagram 2-192. Hac

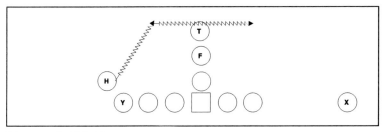

Diagram 2-193. Harc

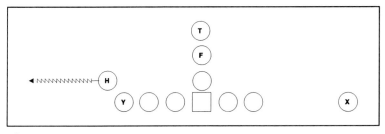

Diagram 2-194. Hout

Shifts

Offenses use shifts of running backs or receivers to compliment multiple-formation schemes, to control coverage and run support, or to create mismatches. For identification purposes, use the shift back's position and name the formation he moved to. Diagrams 2-195 and 2-196 are examples of back shifts and move-tos.

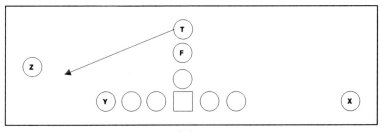

Diagram 2-195. T move to trey left

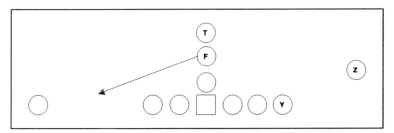

Diagram 2-196. F move to spread left

Any Y shift is called "trade." Diagram 2-197 illustrates a Y trade. In this illustration, the Y trades to a twins-over-right formation.

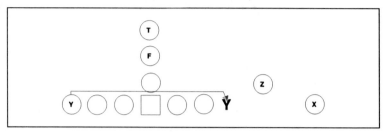

Diagram 2-197. Y trade to twins over right

Tight-End Trade

Some teams choose to trade or walk the tight end opposite his original alignment. The reasons for this are wide and varied. Defensive reactions and adjustments are also wide and varied. Some defenses will "Omaha" the front and realign. Some coordinators will simply cheat their linebackers to the tight end's new alignment. Still other teams choose to slant toward the new strength call. Other teams, at the risk of losing leverage, simply ignore the trade. No matter the adjustment, it should be planned and drilled. A defense can basically play it one of two ways if no blitz is called. The most basic way is to Omaha the front. With an Omaha call, the front, linebackers, and safeties are realigned to the new strength. Diagrams 2-198 and 2-199 illustrate an Omaha call.

The second major way to play a Y trade is to "Yukon" the defense. Defensive linemen, weak outside linebacker (W), and the middle linebacker (S) freeze. The B (or strong) outside linebacker travels. The strong and free safeties stay where they are. Yukon is a good way to play if the offense is mixing in trades and Y motion.

Various ways exist to play Y trades. Included in each week's game plan should be a strategy for trades whether the opponent has showed this wrinkle in the past or not.

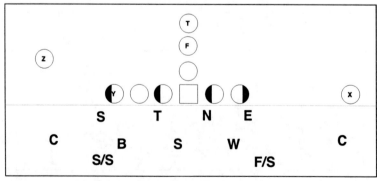

Diagram 2-198. Pre trade

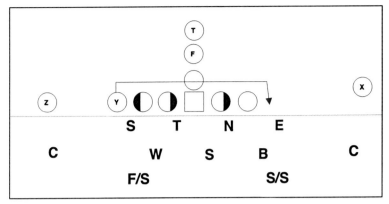

Diagram 2-199. Post trade

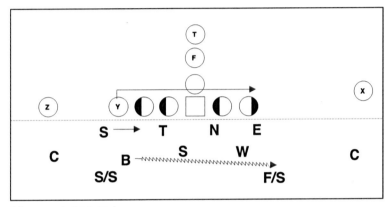

Diagram 2-200. Yukon

Shifting and Motion

Some teams will add more mental pressure on the defense by shifting and motioning on the same play. For identification purposes, the defense can simply tag the shift and then the motion. Diagrams 2-201 and 2-202 are examples of how to call shifts and motion on the same play.

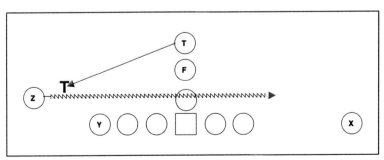

Diagram 2-201. Pro Left–T move to Trey–Zac

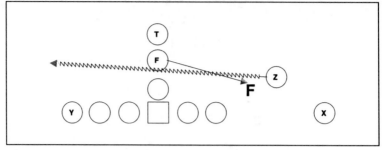

Diagram 2-202. Twins Right–F move to Trips–Zac

Numbering Eligibles

Numerically labeling eligible receivers is desirable when discussing coverage responsibilities. Eligible receivers are numbered outside-in from the widest to the center. Following are three formations illustrating the numbering system.

If a back is in the 3 or 4 position, he cannot be given a definite number until he declares to a particular side by motioning or moving post-snap. For example, F in Diagram 2-205 can be either #4 strong or #2 weak, depending upon which way he steps post-snap. Receiver numbers can change post-snap should two receivers in close proximity cross paths on their release. This possibility might necessitate a banjo or combo call by the defense. On a flow pass, the T becomes #3 and the F becomes #4. The widest man has the lower number (Diagram 2-206).

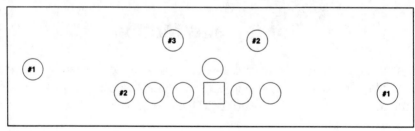

Diagram 2-203. Red pro

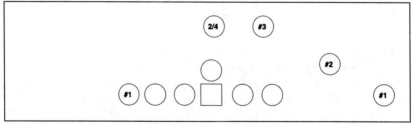

Diagram 2-204. Brown twins

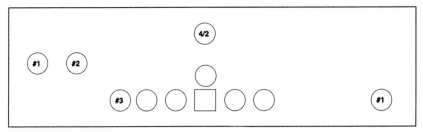

Diagram 2-205. Trey

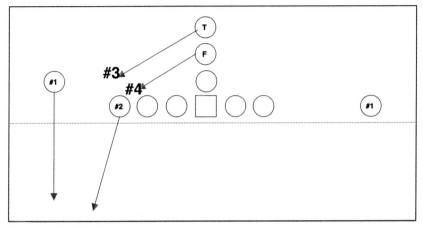

Diagram 2-206. Flow pass

Unbalanced, Overloaded, and Group Formations

In addition to the basic formations an opponent uses, defensive coordinators should be prepared to adjust to unconventional and/or unbalanced formations. If unbalanced sets have been seen through film study or scouting of the opponent, the defense will have an idea what to expect. However, the opponent may use a different style of unbalanced formation or a previously unseen overloaded formation. Regardless of past history, the defense should be exposed to unbalanced sets periodically throughout the year so they will be prepared when the need to adjust arises. Overloads can be accomplished in a variety of ways. A common practice involves bringing X over to the tight-end side. Diagrams 2-207 through 2-209 give three examples of X-over formations.

X can align overloaded, or he can motion to the overload. X-motion can be used only with one- or two-back sets. Three-back sets are not conducive to X-motion, since X-motion would result in the offense having only six men on the line of scrimmage. Another common tactic involves trading Y to X's side. Doing so would serve the same purpose as motion (Diagram 2-210).

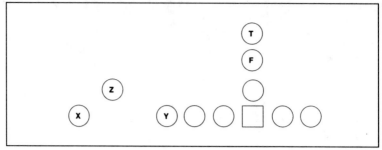
Diagram 2-207. Pro–X over

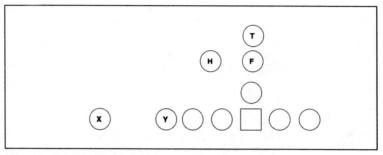
Diagram 2-208. Power I–X over

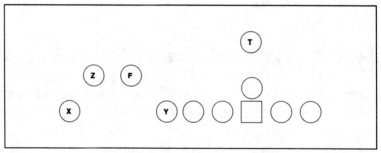
Diagram 2-209. Trey–X over (quads)

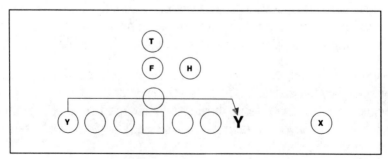
Diagram 2-210. Y Trade to x over

Another way to gain an overload is to bring a tackle over to the tight-end position and place him next to the other offensive tackle. The tight end, in turn, would line up to the weakside, or nub side (Diagram 2-211).

Care must be taken to adjust to the running strength of the formation, while ensuring that Y isn't uncovered. Another common way to get an overload is to add a fourth gap to the tight-end side through substitution or placing a receiver on the line outside Y. A basic adjustment to this overload is to move one man to the overload and treat the strong guard as the center. Doing so would result in the formation being played as a two-tight-end formation (Diagram 2-212).

This simple reaction allows the defense to play the front and coverage called without being leveraged by the overload. Obviously, adjustment can be made in other ways . Some coaches may cheat linebackers, slant the line, stunt, or simply ignore the overload. Whatever method is used, it is advantageous to recognize the overload. Recognition starts with huddle awareness. Outside linebackers can key the tackle to their side while the offense is still in the huddle. Tackles crossing the ball are easily recognized (Diagram 2-213). For example, if Bandit's (B) tackle goes away, he simply makes a "tackle over" call and declares "rip," which is a right strength call (Diagram 2-214). Should Will's (W) tackle go over, he declares "Liz," which is a left strength call (Diagram 2-215).

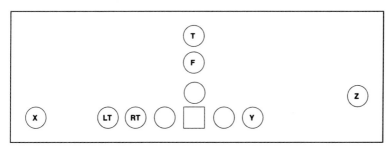

Diagram 2-211. Tackle over

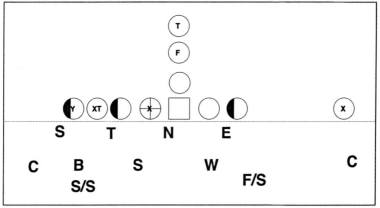

Diagram 2-212. Move one man

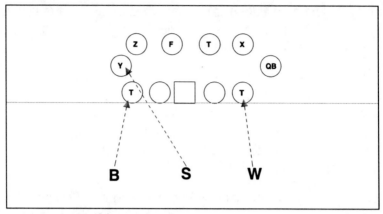

Diagram 2-213. Huddle awareness

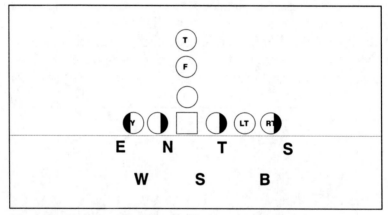

Diagram 2-214. Bandit (B) Calls "Tackle Over–Rip"

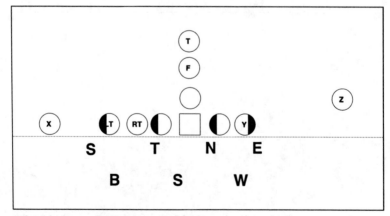

Diagram 2-215. Will (W) calls "Tackle Over–Liz"

Another common way to gain an overload is to go unbalanced with substitute personnel. This alignment serves to add another gap to the front. Unless the defense adjusts, it can be outmanned to the overload. Substitutions can be seen from the box and communicated downstairs. Defensive responses should be built into the game plan.

While contemplating a defensive blueprint, the defensive coordinator should foretell offensive intentions when they go unbalanced.

- Is the offense trying to gain a numbers advantage?
- Is the offense seeking to attack away from the defensive adjustment?
- Is the offense trying to sneak in an eligible receiver at the tackle position on the weak (or nub) side?

Obviously, overloads have inherent advantages. However, one possible drawback is that the Y may be covered up and ineligible. The defense should game plan and take advantage of this. A defensive back should be schemed to be more involved in the run defense. It is the defensive coordinator's job to find work for the extra defender.

Other defensive tactics:

- Cheat linebackers to the overload.
- Stunt linebackers to the overload. If this choice is made, the next decision is whether to stunt into base stunt paths, or move one man to the overload and stunt those gaps.
- Drop someone down out of the secondary.
- Slant to the overload or unbalance.
- Declare the strong guard as the center and move the front one man to the overload.
- Check the end man to the weak (or nub) side for eligibility. Don't uncover an eligible receiver.

No matter the preferred adjustment, it should be well-defined, understood, and practiced periodically.

Defensing Group Formations

A group formation is an unusual or exotic formation that split out offensive linemen. Group formation defenses should always be included in the weekly game plan and reviewed weekly. It is recommended that group formations be inserted into team periods throughout the week and covered in walk-through periods.

3

Defending the Run Game

Whether the offense is known as a throwing offense, running offense, or has a 50/50 balance, the defense's first consideration should be to stop the run and make the opponent one dimensional The old saying "Some teams can beat you though the air but every team can beat you on the ground" has been repeated many times. Statistical analysis of most bowl games and NFL playoff games reveal that the teams that have more rushes win most of the games. Further study divulges that teams with a 100-yard rusher also win most of the time. Even passing teams feel they need to be able to run the ball to some extent to be successful. One coaching philosophy is that to be successful defensively, a team must stop the opponent's bread-and-butter running plays. Furthermore, a defense should not try to stop everything or it won't be able to stop anything. Run defense, at its most rudimentary level, involves finding the best runner and his best running play and stopping it. Thus, the offense should have to try to beat the defense with other runs that they normally aren't as proficient at. By the same token, teams that run the ball effectively have some peripheral advantages over the defense. One of those advantages is that when teams run the ball effectively, their opponent finds it hard to mount a pass rush when they do throw the ball.

Stopping an opponent's run game can be done through physical dominance or a scheme that overpowers it with numbers. An added benefit or by-product of stalling the opponent's run game is that it serves to nullify their play-action pass game. Should this happen, the opposition will be left with only a dropback pass game. Again, take the run away and force them to try to win with the pass. Psychologically, it is very important that the opponent not be able to effectively run the ball. An offense that successfully runs the ball can control the clock, dictate the tempo, keep their defense fresh, and psychologically cripple not only the opposing defense but their offense as well. An offense whose defense is giving up points and long drives feels added pressure to score each time it gets the ball. Most offenses don't like to be involved in a scoring battle. Teams that run the ball with great effect can impose their will on the opposition. Statistically, teams that win the "time of possession" battle win most games. It is evident that the best way to control the clock and wear down the opponent is through a highly effective run game.

Game planning begins with discerning the opponent's basic philosophy of offense. Does the offense rely on a system, particularly talented player(s) (quarterback, receiver, running back), or on a process of outmuscling an opponent to be successful? How involved is the quarterback in the run game? Does the quarterback carry by design (i.e., sneak, option, draw), or are his carries out of necessity (i.e., broken plays and scrambles)? Does the offense present a balanced attack with a good ratio of both passes and runs, or are they schematically one-dimensional? No matter the philosophical approach your opponent takes, the successful offenses follow these basic tenets:

- Formational variations: few plays with multiple formations
- Use of motion/shifts: force defensive adjustments
- Package running plays with play-action passes off of these runs
- Use of gadget or special plays
- Seek a numerical advantage at the point of attack
- Use of blocking angles
- Slow or block run support through shifts and/or motions
- Look for favorable physical match-ups
- Exploit defensive tendencies
- Use an effective audible system to get out of bad plays
- Attack defensive weaknesses and avoid defensive strength

The most basic question that must be answered in game preparation is: what type of run game does your opponent employ? A cursory film study will answer that basic question. It can be readily discerned through film study whether the opponent is an option, power, wing-T, or pro-style offense. Further study, however, may reveal some intricacies that are not so readily visible. Film study will allow the defensive coordinator to figure out a way to cheat the defense to take away what the offense likes to do by formation, down-and-distance, field zone, and so forth. Game plans should start with basic adjustments that will defeat the offense's best three runs. The opponent's three favorite run plays may have to be determined by sifting through a smoke screen of multiple formations, shifts, and motions. A well-prepared defense can attack the offense by varying shades or linebacker adjustments. Defenses should be flexible in order to expand or contract according to the tactical situation. Linemen and linebackers should possess the ability to adjust horizontally and vertically to be effective in stopping the run game. The ability to move safeties in and out of the box serves to enhance chances of successfully stopping an opponent's running game.

A defense's own history is of particular importance in game planning. Film exchange enables the opponent to know where the last two or three opponents hurt the defense and where it was the weakest. Particular plays or points of attack have a habit of showing up if past problems have existed. Correcting past problems should be an integral part of game preparation. Opponents will scout and identify from film study, formations, or situations that get a particular response and will seek to exploit that knowledge. Unpredictability is a must in defensive game planning.

Paradoxically, defense success against the run may depend upon pass coverage. How do the corners match up with their wideouts? If the corners match up well with the opponent's receivers and can cover them with little or no help, a whole world of possibilities opens up on what the defense can do to stop the run. For example, safeties can be committed to the run and be inserted into the box.

After developing a good feel for the type of offense to be faced, in-depth film study will reveal its approach to run blocking. Most offenses can be labeled as one of the following types of offenses:

- Finesse
- Power
- Option
- Zone
- Gun

It should be understood, however, that most offenses may utilize one or more of these philosophies or extensive overlap may exist. In truth, it may not be so easy to compartmentalize a certain offense as one thing or another. Nevertheless, all successful offenses are known for something. A basic philosophy guides them and gives them something to "hang their hat on."

Finesse Offenses

In many cases, this approach is adopted by smaller and quicker teams. The run game is characterized by angle blocks, pulling linemen, influences, and cross blocks. Its success depends upon mobile linemen who can pull, lead, and trap. Traps—whether of the short or long variety—are highly effective. The trap game may use both guard and tackle traps.

Power Offenses

The antithesis to finesse blocking schemes is the more traditional base-blocking scheme. This approach is the preferred mode of operation of large, physical, and less mobile linemen. This style is distinguished by a grind-it-out mentality that makes liberal use of drive, base, double, wedge, lead, and isolation-type blocks.

Option Offenses

Seldom do high school or college teams fully commit to the option game. Many teams, however, will have an option package in place as a change of pace. The lack of option familiarity by defenses makes teams that are committed to the option highly dangerous. Preparing to play option offenses may make radical adjustments necessary for teams who haven't laid the essential groundwork to face option teams. Defenses should play assignment football when facing option teams. Upfield charges and unbridled pursuit can be detrimental to the defense. Film study will reveal the type or types of option(s) to be faced. Game plans should take into account whether the opposition runs a double, triple, lead, or counter option game. In most cases, an option offense will run a variety of option packages. Is the option offense a one-, two-, or three-back attack? This very crucial question needs to be asked as the defense prepares to face an option team. Option responsibilities have to be defined and assigned for each front or stunt. Assignments should be clearly defined and technique perfected in game planning and practice time during the week.

Zone Offenses

Many zone-running teams are pass-oriented. They seek to keep their run game simple, which in turn allows more flexibility and quality in the pass game. Run schemes are usually simple to allow more practice time to be spent on the passing game.

Gun Offenses

Some teams use the shotgun to run the ball effectively. These teams are able to take advantage of the upfield pass-rush mindset of defenses. Options, shuffle passes, and misdirection with the quarterback as a running threat can be proven highly effective.

No matter the style of offense being faced, an identification system is needed for communication purposes. This section will establish nomenclature pertaining to the running game. Included will be a hole-numbering system, play-naming system, play description, run-blocking schemes, individual and combination blocking schemes by linemen, running-back blocks, and receiver blocks. Also included will be a discussion of run force. Run force is an integral part of any blueprint in defeating an opponent's running game. Advice on how to analyze and break down your opponent's run game is also included.

Hole-Numbering System

Hole numbers are designated directly over offensive linemen (Diagrams 3-1 and 3-2). Gaps are also labeled to further distinguish points of attack. Most offenses use even numbers to their right and odd numbers to their left. Doing so allows carryover from the offense.

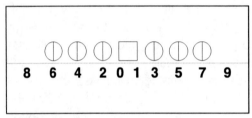

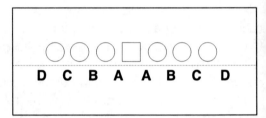

Diagram 3-1. Holes   Diagram 3-2. Gaps

Holes

0, 1 (Midline): Tight off the center. These holes are used for traps, cutbacks, options, isolations, and draw-type plays.

2, 3 (A gap): Outside leg of the center to the outside leg of the guard. This area is used for isolations, traps, and options.

4, 5 (B gap): Outside leg of guard to the outside leg of the tackle. Conducive for zones, veer options, leads, and play-action passes.

6, 7 (C gap): Outside leg of tackle to the outside leg of Y. Domain for counters (guard-tackle/fullback-guard), and power plays.

8, 9 (D gap): Outside leg of Y or ghost Y to the sideline. The intent of this play is to outflank the defense. Quick pitches, sweeps, lead options, and reverses are plays executed in this area.

Play-Numbering System

Play description is a simple matter. Simply assign the ballcarrier's backfield numerical position with the point of attack. Descriptive terms such as option, counter, mesh, and so forth can also be used. The quarterback's actions (Diagrams 3-3 through 3-6) are also included in the call. Diagrams 3-7 and 3-8 give examples of the play-numbering system.

Quarterback actions:

- Open: Quarterback faces out to the ballcarrier with a direct handoff (Diagram 3-3).
- Roll: Quarterback pivots or reverses out to the ballcarrier with a direct handoff (Diagram 3-4).
- Sprint: Quarterback faces out at a 45-degree angle to the line of scrimmage with a direct handoff (Diagram 3-5).
- Toss: Quarterback airmails the ball to the ballcarrier (Diagram 3-6).

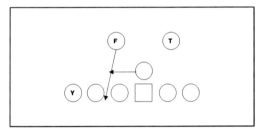

Diagram 3-3. Open

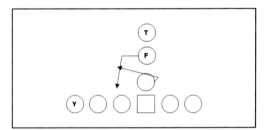

Diagram 3-4. Roll

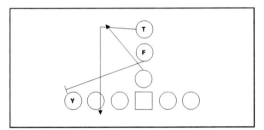

Diagram 3-5. Sprint

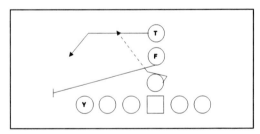

Diagram 3-6. Toss

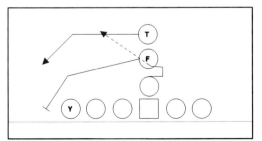

Diagram 3-7. 48 toss sweep

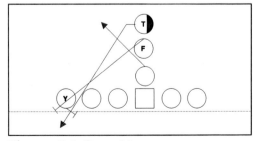

Diagram 3-8. Open 46 power

Play Description

Following is a list of play types, specific plays, and blocking schemes. Abbreviations are presented which allow for brevity in communication as well as a space-saver during film breakdown.

Option Plays

The play is numbered by the first man in the hole. Descriptive terms are used to denote the blocking scheme.

Types of Options

- Dive Option (DOP): Playside back dives into the line of scrimmage with the off back running a pitch track.
- Freeze Option (FOP): The F hits the midline and the T freezes or delays.
- Load Option (LOP): A blocker is assigned to the defender responsible for the quarterback.
- G/LO: Guard seeks to load.
- B/LO: Back seeks to load.
- Y/LO:Y seeks to load.
- LB/LO: Back seeks to load an off-the-line linebacker.
- Speed Option (SOP): The quarterback immediately takes the ball to the perimeter with a back assigned to either the primary or secondary force man.
- Trap Option (TOP): Option that comes off trap action by the F.

Dive Option Blocking

Compartmentalized option-blocking schemes:

- Double (D): Double-team on 3 or 4i technique.
- Man (M): Offensive linemen blocking man on.
- Round (R): 4i defender is left unblocked.
- Veer (V): Down or angle blocking with Y (if run to strongside) arcing on support.

  Descriptive terms used in breaking down the offense's non-option running plays:

- Belly (Be): Quarterback rolls to ballcarrier on a full flow play
- Bounce (Bo): Ballcarrier shows an off-tackle angle but bounces outside. This play is designed to go wide with no cutback option.
- Counter (Ctr): Misdirection play. Should always be called to the point of attack.

Terms to use in describing the counter-blocking scheme:

- GT: Counter with guard and tackle pulling
- FG: Counter with fullback and guard pulling
- TY: Counter with tackle and Y pulling
- GY: Counter with guard and Y pulling
- Cutback (Cb): Ballcarrier winds back underneath an unblocked lineman, or a lineman is brush blocked.
- Dive (Di): Ballcarrier takes a straight path to the point of attack. Full flow is employed with no lead back.
- Influence Trap (In/Tr): Trap with trapee influenced to step outside or run upfield.
- Isolation (Iso): The lead back blocks on the inside linebacker. The ballcarrier follows him.

Terms to use in describing isolation types:

- Bear: Pull backside guard up into isolation gap.
- Fan: Defenders at the point of attack are turned outside by offensive linemen.
- Carolina: Lead back and ballcarrier slide step before hitting the point of attack.
- Draw: Defensive linemen are invited upfield at what they perceive to be a pass play.

Terms used in describing draw types:

- Shuffle: Ballcarrier slides or crow hops to the handoff.
- Lead: Draw action with another back heading to the point of attack.
- Split Lead: Backs divide with the ballcarrier receiving the ball and countering back behind the lead back to the point of attack
- Steeler: One-back draw
- Ram: Isolation that starts out with flow away from the point of attack.
- Split Ram: Isolation that starts out with split flow and the tailback ends up behind the fullback's lead block.
- Isolation Toss (Iso/To): Iso play with toss to the ballcarrier.
- Power (Pwr): Off-tackle point of attack with down block by end-of-line offensive man, followed by a kickout block by the near back. Can be followed by a guard pull (G).
- Reverse (Rev): Play which seeks to hit wide to the side away from the initial flow. The call will denote the initial play that preceded the reverse action.
- Shovel (Shvl): Dropback action with the quarterback underhanding or passing the ball to a back behind the line of scrimmage.

- Split Dive (Sp/Di): Dive play with remaining back going opposite the ballcarrier.
- Sprint Draw (Sp/Drw): T gets the ball off full flow.
- Stretch (Str): One-back run which seeks to flank the defense.
- Stud (St): Defensive lineman at the point of attack is blocked by a receiver (or receivers).
- Sweep (Swp): Play attacking the 8 and 9 holes initiated with a direct handoff to the ballcarrier
- Toss (To): Quarterback airmails the ball to the ballcarrier. Play can be off-tackle or attacks wide at the 8 or 9 holes.
- Trap (Tr): Usually attacks the 0 and 1 holes. Ballcarrier runs 0 or 1 angle with the pulling guard blocking a down lineman.
- Wham (Whm): Used in three-back sets. The ballcarrier follows a two-back lead.
- Zone (Zn): One-back run to daylight. Cutbacks are a distinct possibility.

Alphabetical Descriptive Terms Play List

- Belly (Be)
- Counter (Ctr)
- Dive (Di)
- Draw (Dr)
- Influence Trap (In/Tr)
- Isolation (Iso)
- Isolation Toss (Iso/To)

- Lead Draw Led/Drw)
- Power (Pwr)
- Reverse (Rev)
- Shovel (Shvl)
- Split Dive (Sp/Di)
- Sprint Draw (Sp/Drw)
- Stud (St)

- Stretch (Str)
- Sweep (Swp)
- Toss (To)
- Trap (Tr)
- Wham (Whm)
- Zone (Zn)

Run-Blocking Schemes

Run types are affected by the blocking schemes used. Most blocking schemes fall into one of two categories.

- Man Schemes: This scheme, of course, involves one-on-one match-ups. Teams that subscribe to a man-on-man philosophy must have above-average personnel at the fullback and tight-end positions.
- Zone Schemes: Blockers are assigned an area rather than a particular man. Zone schemes are more effective against stunts and overloaded fronts.

When scouting the opponent's run game and game planning to defend it, nomenclature should be established to describe the various offensive-blocking schemes. This terminology is used during coach-to-coach communication as well as coach-to-player interaction during meetings, practice, or on the sideline during games. Linemen blocks will be broken down into two categories: individual run blocks and combination run blocks.

Individual Run Blocks

Base (Diagram 3-9): The base is the first block the defense should defeat. The defense cannot trade one for one. The winner of this battle has the upper hand.

Cutoff (Diagram 3-10): The cutoff is used by offensive linemen to establish an inside-out ball-side relationship on the defender. If the defender is in an inside shade, it is referred to as a shoeshine block. If the offensive man works high on the cutoff, it is referred to it as a "high wall" block.

Veer (Diagram 3-11): This scheme is commonly used to trap or read a defender.

Head-Fake Veer (Diagram 3-12): This scheme is an influence-type block. It starts out like a reach block, but turns into a down or veer technique.

Influence (Diagram 3-13): In the initial stage, this block appears to be a pass set. In reality, it serves to invite the defender upfield with a trap or wham block coming inside-out.

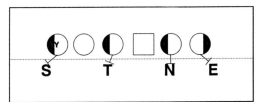
Diagram 3-9. Base

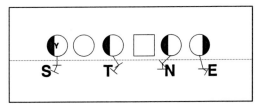
Diagram 3-10. Cutoff

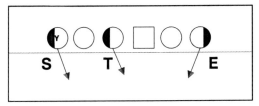
Diagram 3-11. Veer

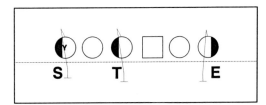
Diagram 3-12. Head-fake veer

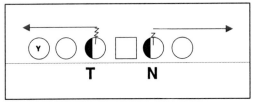
Diagram 3-13. Influence

Drive Turnout (Diagram 3-14): This block is designed to place the offensive man inside a defender with the ball in the immediate area.

Reach (Diagram 3-15): The offensive objective is to gain outside position on a defender who is aligned outside the blocker.

High Wall (Diagram 3-16): This scheme is a form of the cutoff block described previously. It seeks to gain inside position on a defensive lineman with the ball two or more gaps removed.

Slam (Diagram 3-17): This scheme is a base block at the onset followed by a veer release. This block is designed to prevent penetration by the defender while working to the second level.

Influence Veer (Diagram 3-18): Designed to invite defenders upfield by giving the illusion of a pass play and then slipping the ball inside them.

Draw (Diagram 3-19): This block seeks to take advantage of an upfield change. Vertical defensive movement is desired so the running back can exploit seams in the front.

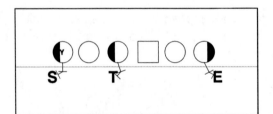

Diagram 3-14. Drive turnout

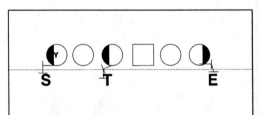

Diagram 3-15. Reach

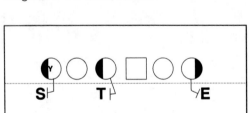

Diagram 3-16. High wall

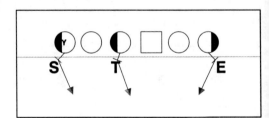

Diagram 3-17. Slam

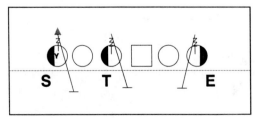

Diagram 3-18. Influence veer

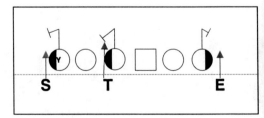

Diagram 3-19. Draw

Pull (Diagram 3-20): This block usually entails a down or turn-back block by the next offensive lineman to the pullside.

Tess (Diagram 3-21): Offensive tackle blocks support.

Gess (Diagram 3-22): Offensive guard blocks support.

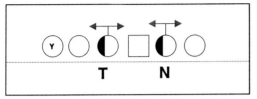

Diagram 3-20. Pull

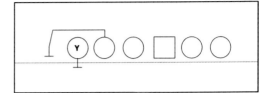

Diagram 3-21. Tess

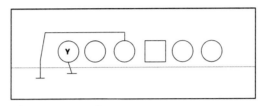

Diagram 3-22. Gess

Combination Blocks

Down-Down (Diagram 3-23): This scheme seeks to take advantage of angles.

Power Scrape (Diagram 3-24): Two-on-one combination block with the offensive man to the playside assigned to work up to the second level.

Power Slam (Diagram 3-25): Similar to the down-down scheme, this block doesn't allow penetration by the defender to be down-blocked.

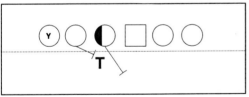

Diagram 3-23. Down-down

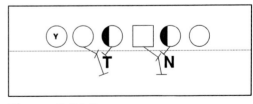

Diagram 3-24. Power scrape

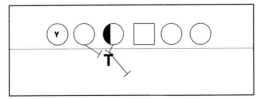

Diagram 3-25. Power slam

Scoop (Diagram 3-26): This combo block involves a jump-through by the playside lineman followed by a zone scoop by the adjoining lineman.

Power Slip (Diagram 3-27): Similar to the scoop, but in this case the playside lineman sets up the scoop by the adjoining lineman.

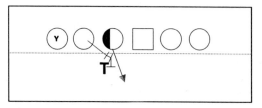

Diagram 3-26. Scoop

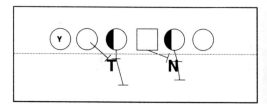

Diagram 3-27. Power slip

Fold Blocks

Fold blocks involve an angle block by one blocker and a pull by an adjoining offensive lineman. Tom and George involve an offensive guard and an offensive tackle.

Tom Block (Diagram 3-28): A Tom block has the tackle blocking down while the guard pulls around.

George Block (Diagram 3-29): A George block has the guard blocking out while the tackle folds inside.

Eat (Diagram 3-30): The eat and tater schemes involve the offensive tackle and tight end. The eat scheme is a fold between the Y and the tackle. The eat is a staple of midline option teams.

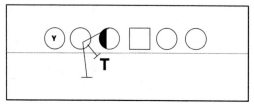

Diagram 3-28. Tom block

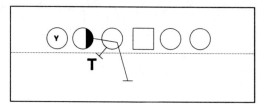

Diagram 3-29. George block

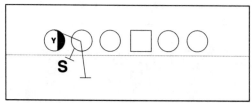

Diagram 3-30. Eat

Tater (Diagram 3-31): This scheme is also performed by the Y and tackle. In this case, the Y blocks the first defensive lineman inside while the tackle folds and pins the first defender to the outside. It is commonly used against a 5 and a 9 technique.

Charlie (Diagram 3-32): The Charlie, Clyde, squeeze, and influence schemes involve the center and guard. The Charlie scheme can be used against an outstanding nose where a power-scrape combo might be ineffective. The center has the angle on the nose.

Clyde (Diagram 3-33): The same principle of the Charlie block is applied here. The guard has the angle on a troublesome nose. For this block to be effective, however, the center should be somewhat athletic.

Squeeze (Diagram 3-34): This scheme improves the chances of getting a level-two defender blocked. The center works from the down lineman up to the second level, while the offensive lineman two men removed takes over the block.

Influence Trap (Diagram 3-35): This trap takes advantage of a defender who is working vertically to what he assumes is a pass play. His penetration makes the trap block more effective.

Wham Trap (Diagram 3-36): This trap involves an off-the-line offensive man. Commonly, the trapper will be a tight end, a back, or a receiver.

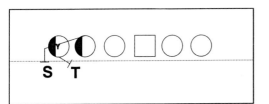

Diagram 3-31. Tater

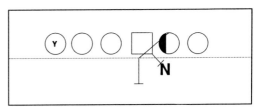

Diagram 3-32. Charlie

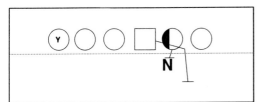

Diagram 3-33. Clyde

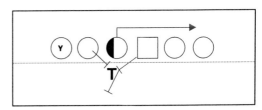

Diagram 3-34. Squeeze

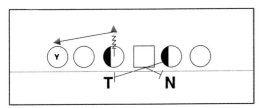

Diagram 3-35. Influence trap

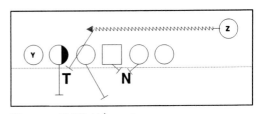

Diagram 3-36. Wham trap

X Block (Diagram 3-37): This block involves two adjoining offensive linemen cross-blocking, with the outside man going first. The play is designed to attack between the two linemen.

Back (Diagram 3-38): This block has the center filling for a pulling lineman by blocking the man lined up over the puller.

Veer Trap (Diagram 3-39): An offensive lineman who is covered by a defender with an outside shade blocks down followed by a trap block on the defender.

Sucker Trap (Diagram 3-40): This play is designed to trap a defender in an inside shade. The covered offensive lineman will release outside to the second level. This release will set up a trap block coming inside-out.

Power (Diagram 3-41): This play is used on off-tackle-type plays where the back kicks out an end-of-the-line defender.

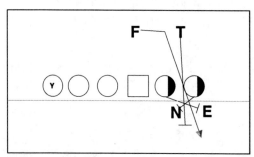

Diagram 3-37. X block

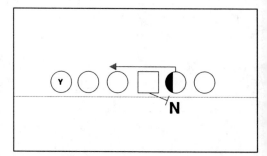

Diagram 3-38. Back

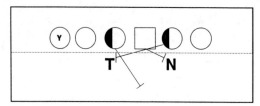

Diagram 3-39. Veer trap

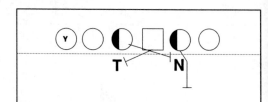

Diagram 3-40. Sucker trap

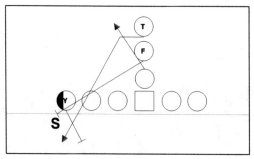

Diagram 3-41. Power

Fill (Diagram 3-42): This play is typically used on counter GT plays when the offense pulls both the guard and the tackle to playside. The back fills for the vacating linemen.

Pull Through (Diagram 3-43): Teams that don't choose to pull the tackle on counter plays can instead replace him with the back.

Bob (Diagram 3-44): This block places the back on a linebacker. It is commonly used on outside running plays.

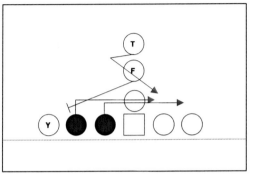

Diagram 3-42. Fill

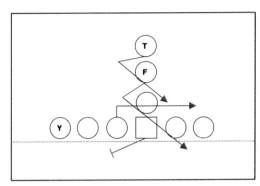

Diagram 3-43. Pull through

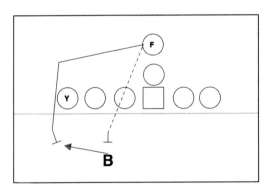

Diagram 3-44. Bob

True double-team blocks are designed to drive a defender vertically off the line of scrimmage. They don't entail an offensive man working off on another defender (see Diagrams 3-45 through 3-49).

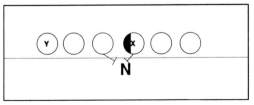

Diagram 3-45. Deal 0

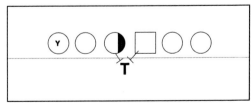

Diagram 3-46. Deal 2

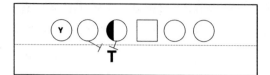

Diagram 3-47. Deal 3   Diagram 3-48. Deal 4

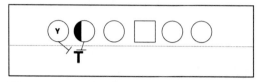

Diagram 3-49. Deal 5

Running-Back Blocks

Lead (Diagram 3-50): Typically performed on isolation-type plays when the back blocks a linebacker.

Boss (Diagram 3-51): A boss block places the back on a safety. It is similar to a Bob block in that it usually entails an outside running play.

Buc (Diagram 3-52): A buc has the back blocking the cornerback. It may involve a crossing action with a wideout on a crack, or it may be a block on a corner to the closed side of the formation.

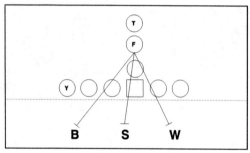

Diagram 3-50. Lead

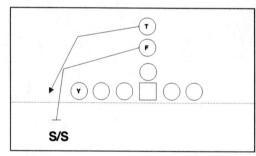

Diagram 3-51. Boss

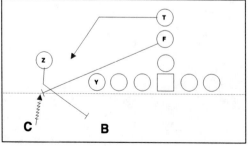

Diagram 3-52. Buc

Receiver Blocks

Arc (Diagram 3-53): Y seeks to block the force man. He will take an outside release.

Stalk (Diagram 3-54): This block is used to the same side of the formation as the receiver's alignment. The receiver seeks to gain an inside-out position on the defensive back.

Dig Out (Diagram 3-55): This block is used when the wideout tries to gain inside leverage on a defensive back or linebacker on inside running plays to his alignment side.

Cutoff (Diagram 3-56): The receiver's alignment on a cutoff block is usually on the side of the formation away from the run play. The defensive back will normally flow to a deep cutoff angle on this type of play. As a result, the receiver should really lead the defensive back to gain leverage.

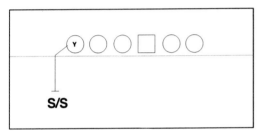

Diagram 3-53. Arc

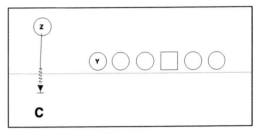

Diagram 3-54. Stalk

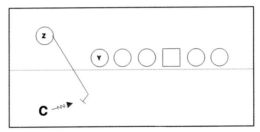

Diagram 3-55. Dig out

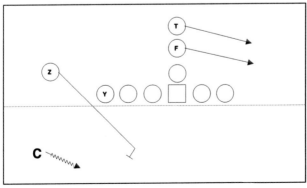

Diagram 3-56. Cutoff

Crack (Diagram 3-57): A crack occurs whenever the receiver blocks a defender inside his alignment. Usually the running play is designed to attack the corner. His target may be a defender on or off the line of scrimmage. Motion may be used in the execution of his assignment.

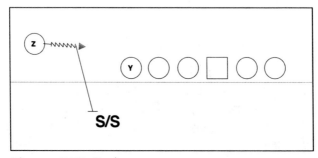

Diagram 3-57. Crack

Run-Force Basics

One of the main considerations for a defensive coach when he designs a defensive game plan is run force. He should tie in force with pass coverage. The opponent's outside runs should be analyzed and their basic blocking schemes understood. Force assignments can then be assigned and perfected. Force responsibilities should be drilled versus stalk, crack, run-off, or crossing blocks on perimeter runs. No matter the scheme used, the defense should have three elements of pursuit in place to meet the end run in its formative stage. A sound defensive scheme will have a primary force man, a cutback man, and a secondary-support defender in place to play a run-pass before he comes up.

- *Primary Force*: This defender should make the tackle, force the cutback, or drive the ball deep.

- *Cutback*: This defender will fit between the force man and the first inside-pursuit defender.

- *Secondary Support*: This defender never crosses the line of scrimmage or comes up on a run until the ball crosses the line of scrimmage, or until he replaces a defender who is being cracked. He is responsible for a run-pass. A good rule of thumb is to really focus on play-pass in a definite run situation.

Game-plan considerations and defensive calls enter into determining which player has force. Outside offensive plays should be broken down and force responsibilities given. Force calls can vary. They can be influenced by the type of coverage, offensive personnel in the game, offensive formations, and down-and-distance. Force calls usually involve three people on each side of the ball—the outside linebacker, the safety, and the corner. However, some calls might even include the defensive end. Occasionally, the end may be involved in a pre-determined "easy" force scheme or a read force. As a basic rule, the four major types of force would include cloud, sky, bronco, or easy force schemes.

The defensive coordinator should plan for run force whether it is a zone, man, or blitz situation. Communication is a must. Demand that defenders communicate force calls verbally and visually on each play. Outside linebackers can make a "you" or "me" call to the safety on every play. Should the outside linebacker be on an upfield stunt, he will give the safety a "me" call. If the end has force, he will give a "me" call to the safety. If the outside linebacker isn't on an outside stunt or is on an inside stunt, he will give the safety a "you" call. A "you" call informs the safety that he (the safety) has force. A "me" call tags the outside linebacker as the force man. Option responsibilities should be clearly defined and understood. No matter the defensive call, someone must be assigned to the dive, quarterback, pitch, and play-pass.

Receiver Splits

A very important question that needs to be answered is the opponent's basic split rules for the wideouts. The width of a receiver often tips off offensive intentions. A reduced split may signal a crack or outside pass route. A wide split may signal an inside run or an inside pass route. With the ball in the middle of the field, use the top of the numbers as a reference point. Should the receiver be two yards outside the numbers, he is referred to as a numbers +2 receiver. Should he be two yards inside the numbers, tag him as a numbers -2 receiver. Plus signifies going away from the ball and minus means toward the ball. If the ball is on or near the hash, use the opposite hash as the reference point. A receiver five yards outside the hash is a hash +5 wideout. Conversely, a receiver five yards inside the hash is a hash -5 receiver. Using this system allows you to get a feel for the play.

Cracks, by wideouts, can cause a change in force pre-snap as well as post-snap. Sound scouting techniques and game planning techniques can determine the best force by formation and/or receiver alignments. Receiver splits will usually determine the type of force desired. A minus split will usually trigger a cloud call. The corner would have pitch/force responsibilities. A sky call may be necessitated should the receiver take a plus split. With a sky call, the safety would have pitch/force. Bronco (outside linebacker) force assigns pitch/force to the linebacker. Film breakdown may indicate a check to Bronco force versus a minus split. To be sound defensively, primary force, cutback, and secondary support responsibilities should be understood and communicated for each play.

Run Breakdowns

The following variables should be scouted and charted for each opponent. This information will allow the coach to gain a handle on the opponent's running game, which will lead to the construction of an effective game plan to defeat their running game.

Formations

Break down and develop a hit chart for each formation. Doing so will help cheat the defense to take away their best running plays for each formation.

Down-and-Distance

Finding favorite run plays by down-and-distance allows the defensive coordinator to play percentages.

Hash

Hash consideration in game planning depends upon the level of play. Pro hashes, which are 70' 9", make a wideside or shortside distinction almost non-existent. College hashes, which are 60' from the sideline, do break the field into short and wide sides. High school hashes are located at 53' 4", which basically divides the field into thirds. If the ball is on a hash, the offense can either work to the third of the field or to the two thirds of the field that constitute the wideside. Hash marks should also be used to scout the split of wideouts. Game planning should seek to decipher the rhyme and reason for receiver splits. A commonly used measure is to denote a receiver's split through the use of a plus (+) or minus (-) designation, as previously discussed in this chapter.

Field Zone

Running plays should be categorized by field zone. Scouting your opponent will reveal their favorite run plays by field position.

Inside Runs

These plays should be broken down and blocking schemes studied. These plays should be further divided into strongside and weakside runs.

Outside Runs

How does the opponent block force? Do they stalk, run off, crack, or cross block? Force will be designed from this information.

Individual Blocks

These blocks should be charted to determine how the opponent will attack individual defenders. Break them down into the following packages:

- Line blocks
- Back blocks
- Receiver blocks
- Line-combination blocks
- Receiver-combination blocks

4

Defending the Passing Game

uccessful pass defense epitomizes the team concept at its best. Successful pass defense includes contributions from all parts of the defense. Each part is interdependent. The line must rush and apply pressure. The secondary and linebackers must cover. Each unit feeds off the other units. To be successful in the secondary, the line must pressure and harass the quarterback and not allow him to hold the ball and wait for the receiver to come open. Conversely, the secondary can force the quarterback to hold the ball longer with good coverage, which allows the rushers to get to him. Simply stated, the more effective the rush, the better the coverage (and the more effective the coverage, the better the rush). To the layman, a defensive lineman is judged by his sack total. Even though a sack is the ultimate goal of every rusher, he doesn't necessarily have to sack the quarterback to be effective. If a lineman tips the ball, hurries the pass, obstructs the quarterback's view, or flushes the quarterback, he has done his job.

The first priority in game planning for pass defense is the pass rush. One of the first questions to be asked is: can the defense get pressure with a base rush? If the answer is yes, the defense has a good start in defending the opponent's pass game. If the defense is unable to apply pressure with the front, it will have to blitz to apply pressure. Obviously, blitzing opens up big play potential for the offense. However, blitzing is highly beneficial when it is judiciously used. Most coaches don't want to go into a game and have to blitz to get pressure. A base rush that pressures the quarterback allows the defense to be in charge. Teams that are consistently able to apply pressure with a vanilla rush scheme have speed and quickness on the corners and power and strength inside.

Film study and analysis will allow the coaches to distinguish the opponent's passing game philosophy. Do they gravitate toward a particular style of passing game? Do they incorporate the full gamut? Do they use the whole arsenal—including three-step, five-step, and seven-step drops? Does the opponent use sprint, dash, play-action, boots, and counter boots? How skillful are they with their screen-and-draw game? Regardless which components they use, they will not be proficient in all. It is the coaches' job to focus on stopping what they do best. Is the opponent's pass offense simple or complex? Do they force the defense to cover the entire field and each position? Will they allow the defense to zero in on a particular player or players, or does everyone get a touch? Film study will reveal formational tendencies as well as wideside/shortside preferences. Questions to be answered from film study include:

- Does the offense prefer combo routes where two or three receivers execute the route?
- Does the offense prefer one-receiver routes?
- Does the offense run mirrored routes from balanced formations?
- Does the offense motion or shift to get a particular defensive shell or match-up?
- Do splits offer a tip-off on routes?

This chapter deals with all aspects of a well-rounded passing game. Included will be an established nomenclature to describe protections, different pass actions, routes, motion, screens, and draws. Also included will be advice on how to effectively break down offensive positions to gain an edge in defending the pass game. The chapter will conclude with defensive strategies and their inherent strengths and weaknesses. Before getting into the nuts and bolts of pass offense, some universal truths about the passing game should be identified. These statements hold true no matter the opponent's passing-game philosophy. Offenses will:

- Try to hit X, Y, or Z on deep routes early to help loosen coverage.
- Try to hit post and up routes if the defense crowds the receivers.
- Try to complete outs, comebacks, hitches, and slants if the defense is loose.
- Try to complete passes wide to outside receivers, which opens up inside routes.
- Try to throw deep versus blitzes.
- Periodically max protect on obvious passing downs.
- Send a man deep with a short route behind it.
- Send a man inside with another receiver running outside.

Pass Protection

The trademark of a competent offensive coach is that he begins with pass protection when developing pass plays. How many offensive coaches at clinics draw up elaborate patterns but neglect the most important element of a pass play: the protection? Protection makes or breaks an offense's passing game. The effectiveness of the protection scheme limits or expands the passing-game package. Bill Walsh states that a fully functional protection scheme:

- Neutralizes the rush.

- Allows the offense to throw hot.

- Gets five receivers out.

- Has the ability to max protect.

- Uses checkdowns or dump-offs to backs.

- Is able to block all fronts without drastic week-to-week change-ups.

- Is able to pass block with man, zone, or combination schemes.

- Is adaptable to the different depths of quarterback drops.

- Is flexible enough to double-team a particular pass rusher.

As was shown in Chapter 3 with the running game, a working nomenclature for the passing game will be established. Included will be pass actions, defensive counter measures, protections, routes, screens, and draws (even though a draw play is a run, it seeks to take advantage of the pass rush). This chapter will help defend the opponent's pass game with general and specific advice—including adjustments, personnel breakdowns, underneath coverage, coverage decisions, and scouting receiver splits.

Pass Actions

60 Series (Full Sprint/Half Roll)

The quarterback will full sprint or half roll. 61 signals the quarterback half rolled to the open side behind both backs. A 62 denotes a pull-up to the closed or strongside. A full sprint to the closed side with a two-back lead is called 68. 69 signals that both backs and the quarterback attacked the corner to the open side. 66 communicates that the backs divided with a quarterback pull-up to the closed side and a 67 call signals the quarterback pulled up, with backs dividing, to the open side (Diagrams 4-1 through 4-6).

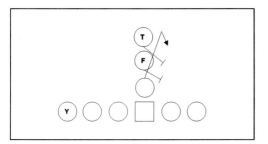
Diagram 4-1. 61

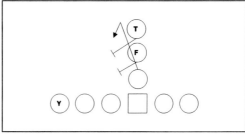
Diagram 4-2. 62

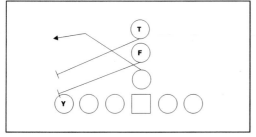
Diagram 4-3. 68

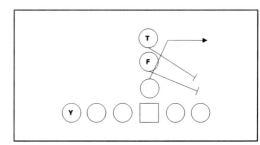
Diagram 4-4. 69

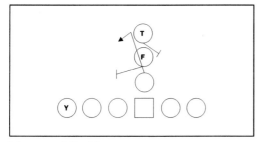
Diagram 4-5. 66

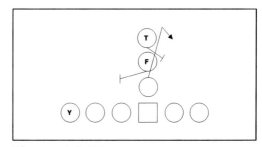
Diagram 4-6. 67

Full Sprint /Half Roll

Teams that prefer this type of pass action usually have a mobile athletic passer. In many cases, he may not be as tall or possess the arm strength of a pure dropback passer. One of the first things to be discerned in game planning is in what order does the offense approach this play? Is the quarterback thinking run or pass as the first option? In other words, does the quarterback look to run the ball, and is he coached to throw if the run isn't there, or is he schooled to throw the ball but run if the pass is covered? Close observation of the quarterback's track can disclose the intentions of the quarterback. If his aim point on the sprint is seven to nine yards deep and wider than off-tackle, he is thinking run first. If his aim point is six to seven yards deep and directly behind the offensive tackle, he is thinking pass first and run second. Teams that full sprint have difficulty throwing back away from the flow. Teams that half sprint leave open the possibility of backside routes.

Benefits of a sprint passing attack include:

- Fewer defenders in the quarterback's face, which creates a clutter-free throw lane.
- Reduces the number of potential blitzers.
- The quarterback is moving toward potential receivers.
- Shortens the distance of the throw.
- If the hole player is fast flowing, the backside post is open.
- The quarterback reads the corner. If the corner stays back, he simply tosses to a receiver in front of the corner. If the corner comes up, he will throw it over his head.
- It stretches the perimeter defense.
- The quarterback learns a simple deep-to-short-to-run progression. It creates vertical and horizontal stretch in a small area.
- Limits turnovers.
- Pass protection is simplified.

Many teams with inferior pass-protection skills can be successful with turnback protection on sprint action. This passing style can be used to avoid inside pressure or blitzing linebackers. Sprint-pass plays simply run away from inside pressure. Line games are futile against this pass action. Defensive linemen are at a disadvantage because offensive linemen usually have the benefit of angles with turnback protection. Even though this type of passing style has many advantages, it does have some limitations. The biggest drawback is that this pass action usually attacks only one side of the formation or field. It can only attack in a limited area. It is hard to get backs involved in the pass game because they are usually blocking. One half of the formation is usually wasted. However, care must be taken that a strong-armed quarterback not hurt the defense with a possible post-wheel route away from the sprint.

Defensive adjustments to combat the sprint game would include bringing pressure from outside-in from the wideside of the field and/or to the quarterback's throwing arm. Bringing outside pressure along with running one or more linebackers through gaps can be highly effective. Inserting a linebacker or linebackers can result in the defense outnumbering blockers at the point of attack. These linebackers are able to discourage the run-first mentality, and they also exert added pressure on a pass-first scenario. Linebackers not assigned to run through will sling or work the coverage to the sprintside. These linebackers will enable the defense to outnumber receivers to the playside. Roll coverage is highly effective against teams that subscribe to the sprint game. Some defenses will kick the coverage to the sprint and cover the backside with a defender who is responsible for two-thirds of the field.

Many sprint teams choose to pass protect one of two ways. Some teams elect to reach protect toward the sprint. Other teams will turnback protect on sprint passes. Defensive linemen should work off the edge of reach blocks. They basically play it like a run-game reach block. Defensive linemen, when faced with turnback protection, should use a "play-the-piano" technique. Rather than penetrate and allow the blocker the advantage of position, defensive linemen should try to crossface the initial block and turn up the first available seam to the quarterback. The worst thing a rusher can do is to allow the blocker to lock on his playside shoulder and ride him upfield.

Turnback protection has linemen blocking their backside gap with both backs attacking the corner of the defense. The fullback takes the first threat off the offensive tackle's hip and the tailback takes the first threat off the fullback's outside hip (Diagram 4-7).

Turnback protection with a guard pulling is similar to the protection scheme illustrated in Diagram 4-7, except it is executed in a one-back set. The onside guard pulls and pins the first man outside the tackle's block. In essence, he replaces the lead back in the two-back sprint. The single back will block the first thing that shows off the guard's hip (Diagram 4-8).

Another favorite blocking scheme has offensive linemen reaching the first man to the sprintside instead of turning back. Some teams will insert a back into the backside C gap to shore up the quarterback's backside (Diagram 4-9).

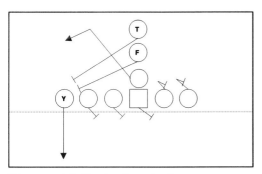

Diagram 4-7. Turnback protection

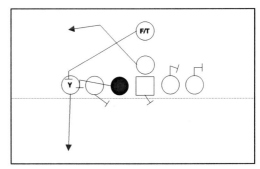

Diagram 4-8. Turnback protection with a guard pulling

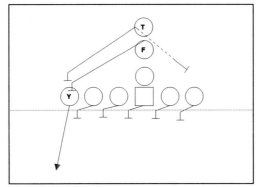

Diagram 4-9. Full reach protection

100 Series (Play-Action)

This passing scheme is tailored to take advantage of defensive reactions to a pass that is designed to look like a run. The backfield will fake a running play and the quarterback sets up behind the backfield action within the tackle box. After selling the fake, backs can have a blocking assignment or a release, depending upon the play design. If the fake is to the closed side with Y dragging, it is referred to as fire action (Diagram 4-10). Flow action involves a run fake to the closed side with Y vertical (Diagram 4-11). Flood action has both backs faking to the open side with leakage by one or both backs and Y blocking or releasing to the closed side (Diagram 4-12).

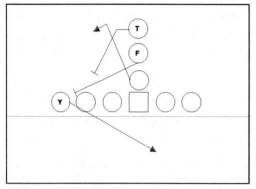

Diagram 4-10. Fire action

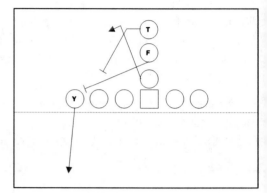

Diagram 4-11. Flow action

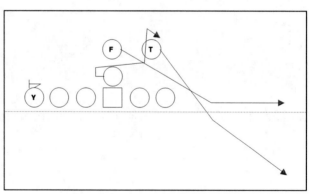

Diagram 4-12. Flood action

Play-action schemes have the quarterback throwing the ball into vacated areas after a run fake. Play-action passes usually are designed to be placed behind the linebackers and in front of the defensive backs. Another tactic quarterbacks use is to throw over the top of the coverage after a run fake. Even though this scheme is highly effective, it does have some major flaws or drawbacks. Play-action passes should not be effective on obvious passing downs. Its strength is its use on rundowns, such as early downs and normal down-and-distance situations when runs are more believable. Third-and-short or on the goal line are prime times for running teams to execute play-action. However, the best play-action down might be first-and-10. The pass will usually come off the offense's best running play. However, if a play-action pass fails on first down, the offensive play caller will be faced with second-and-long—which may be the best defensive down in football. Defensive scouting reports should reveal how much passing the opponent does on first down. Another drawback of play-action passes is that they are not as effective if the offense is behind on the scoreboard.

Play-action pass protections are predicted on run fakes. Offensive linemen will make it appear as if they are executing a run block. They will fire out and contact defenders in their assigned area. However, because the play is a pass instead of run there are tip-offs to a well-schooled defense that the play is a pass. The play will not sound like a run. One coach has made the point that his defensive backs who were not actively involved in a particular scrimmage could close their eyes and discern—through sound waves—if the play was a run or pass. Play-action passes will not sound like a run. Another clue that the play isn't actually a run is that offensive linemen will not be downfield on the play. High offensive helmets also offer clues that the play is a pass. Probably the best tip-off of all is uncovered offensive linemen will show pass even though, from all appearances, a run has been called.

The defense should identify play-action passes with the running action by the backs. For example, Diagram 4-13 shows a play-action pass off isolation action. F and T can leak out if their assigned defenders drop.

Diagram 4-14 illustrates protection similar to sprint turnback protection. Running backs block just like they do on sprint action. The only difference is they do it from level 1 (down-the-line) action.

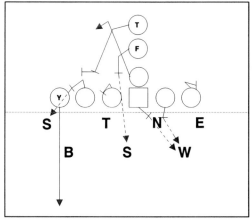

Diagram 4-13. 144 play pass

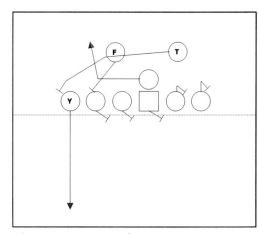

Diagram 4-14. 133 play pass

200 Series (Play-Action)

The back(s) fakes a running play with the quarterback faking and rolling out behind the fake and pressuring the corner. 200 passes have the quarterback outside the tackle box. In many cases, the quarterback has a run or throw option (Diagram 4-15).

300 Series (Play-Action)

300 action has the quarterback going opposite the run fake. If backs full flow, the pass is referred to as a bootleg. If the backs divide, the action is referred to as a counter boot. Many times, the counter boot is a run or pass option. Identify the call with whoever pulls (Diagram 4-16).

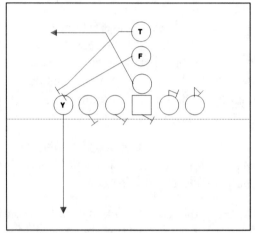

Diagram 4-15. 246 play pass

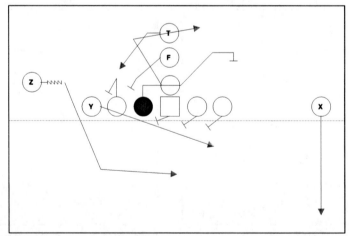

Diagram 4-16. 346 bootleg G

Types of Boots and Counter Boots (Diagrams 4-17 through 4-22)

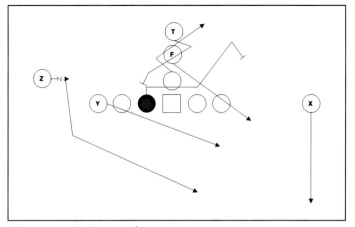

Diagram 4-17. Counter boot

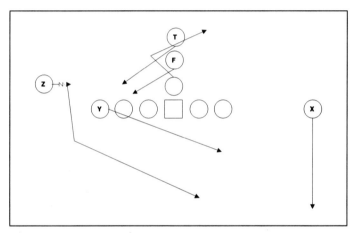

Diagram 4-18. Power boot

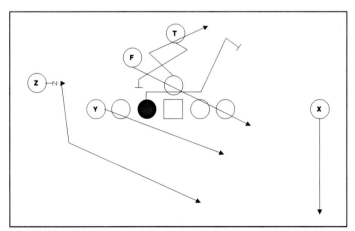

Diagram 4-19. Packer counter boot

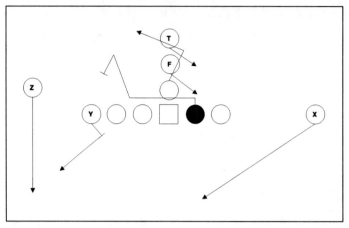

Diagram 4-20. Belly boot

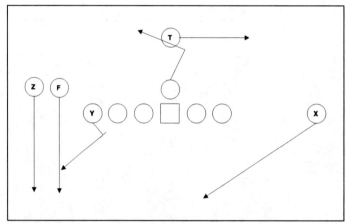

Diagram 4-21. Toss counter boot

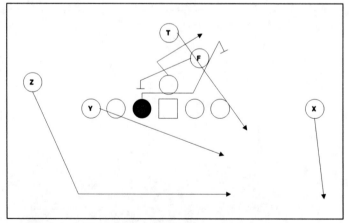

Diagram 4-22. Swap counter boot

400 Series (Play-Action)

This series has the running back throwing the pass off of run action. Diagram 4-23 illustrates a back throwing a play-action after receiving a toss from the quarterback.

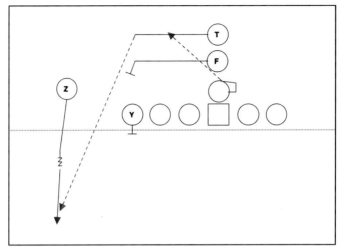

Diagram 4-23. 448 halfback pass

500 Series (Screen Passes)

The first digit denotes screen. The second digit identifies the back or receiver. If the screen is to the back, give the number of his position. If the recipient is a receiver, use their designation (X, Y, Z, S, R, etc.). The third digit gives the point of attack. Since screens are attempted behind the line of scrimmage, list the point of attack using run holes. Also identify the screen with descriptive terms such as slip, quick, read, flare, rocket, middle, double, throwback, bubble, and checkdown screens.

Screen Categories (Diagrams 4-24 through 4-33)

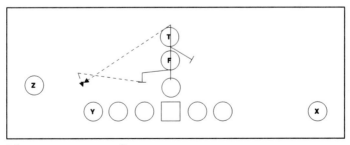

Diagram 4-24. 538 slip

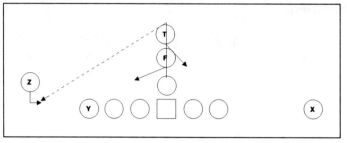

Diagram 4-25. 5Z8 quick

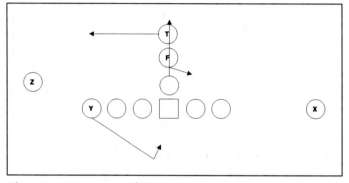

Diagram 4-26. 548 read

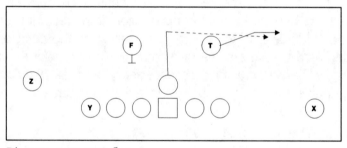

Diagram 4-27. 559 flare

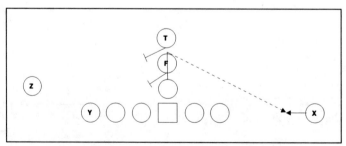

Diagram 4-28. 5X9 rocket

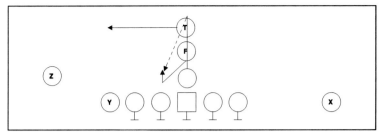

Diagram 4-29. 532 middle

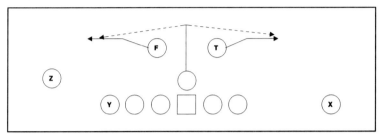

Diagram 4-30. 528 double

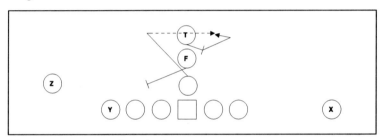

Diagram 4-31. 549 throwback

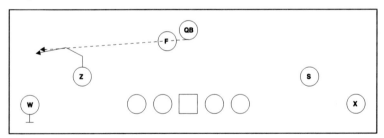

Diagram 4-32. 5Z8 bubble

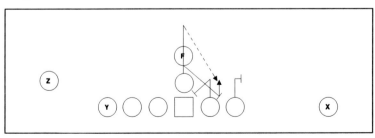

Diagram 4-33. 533 checkdown

600 Series (Dash Drop)

A highly effective type of pass drop is the moving pocket. This action involves the quarterback dropping straight back before he rolls to one side of the formation. This system affords the linemen the advantage of angles. By moving the pocket, the quarterback can run away from pressure. The dash series has many of the same advantages as the sprint series.

600 Series (Diagrams 4-34 through 4-39)

- 631–three-step dash to open side
- 632–three-step dash to closed side
- 651–five-step dash to open side
- 652–five-step dash to closed side
- 671–seven-step dash to open side
- 672–seven-step dash to closed side

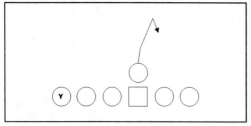

Diagram 4-34. 631

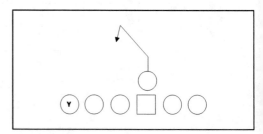

Diagram 4-35. 632

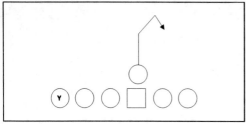

Diagram 4-36. 651

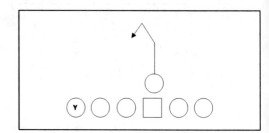

Diagram 4-37. 652

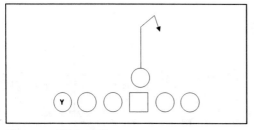

Diagram 4-38. 671

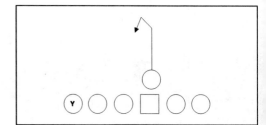

Diagram 4-39. 672

700 Series (Quarterback Sprint)

The quarterback sprints away from backfield flow with no run fake involved. It is assumed the guard will pull to block contain. Should someone other than the guard pull, it should be noted. If no one pulls, refer to it as "naked" (Diagram 4-40).

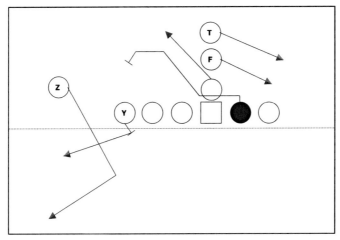

Diagram 4-40. 749

830 Series (Three Step Drop)

Level-3 action (quarterback straight back), where the quarterback drops a maximum of three steps, is called 830 action. 8 denotes dropback action and 3 signals a three-step drop.

830 Series (Diagrams 4-41 through 4-43)

- 830–three-step drop with backs on a divide
- 831–three-step drop with both backs to the open side
- 832–three-step drop with both backs to the closed side

The quarterback may take only one or two steps, but the action falls into the 830 category. This pass series is out of the quarterback's hand quickly. Most offenses want to get the ball snapped and thrown in 0.7 seconds. Three-step drops are highly effective when receivers are given cushion. Soft coverages are vulnerable to quick passes. Many teams audible to the three-step game to negate pressure defenses. Three-step passing attacks seek to throw in front of defenders or over the top. Not too many intermediate routes tend to be involved. A high completion rate is expected. Three-step-drop attacks are defined as "ball-control" offenses. Offenses, with limited talent, can be successful with this type of passing game. The quick passing game makes

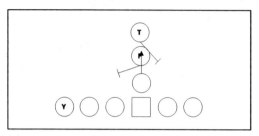

Diagram 4-41. 830

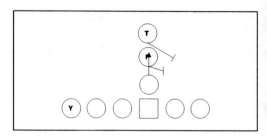

Diagram 4-42. 831

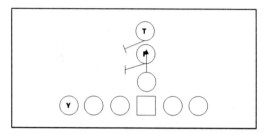

Diagram 4-43. 832

liberal use of streaks, quicks, and slant routes. Bill Walsh states that the slant is the best route in football. It serves the effectiveness of quick routes if the stem of the route looks like a go route.

Three-step routes are timing oriented. The quarterback and receiver must be on the same page. Most receivers will run a prescribed number of steps or work to a particular landmark, and then work back to the ball. Most three-step routes are run in a six-yard area. A quick pass game is a good call if the play caller has the luxury of playing a defense with definite coverage tendencies by down-and-distance or formation. The quick pass game is a great antidote for blitzing defenses. A three-step drop can incorporate an eight-man protection scheme. Passes can be easily thrown to either the wide or short side. Another distinct advantage of the quick game is that offensive linemen don't have to be accomplished pass protectors. The quick game is a great alternative if pass-protection skills are lacking. Quick-game protection is an aggressive scheme, which can employ man or zone principles. Offensive linemen may fire out low to get the defense's hands down. Offenses can easily check into or check out of the quick route.

Film study will reveal if and how the opponent audibles to the quick game if faced with a pressure defense. A common defensive tactic when facing the quick game is to disrupt the route. Since most three-step routes are predicated on timing, it would serve the defense to disrupt that timing. Getting hands on the receiver will spoil the timing of the route. A five-under, two-deep zone or man scheme disrupts the quick game. A five-under, two-deep concept allows the defense to get a bang on receivers (Diagram 4-44). Drop loaded coverages are also highly effective. Diagram 4-45 shows a seven-to-five cover-men-to-receiver ratio.

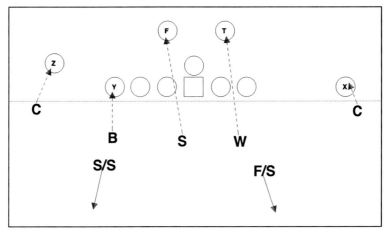

Diagram 4-44. Five-under, two-deep

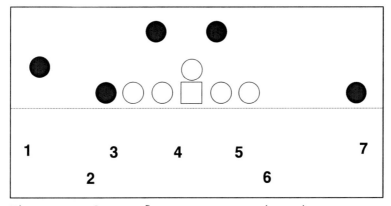

Diagram 4-45. Seven-to-five cover-men-to-receiver ratio

Corners, as a basic technique, should be taught on their initial backpedal to key the three-step drop. Corners should play games with vertical cushion on wideouts. Additionally, cornerbacks should be sure tacklers. A five-yard reception could turn into a big gainer should a corner miss a tackle. Sure tackles would limit yards after the catch. On a thrown ball, the corner should go through the receiver's outside shoulder to force the receiver back inside where he has help. Inside defenders should fly inside out to the ball. That a big hit and/or a turnover will be the result is a distinct possibility.

Because it is so hard to pressure the quarterback on a three-step throw, it might be advisable to load up the coverage. If pressure is desired, it is best to bring it through A gap or off the corner. Pressure off the corner can place defenders in the outside throw lanes. Another effective tactic would involve getting an inside push with interior linemen. Defenders should attack the blocker with a two-hand power move. Not enough time exists for finesse moves. Bull rushes or push-pull moves are more desirable. Rips should be avoided, since this will make it difficult for the rusher to get his hands up. After rushers get a push, they should then get their hands up. Delayed twists and lane exchanges are probably a waste of time. Strategically, it is always a good idea to make an offense go the long way. It is especially effective against the three-step pass game because they will have to nickel and dime their way downfield.

850 Series (Five Step Drop) (Diagrams 4-46 through 4-48)

The quarterback takes a five-step drop.

- 850–Five-step drop with backs on a divide
- 851–Five-step drop with both backs to open side
- 852–Five-step drop with both backs to closed side

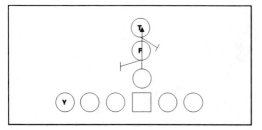

Diagram 4-46. 850

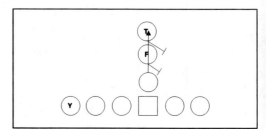

Diagram 4-47. 851

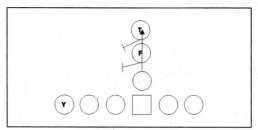

Diagram 4-48. 852

The five-step drop is the staple of the West Coast offense. It is a timing-oriented package. This scheme is characterized by short passes to wideouts and backs. The ball comes out in around 1.2 seconds. Attacking underneath coverage, specifically linebackers, is a priority. It has also been commonly referred to as a possession passing game. It has also been criticized as a dink-and-dunk, nickel-and-dime offense. History, however, has proved it to be a very successful approach. The West Coast offense makes effective use of crossing routes, timing, picks, and middle passes to the tight end. Success hinges on discipline and great execution. Quarterbacks seek to attack vertical and horizontal seams or dead areas in zones. Many passes are considered to be similar to a long handoff. The five-step approach has many of the same advantages as the three-step scheme. Since the ball is launched so quickly, it is difficult to apply delayed pressure. Lane exchanges may be futile if the ball is thrown on time. Unlike the three-step game, more and varied routes are available. Routes that attack zone seams are highly effective. Should a team elect to play man coverage, they will be faced with pick routes and crossing routes where the receiver will seek to outrun the defender horizontally. Defensive linemen simply getting a push and then throwing their hands up is not as effective against a five-step drop as it is against a three-step drop. Linemen should also be aware that the rush angle is sharper for a five-step drop than a seven-step drop. Edge players can't get as wide against a five-step quarterback as they can against a seven-step dropper.

870 Series (Seven-Step Drop) (Diagrams 4-49 through 4-51)

The quarterback takes a seven-step drop

- 870–Seven-step drop with both backs on a divide
- 871–Seven-step drop with both backs to the open side
- 872–Seven-step drop with both backs to closed side

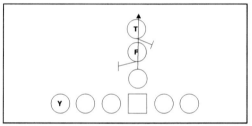
Diagram 4-49. 870

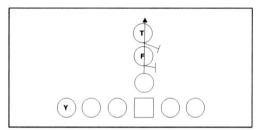
Diagram 4-50. 871

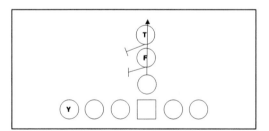
Diagram 4-51. 872

Quarterbacks who use the seven-step drop usually possess good arm strength. They also tend to be taller and, in many cases, less athletic than quarterbacks who use shorter types of drops. Teams that employ a seven-step drop must possess an offensive line, which is highly effective in pass protection. The quarterback will hold the ball longer than a three- or five-step drop. The seven-step-drop system is better able to attack downfield. Routes designed for seven-step drops tend to take longer to develop.

Double moves and crossfield routes are very effective in this scheme. Routes are predicated on a progression, which must be read by the quarterback. Teams that subscribe to the seven-step scheme effectively use the vertical pass game. These teams are able to isolate one or more receivers downfield. Speed receivers are highly desirable in this scheme. Seven-step-drop routes allow receivers to take advantage of mismatches. Receivers also have time to gain separation and exploit space. A seven-step drop allows the tight end and backs to free themselves in the intermediate areas. The quarterback's drop and delivery should be exact. The ball should be thrown in 1.5 seconds. A seven-step drop will take the quarterback approximately 10 yards off the line of scrimmage. The quarterback should be able to drop, set, and deliver the ball on time. Teams that use a seven-step pass game are obviously more proficient throwing the ball than other types of pass actions (i.e., three-step drops or sprint passes).

Unlike defending quick or sprint-type passes, defenses can use a wide variety of defensive tactics to attack the seven-step game. Pass rush moves can involve more finesse. Lane exchanges, snap exchanges, or delayed exchanges, are highly effective versus seven-step systems, whereas they are practically useless against three-step or sprint schemes. When game planning to play a seven-step quarterback, the defensive coordinator can attack specific offensive linemen and/or the protection scheme. Multiple coverages with good disguise are needed when facing a good seven-step passing scheme. Pressure is tough to apply against sprint or quick passes, however, seven-step protections can be affected by pressure packages. Zone blitzes, which can be negated by quick or sprint passes, can be highly effective against the seven-step system.

Protection Schemes

Dropback pass-protection schemes vary from team to team. Film study will reveal the opponent's preferred methods. Pass protections can be broken down into two-back and one-back schemes. It is impossible to list all the possible protection schemes. Protection schemes are limited only by the offensive coordinator's imagination. Included will be some of the more popular schemes.

Two-Back Schemes

Rip/Liz Protection (Diagrams 4-52 and 4-53)

Rip has the offensive linemen sliding to their right with backs protecting away from the slide. Sliding left is called Liz.

Big on Big (Diagrams 4-54 and 4-55)

Offensive linemen on defensive linemen (big-on-big) is a great way for offenses to

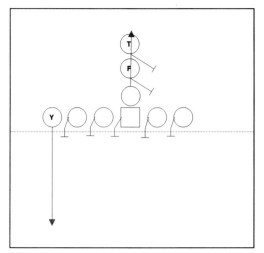

Diagram 4-52. Rip protection

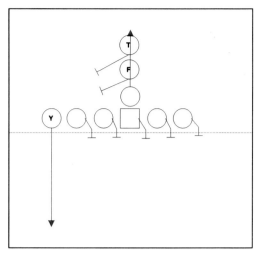

Diagram 4-53. Liz protection

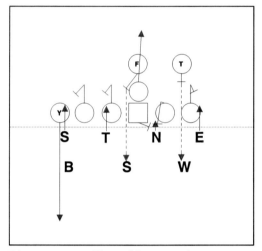

Diagram 4-54. Big-on-big protection

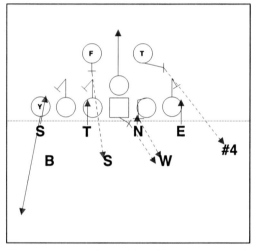

Diagram 4-55. Big-on-big with T on #4 weak

avoid size mismatches. Backs match up with linebackers. Diagram 4-55 shows a big-on-big concept with the center and weak guard reading W and placing T on #4 weak.

Diamond Protection (Diagram 4-56)

Diamond is an eight-man protection. Diamond allows for maximum protection should a blitz occur. This eight-man blitz protection limits the pattern to two receivers. However, these two receivers have an opportunity to make a big play because they should have time to get deep or make a double move, which is highly dangerous to blitz coverages if the quarterback has time to throw. If their assigned man drops, each eligible receiver can release.

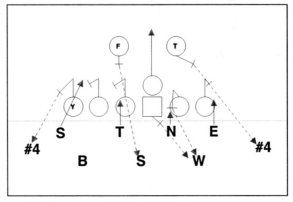

Diagram 4-56. Diamond protection

One-Back Schemes

- Diagram 4-57 has Y releasing in a six-man protection. The single back dual- or double-reads from #1 to #2 inside out to Y's side. If both come, the quarterback throws hot.

- Diagram 4-58 has Y on a release in a six-man protection. The back again duals or double-reads from #1 to #2 inside out to the open end.

- Diagram 4-59 has Y on a pass release with a six-man protection. Uncovered linemen dual- or double-read with the back checking #4 strong.

- Diagram 4-60 has a scheme that is similar to the protection in Diagram 4-59. All assignments are the same except the back checks #4 weak.

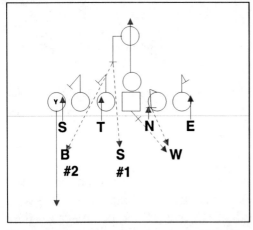

Diagram 4-57. Six-man protection with back dual read inside

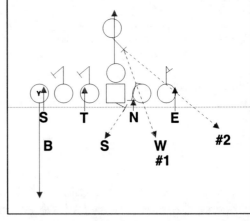

Diagram 4-58. Six-man protection with back dual read to open side

- Diagram 4-61 has a big-on-big philosophy with the back dualing on the most dangerous inside linebacker.

- One-back rip protection has slide protection, which is similar to the previously described two-back protection. The only difference is one back (instead of two) fills away from the slide. The back will take the first man to show off the tackle's hip (Diagram 4-62).

- Diagram 4-63 illustrates a seven-man scheme. The single back eyeballs the linebacker to the strongside. Y has #4 strong with the center and weak guard keying the weakside linebacker.

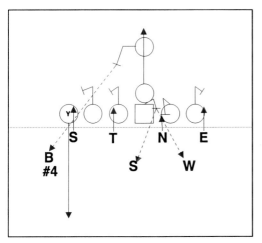

Diagram 4-59. Six-man protection with back read #4 strong

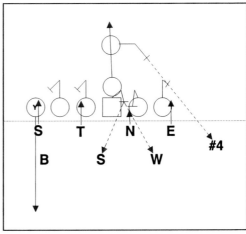

Diagram 4-60. Six-man protection with back read #4 weak

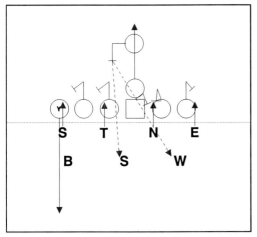

Diagram 4-61. Six-man protection with back dual-read inside linebackers

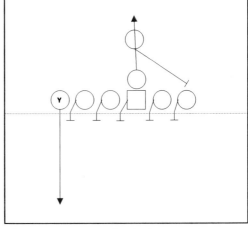

Diagram 4-62. One-back rip protection

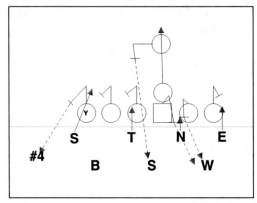

Diagram 4-63. Seven-man protection with back read inside linebacker

Routes

This section will illustrate basic pass routes used in an offense's passing game.

Three-Step Route Package

- *Receiver Quick-Game Routes* (Diagrams 4-64 through 4-73)
- *Y Quick-Game Routes* (Diagrams 4-74 through 4-77)
- *Back Quick-Game Routes* (Diagrams 4-78 through 4-80)

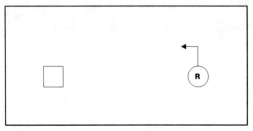

Diagram 4-64. Quick screen

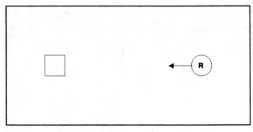

Diagram 4-65. Rocket screen

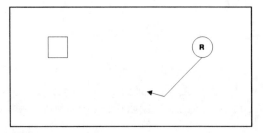

Diagram 4-66. Stop

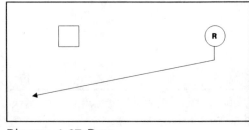

Diagram 4-67. Drag

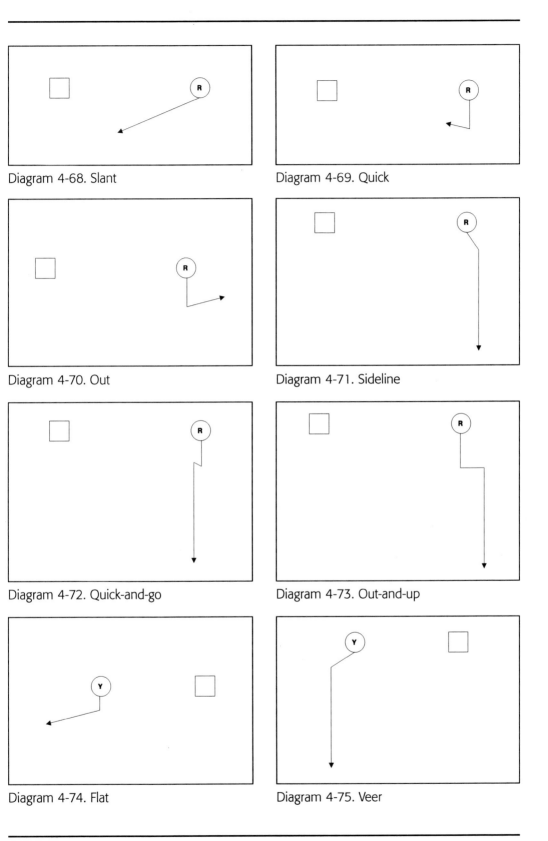

Diagram 4-68. Slant

Diagram 4-69. Quick

Diagram 4-70. Out

Diagram 4-71. Sideline

Diagram 4-72. Quick-and-go

Diagram 4-73. Out-and-up

Diagram 4-74. Flat

Diagram 4-75. Veer

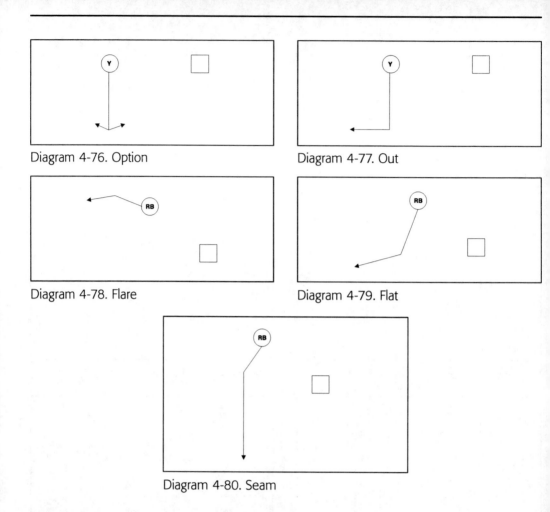

Diagram 4-76. Option

Diagram 4-77. Out

Diagram 4-78. Flare

Diagram 4-79. Flat

Diagram 4-80. Seam

Intermediate- and Deep-Route Package

These routes are applicable to either five- or seven-step drops.

- Receiver intermediate and deep routes (Diagrams 4-81 through 4-92)
- Y intermediate and deep routes (Diagrams 4-93 through 4-108)
- Back intermediate and deep routes (Diagrams 4-109 through 4-120)

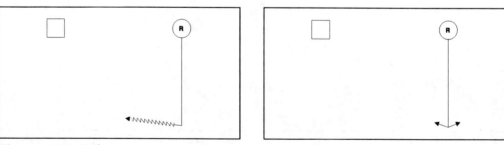

Diagram 4-81. Curl

Diagram 4-82. Hook

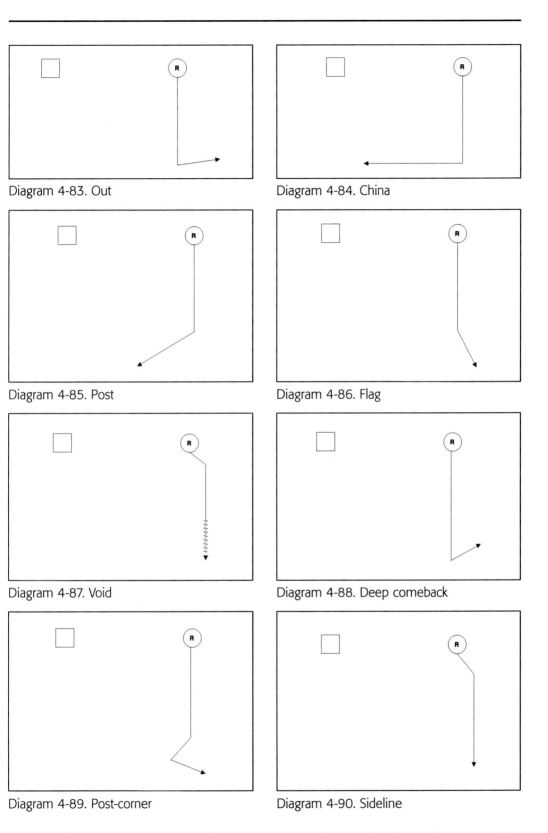

Diagram 4-83. Out

Diagram 4-84. China

Diagram 4-85. Post

Diagram 4-86. Flag

Diagram 4-87. Void

Diagram 4-88. Deep comeback

Diagram 4-89. Post-corner

Diagram 4-90. Sideline

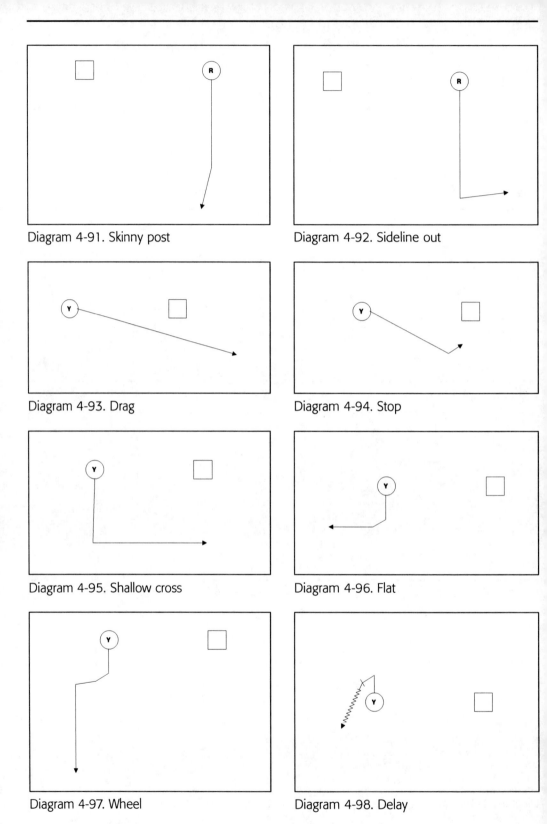

Diagram 4-91. Skinny post

Diagram 4-92. Sideline out

Diagram 4-93. Drag

Diagram 4-94. Stop

Diagram 4-95. Shallow cross

Diagram 4-96. Flat

Diagram 4-97. Wheel

Diagram 4-98. Delay

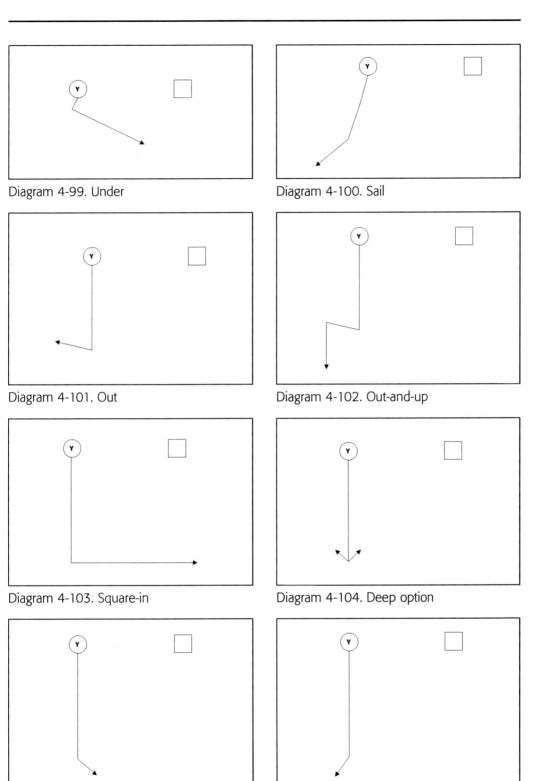

Diagram 4-99. Under

Diagram 4-100. Sail

Diagram 4-101. Out

Diagram 4-102. Out-and-up

Diagram 4-103. Square-in

Diagram 4-104. Deep option

Diagram 4-105. Post

Diagram 4-106. Flag

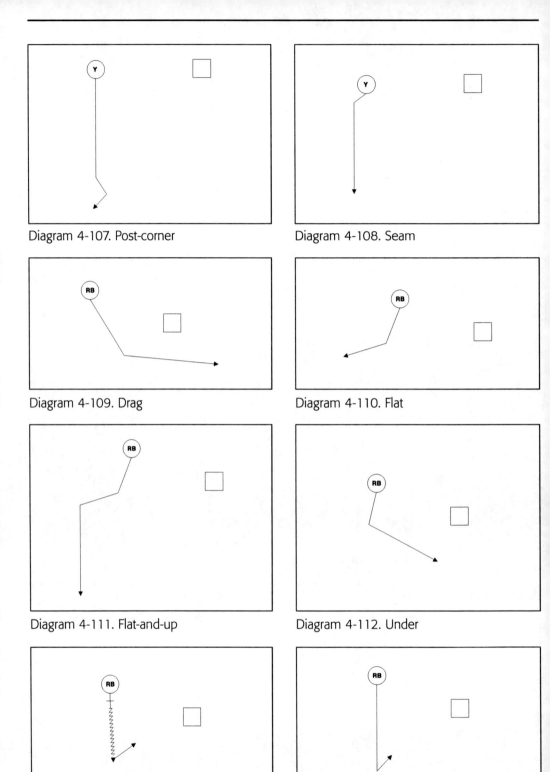

Diagram 4-107. Post-corner

Diagram 4-108. Seam

Diagram 4-109. Drag

Diagram 4-110. Flat

Diagram 4-111. Flat-and-up

Diagram 4-112. Under

Diagram 4-113. Delay

Diagram 4-114. Hook

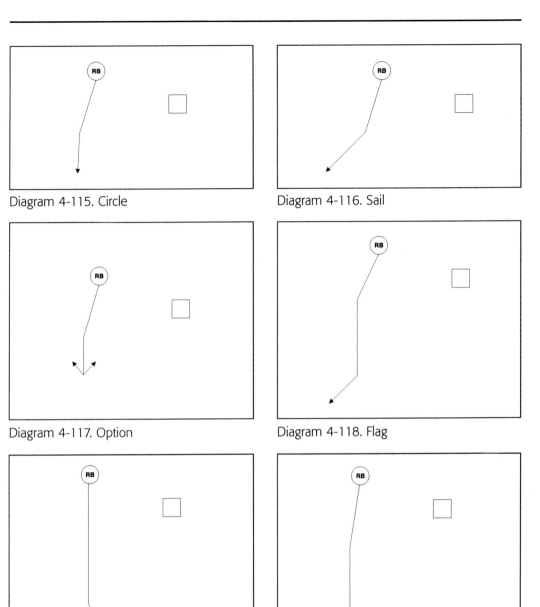

Diagram 4-115. Circle

Diagram 4-116. Sail

Diagram 4-117. Option

Diagram 4-118. Flag

Diagram 4-119. Post

Diagram 4-120. Takeoff

Combination Routes

- Commonly-used combination routes to the Y and Z side (Diagrams 4-121 through 4-130)

- Commonly-used route combinations to the weakside (Diagrams 4-131 through 4-138)

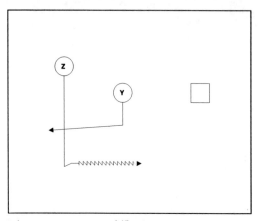

Diagram 4-121. Curl/flat

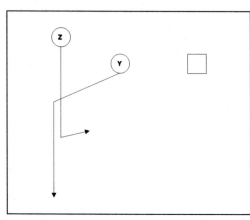

Diagram 4-122. Wheel

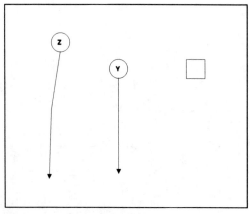

Diagram 4-123. All vertical

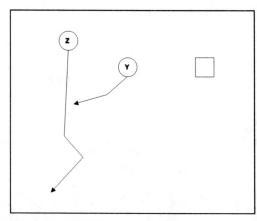

Diagram 4-124. Post-corner/flat

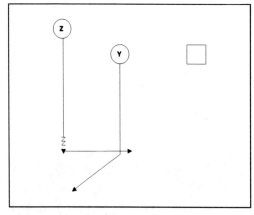

Diagram 4-125. China

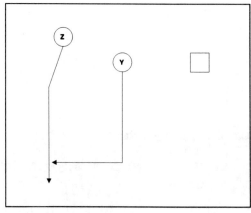

Diagram 4-126. Option

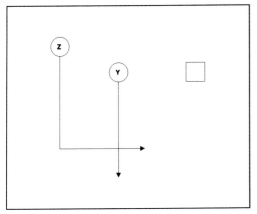

Diagram 4-127. Vertical/dig

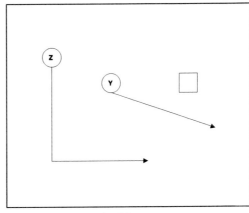

Diagram 4-128. Fire/dig

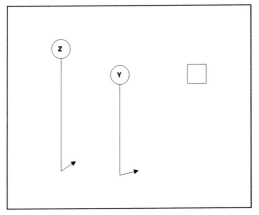

Diagram 4-129. All hook

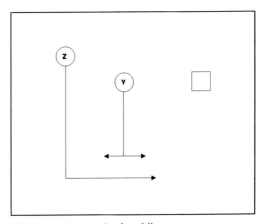

Diagram 4-130. Option/dig

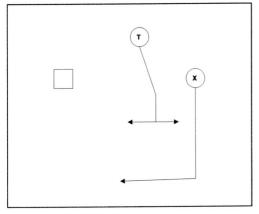

Diagram 4-131. Spin

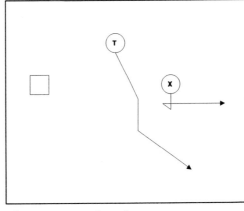

Diagram 4-132. Smash

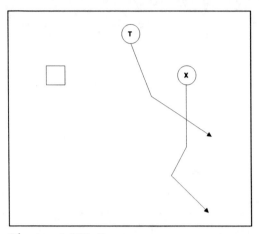

Diagram 4-133. X-corner

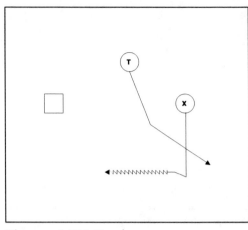

Diagram 4-134. X-curl

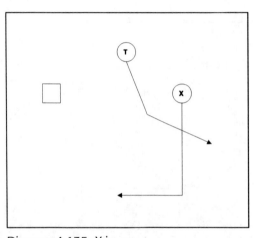

Diagram 4-135. X-in

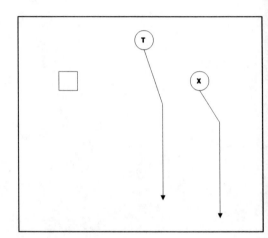

Diagram 4-136. T-seam

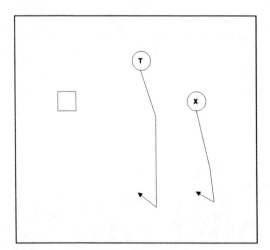

Diagram 4-137. All hook

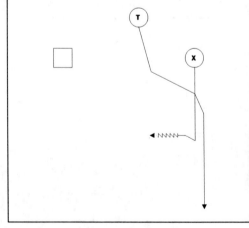

Diagram 4-138. T-wheel

Screens and Draws

Any defensive game plan would not be complete without making provisions to counter the offense's screen and draw plays. Screens and draws are designed to take advantage of the defense's pass rush. Screens try to draw the rushers to the quarterback and then throw the ball over their head. Screens serve to control and exploit the pass rush. Draws are also designed to invite defenders upfield and then hand the ball to a back who takes advantage of seams in the defense.

Defensing Screens

Screens can usually be defeated by defensive recognition. Linemen who read a shoddy pass block or read the quarterback taking a deeper-than-normal drop can be a "fly in the ointment." It is abnormal for the quarterback to take a five-step drop and then drift on a normal pass play. Ends who read a poor pass block can end up in the throw lane on rocket, hitch, and slip screens. Defensive linemen who read an excessive drop (or notice that an offensive lineman doesn't move his feet) can disrupt a screen play.

Assigning screen responsibilities is a sound tactic. Defenders who have been assigned screen responsibilities "mush" rush the quarterback as they sniff out screens. Defenders who have rush responsibilities should do so with maximum effort until they read screen. Care should be taken that rushers do one or the other. They can't be effective rushing the quarterback *and* playing screen. Rushers should rush and then react to screen. Rushers who have gotten in too deeply on a screen play should continue rushing the quarterback even if they read screen. It is better, at this point, to pressure the quarterback instead of trying to fall back to the screen point. If the rusher peels off after he is committed to the quarterback, he is unhelpful either way. It is advantageous when playing man-to-man coverage to insert or hug a back who blocks with the defender who is assigned to him. A linebacker inserting on the back can better cover the running back should he try to slip out on a screen. Green-dogging the back places the defender behind the line scrimmage and, as a result, behind blockers.

Defensing Draws

In addition to an offense's screen game, its draw game is also designed to take advantage of the defensive linemen's attempt to get to the quarterback and linebackers reacting to pass keys. Draw plays serve several purposes. They take advantage of vertical seams in the defense when pass rushers explode upfield on a perceived pass play. Also, the threat of a draw play can serve to slow down the rush on a called pass play.

Draws are also designed to slow down linebackers' pass drops. This concept seeks to exploit the void between defensive backs and the linebackers. Draws, like screens, can be suppressed by astute defensive recognition. It is beneficial for defenses to ascertain the primary blocking scheme the opponent prefers on draw plays. Some teams trap, turnout, or fold on their draw plays, while others simply run vertical defenders up the field and run in the vacated area. Even though offensive linemen are showing pass, it isn't quite the same as a real pass-protection block. Pass protectors, on a draw play, may exhibit overly-active hands and give up the edge or corner too easily. Also, uncovered linemen release downfield. Other tip-offs include the running back standing up from his stance to receive the ball. When defensive linemen read draw, they should yell, "Draw" and retrace their steps.

Besides recognition, another common tactic in stopping draw plays is solid defensive design. Draw (as well as screen) responsibilities can be delegated to particular defenders, while their teammates execute an aggressive pass change. Just as a defender can't effectively rush a passer and play screen, a defender cannot be expected to rush and play draw. Another defensive tactic is to call lane exchanges. It is easier to run draws when the offensive line has an idea of assigned defensive rush lanes. Lane exchanges result in defenders having the capability of filling different and various rush lanes. Varying the depth of lane exchanges is also helpful. It is highly beneficial to the defense if defenders unexpectedly show up in draw lanes.

Defensing the Total Pass Game

In previous sections, tips and advice on how to attack different types of pass actions were given. This section will include more detailed suggestions and proposed antidotes for the opponent's particular pass-game philosophy. Also, the strengths and weaknesses of possible defensive game plans will be highlighted. Whatever the defensive scheme or game plan, it should:

- Fit into the basic scheme.
- Fit the personnel.
- Be teachable.
- Be adjustable to all formations and motions.
- Have sound run support. All the elements should be in place (i.e., primary force, cutback, and secondary support).
- Avoid easy pre-snap reads by the quarterback.
- Be able to take away an offense's best receiver, which can be done through personnel match-ups, double coverage, rolls, or help schemes.
- Pressure and disrupt when desired.

Before a game plan and scheme to defeat the opponent's passing game is developed, the coach should first understand how the offensive signal caller is studying *him.* To be successful against the opponent's passing game, the coach should understand what the offense is looking for and how it will attack. A typical offensive breakdown of the defense would include the following information:

- Basic defensive philosophy
- Coverages by down-and-distance
- Coverages by field zone
- Coverages by offensive formations
- Personnel pass/drop ratios
- Blitz coverages
- Defensive adjustments to motion. How does motion affect factors such as force, coverage, blitzes, and so forth?
- How do wideouts match up with the corners?
- Where is a height or speed mismatch likely?
- Who is the best and worst cover man? The offense will seek profitable match-ups.
- How effective is the underneath coverage?
- How do running backs match up with linebackers?
- Short-yardage coverages
- Two-minute coverages
- Substitution packages
- Five- and ten-cent coverages
- Prevent defense

As the defensive coach develops a game plan on how to attack the opponent's passing game, he should first ask some pertinent questions about offensive personnel.

Quarterback

- How tall is the quarterback? Height may predict the type of pass game employed. Tall and less mobile quarterbacks tend to be pocket passers, while shorter and more athletic passers may run boots, counter boots, dashes, and sprints.
- How good a runner is the quarterback? A poor running quarterback can be flushed from the pocket and run down, whereas a more mobile quarterback should be kept in the pocket. Against an immobile quarterback, the ends can go underneath the tackle's block to flush the quarterback. Do you need to stay in well-defined rush lanes, or are contain responsibilities irrelevant?
- What is the quarterback's maneuverability? To which side does he like to escape? Is there a need to spy him?

- How does the quarterback handle pressure? Does he become frustrated and have happy feet if pressure is applied? Does pressure cause him to throw too quickly?
- Does the quarterback look off the coverage, or does he lock on his primary receiver?
- Does the quarterback pump fake to get the free safety to lean one way or another?
- Does he do an adequate job audibling? Can he be fooled?

Tight End (Y)

- How does the offense use the tight end?
- What routes does he favor?
- Can he be a factor versus a two-deep zone?
- Is he used as a pass blocker? If so, how effective a blocker is he? Can he handle #4 strong? What is their adjustment should #4 present a possible B-gap stunt?
- Does he chip before he releases? If so, how effective is he?

Running Backs

- How are running backs used in the pass game?
- Are they called upon to chip before they release?
- How effective are they as blockers? Is the back's heart into pass blocking? Green dogs are effective if the back is primarily a blocker.
- Do they check down? Does he check a linebacker before he releases into the route in an attempt to manipulate the underneath coverage?

Receivers

- Who is the best receiver?
- What is his forte?
- What is his best route?
- How physical is he?
- How fast is he?

Underneath Coverage

A major component in the game plan is how to play the under coverage against the opponent's passing game. How to play the linebackers is crucial to successfully thwarting the opponent's passing game. Some pertinent questions to ask include:

- How effective will the linebackers be in defending the pass game? Will they have to be replaced with a nickel or dime package on passing downs, or are they competent enough to get the job done?
- How do they match up with the opponent's running backs? Can they cover the backs one-on-one?
- Will offensive formations necessitate banjo (in-out) coverage?
- Should linebackers be run through versus sprint passes? If so, decide which linebackers to send. Is it better for the frontside linebacker or the backside linebacker to force the quarterback?
- Does a need exist to assign a linebacker spy responsibilities against a running quarterback?
- Is it a good idea to stunt a linebacker in the area of a good receiving back to keep him from releasing? If the back is placed over a linebacker who rarely stunts, it is best to be flexible and place the best blitzer to his side.
- Is it better to green dog or hug a running back if he pass blocks? In man-to-man coverage, it is best to have the linebacker assigned to the back to go get him if the offense likes to screen. Green-dogging also keeps a back from checking down. If the offense runs a lot of crossing routes, it might be best to drop a linebacker if his assignment pass blocks.

Coverage Decisions

A vital and crucial decision to be made in game planning revolves around the key decision of what coverages to use. Most coverages fit into one of four basic types: zone, man-to-man, combination, or blitz coverages. This section highlights the advantages and disadvantages of each system. Most defenses have components of each package. However, defenses will usually be more proficient in one area than the others. Also included will be a compendium of offensive thought on how to attack these specific defensive schemes.

Advantages of Zone Coverages

- Defends the field.
- Makes the ball the issue.
- Offers better run support.
- Allows all defenders to better see the ball and break when the ball is thrown.
- May give up completions but shouldn't allow deep completions. Hard to blow the top off of the coverage.

- Makes the offense go the long way. The offense must execute.
- More interceptions than man coverage because all defenders see and rally to the ball.
- Gang tackling is better in zone than man.
- Less talented players can be used.
- Handles crossing routes, picks, and rub-offs better than man coverage. Receivers can be punished on short crossing routes.

Disadvantages of Zone Coverages

- Defenses must get pressure with a base rush.
- Quarterback has time to throw. He can get in a rhythm.
- Allows a high completion rate.
- Pass-protection schemes allow help to be given to weak blockers.
- Zones can be flooded.

Offensive Plan of Attack Against Zones

Offenses will try to:

- Horizontally stretch the defense to attack seams between defenders and force the defense to cover the entire width of the field.
- Place stress on the defense with a high-low or in-out philosophy. The offense will make the defense fashion a decision and then take advantage of that decision.
- Attack horizontally between intermediate and deep coverage (vertical stretch).
- Place receivers underneath intermediate-area defenders who drop quickly to cover the horizontal horizon. The quarterback will work deep, to intermediate, to short.
- Attack inferior defenders. Zone responsibilities usually place these men in predictable areas or positions.
- Screen passes become more effective as the underneath coverage gets more depth.
- Throw to a back after a fake to him.
- Clear an area with a second receiver following the clearing route.

Advantages of Man Coverage

- Doesn't defend grass.
- The ball is the issue.

- Completion rate is lower.

- Defense can use numbers to attack protection schemes.

- Various games and stunts are available.

- Added number of rushers pressures the quarterback. The result is hurried passes and sacks.

- Quarterback may have to hold the ball longer, waiting for the receiver to break free. Makes him pat the ball.

- With tighter coverage, the quarterback must be more accurate. He has to "stick the ball in there."

- Man coverage is better in short and medium down-and-distance situations.

- A linebacker can insert or drop to find work if his assigned man blocks.

- Insertion of a linebacker when his man blocks disrupt screens.

Disadvantages of Man Coverage

- Need more athletic personnel.

- Completions usually mean longer gains.

- Interceptions are less likely because more defenders will have their back to the ball.

- Defenders can be isolated. Mismatches can occur.

- Scrambling quarterback is a problem to underneath defenders. These men usually have their backs to the ball.

- Coverage busts are more costly than zone. There may be no help in man coverage.

- Offenses can use play-action to present a conflict between run/pass responsibilities.

- Mismatches are possible, especially with formational changes or motion.

- The defense must get to the quarterback with pressure or defenders will be hung out.

- The strong safety may give away the coverage by his alignment on the tight end.

- Underthrown deep route is harder to play in man.

Offenses Plan of Attack Against Man Coverages

Offenses will try to:

- Scheme mismatches through use of formations, shifts, or motion.

- Pick or rub defenders with crossing routes.

- Pressure underneath defenders and force players with play-action passes.
- Pass to a back after he has faked a run.

Receiver Splits

Receiver splits may provide insights on potential pass plays. Obviously, receivers will vary alignments so they won't telegraph whether the play is a run or pass. However, down-and-distance tendencies bracketed with receiver splits will give the defense a clue as to the design of the upcoming play. Minus splits on passing downs might indicate out or crossing routes. It also triggers crack alerts. Plus splits suggest inside cuts (such as digs or curls) or deep routes (such as posts and takeoffs).

Defenses can just about rule out crossing routes with large splits. Plus splits are effective against five-under, two-deep zones because it spreads the underneath defenders and really stretches the two-deep safeties. However, plus splits against man-coverage schemes are counterproductive. The wider the split, the easier the corner can force or wall receivers outside. Offensive line splits are also indicative of the upcoming play. Big splits can place blockers on an island and gives the pass rushers more room to maneuver. As a result, line splits are usually tighter on pass plays.

Shotgun

No defensive game plan would be complete without provisions on defending a shotgun passing game. The shotgun has many inherent offensive advantages. First and foremost, the gun allows the quarterback time to read the coverage. A pre-snap setup of five or more yards allows the quarterback a panoramic view of the defense. However, the gun has some negatives. The biggest drawback to the gun might be a limited run game. Effective runs such as draws, shuffle passes, and mesh plays exist. But for the most part, the gun doesn't offer the variety of plays that a quarterback-under-center alignment provides.

Some commonly-used defensive tactics against the gun include placing a rusher on the center's snap hand, or stunting a linebacker over him. Some teams can stem or roll coverages as the quarterback is looking the ball into his hands on the snap. The quarterback must focus on the ball and cannot eyeball the coverage as well as he can when under center. Defensive game plans should answer some pertinent questions concerning the shotgun.

- When does the opponent use it?
- Is it used with normal personnel, or do they send in a receiver-loaded package?

- Does the opponent shift into the gun?
- Do they shift out of the gun?
- What is the defensive plan if the offense shifts into the gun on first-and-ten with normal personnel?

Defending Quarterback Scrambles

A commonly overlooked aspect of defensing an opponent's passing game is defensive reaction to a quarterback scramble. Many big plays result when the quarterback scrambles on a given play. Bill Walsh writes that one in five dropback passes end up with the quarterback scrambling. Well-prepared defenses allot practice time to work on defensive reactions when the quarterback is forced to scramble. It is imperative that defenses know how to react when the quarterback leaves the pocket. Before a coach can tailor a defensive response, he should first understand the offense's basic rules or guidelines on a quarterback scramble.

Some Offensive Guidelines

Different offensive systems use various rules and it is the coach's job to know the rules employed by each opponent. Following are some basic scramble rules:

- Quarterback looks deep to short.
- Quarterback looks to the near sideline.
- The quarterback should avoid leading the receiver. He should throw to a spot.
- The quarterback should avoid throwing across the body.
- The quarterback should avoid throwing late down the middle.
- The quarterback will take a little off the throw because of the added velocity of a ball thrown on the run.
- Receivers will show up in the quarterback's line of sight.
- Receivers will move in the same direction as the quarterback. If a receiver gets close to the sideline, he will work to uncover the sideline.
- Running backs will work parallel to the quarterback and look for an open spot.
- If receivers were assigned a deep route, they will come back.
- If the quarterback scrambles away, the receiver will break parallel toward the quarterback. He will try to stay on the same yard line and work horizontally.
- If receivers were assigned a short route, they will convert to a deep route.
- If a receiver is to the side of the scramble, he will go deep.

- Receivers will remain stationary if open toward the side of the scramble.
- Receivers will go to the ball when it is in the air.
- If the quarterback decides to cross the line of scrimmage he will give a "go" call, which alerts the line that it can cross the line and informs backs and receivers to block.

Defensive Guidelines on Quarterback Scrambles

- Defenders must know which way the quarterback likes to scramble, and whether he usually scrambles to run or to throw.
- Deep defenders must stay deep.
- Pass defenders should stick with their primary assignment and not turn a receiver loose. Defensive backs don't come up until they get a "run" call.
- Rushers should disengage and take sharp pursuit angles.
- Frontside linebackers, if not in man coverage, should supply frontside run through on the quarterback.

5

Down-and-Distance Considerations

One of the most important considerations in defensive or offensive play selection is down-and-distance. Offensive-play calls should be tailored to meet different down-and-distance situations. This chapter will explore fundamental offensive goals for each down-and-distance situation and give possible defensive responses.

First Down

First-and-Long (10 yards)

Many offensive and defensive coaches feel that first down is the most important down in a series. Most offensive and defensive calls made in a game will be first-down calls. NFL statistics reveal that, on the average, 23 to 25 first down calls will be made per game. Forty-five percent of open-field calls will be first-down calls. First-down results determine if the offense stays or falls behind schedule. Most offenses seek to gain four or more yards on first down. First-down success will keep the offense in a make-able third down situation. First-down success allows the offensive coach the ability to call plays that match his personality and philosophy. Generic offensive objectives usually range from getting a first down, gaining successive first downs, position for a convertible third-down call, score, or call an explosive play to gain a score or gain field position. Sixty-five to seventy-five percent of a team's first downs are generated on first and second down. Third-down success rates range only from 25 to 35 percent.

Many offensive coordinators feel first down is the best time to dial up an explosive-type play because the defense is stretched with multiple concerns. It really isn't possible to make a bad offensive call on first down, only better calls. Statistics show that teams with a two-play advantage in explosive plays will win the game 80% to 85% of the time. An explosive play is defined as a play that gains 20 or more yards. Statistics also show that the ability of teams to successfully sustain drives is only 15 to 20 percent. Thus, explosive plays are paramount. Chances of executing a big play are greater on early downs—especially first down. Obviously, defenses seek to keep the offense off schedule and force them into third-and-long situations. Defensive objectives include holding offenses to three yards or less on first down. Sound scouting techniques will reveal the offense's favorite first-down run plays. Prudent defensive coordinators will also expect play-action passes from these run actions. Defensive coordinators should break first-down run plays into inside and outside categories. How much dropback passing does the opponent use on first down? They should determine if draws and screens are a prominent part of the offensive package on first down. If the odds of draw or screen are minimal, the pass rushers can lay their ears back when they read pass. Pressure can be applied without stunting should they read pass. An example would be a delayed pick call, in which linemen play the front call versus run blocks (Diagram 5-1), but exchange lanes if the offense shows pass-protection blocks (Diagram 5-2).

Another great way to get pressure versus passes and an eight-man front against runs is the Bear (or 46) defense (Diagram 5-3). Defensive coaches must be very careful not to allow the offense the luxury of locking in versus a base front and coverage on first-down calls. Offenses will have a distinct advantage if all they see on first down is a base or vanilla look. Defenses should mix fronts but always ensure quick run support. Run stunts are beneficial if good run support is supplied. Care must be taken to match

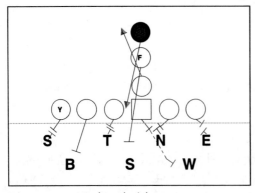

Diagram 5-1. Delayed pick versus un-play technique

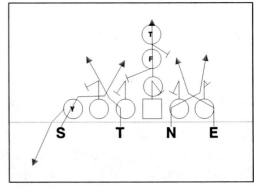

Diagram 5-2. Delayed pick versus pass-lane exchange

defensive personnel with different personnel packages the offense may employ. It might be unwise to play base personnel versus three or four wideout personnel. To be sound on first down, defenses should use calls that are solid against run or pass—especially play-action passes. First down is a good time to dial up a run stunt.

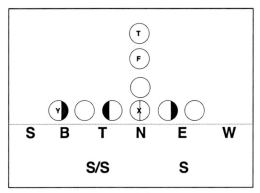

Diagram 5-3. Bear 46 defense

Sudden Change

Within the framework of first-down situations are special situations that need to be explored and planned into the defensive game blueprint. How does the opponent react to his defense intercepting the ball, recovering a fumble, or blocking a kick? Some offensive coaches see this situation as a great opportunity for an explosive play. The defense should be prepared for a home-run-type play in this situation. Play-action passes, reverses, or double passes are distinct possibilities. The defensive coach should discern his opponent's approach in this situation and forewarn his players. He should also include sudden-change situations in the play script during the week's practice.

First-and-Medium (5 yards)

Periodically, a defense may be faced with a first-and-five situation, which usually occurs when the defense is charged with an offside penalty. What is the approach taken in this situation by the opponent? Some offensive signal callers will see this penalty as a free down. If they throw an incomplete pass, they will be faced with a very manageable second-and-medium call. Other coaches may approach this situation as a standard first-down play and get all of the yards they can.

First-and-10+ Yards

This situation usually entails an offensive penalty on the prior play. For example, an illegal-procedure call on first down puts the offense in a first-and-15 situation. In this scenario, most offenses will run a play to get some positive yardage. A holding call on first down may place the offense in a first-and-20-plus, and they will try to get into a second-and-nine or second-and-10 situation. Most teams will run one of their best base plays in which they have a lot of confidence. The worst scenario is to throw incomplete and be faced with a second-and-plus-10 call. However, a passing team may approach this scenario as make-able with a couple of completions.

Other reactive offensive situations should be broken down and studied to see if the offense has tendencies in those areas. Those situations include:

- First down after a rushing first down.
- First down after a passing first down.
- First down after an explosive rush.
- First down after an explosive pass.

Second Down

Second-and-Long (7+ yards)

Second-and-long is usually the result of defensive success on first down. Second-and-long is a crucial down. More often than not, second-and-long is the best blitz down. Should the defense win this down, the offense will be faced with a third-and-long call. Second-and-long should be the best defensive down. On the average, 11 to 12 second-and-long calls will be made per game. An evenly-balanced offense will try to mix in an occasional pass on first down, and if this pass is incomplete, the offense will be faced with a second-and-long decision. Second-and-long is a great time to call a screen or draw. A second-and-long screen or draw would have more of an element of surprise than third-and-long. If the opponent is a big second-down screen team, it might be advantageous to assign a spy (or spies) for screen or draw. A coach can choose from a variety of spy calls. Diagram 5-4 shows a Cobra In call. With this call, the tackles have pass-rush assignments with the ends on a "mush" rush. Diagram 5-5 shows a cobra-out call. With this call, the ends explode upfield with the tackles spying. Diagram 5-6 shows a cobra-man call. With this call, all linemen are on jet charges except the nose, who will spy. Lane exchanges would also be effective if they are contain sound, especially against a mobile quarterback.

Second-and-Medium (3 to 6 yards)

Second-and-medium will arise five to six times per game. Many offensive coaches treat this category as either second-and-long or second-and-short. Film study should clue the defensive coordinator as to how he should approach the call. Aggressive offensive signal callers may see this as a good opportunity to hit a big play. If they take a shot and fail, they would be faced with a make-able third down. Another school of thought is to remain balanced with a good run, pass, or play-action-pass mix.

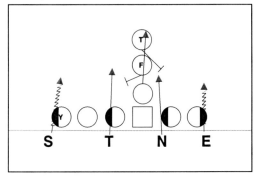

Diagram 5-4. Cobra in

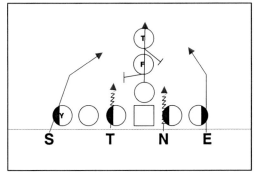

Diagram 5-5. Cobra out

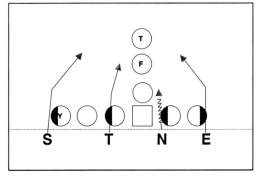

Diagram 5-6. Cobra man

Second-and-Short (1 to 2 yards)

Defensively, this down is very dangerous. The offense has all the advantages. The offensive signal caller can use all his playbook on this down. It is a great time to go for a touchdown on a play-action-type pass. Failure to gain yardage will still leave the offense with a favorable third-and-short call. Defensively, a team cannot be successful facing many of these second-and-short calls. This scenario may indicate the defensive line is being mauled at the line of scrimmage. Defensively, a coach may have to put more men in the box or use fronts that use more down linemen on first down. A good

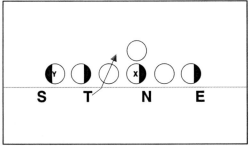

Diagram 5-7. Tab stunt

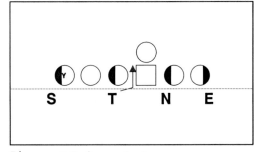

Diagram 5-8. A-gap stunt

second-and-short call might be to use an individual stunt or change by a lineman—which could result in a loss of yardage, which in turn would put the offense in a third-and-medium (or -long) situation. Two effective second-and-short calls are illustrated in Diagrams 5-7 and 5-8. In Diagram 5-7, the 4i technique executes a tab stunt, which beats the offensive tackle. In Diagram 5-8, the 3 technique executes an A-gap stunt, which beats the offensive guard.

Third Down

Third-and-Long (7+ yards)

Statistically, third-and-long will arise 12 to 14 times a game with a third-down conversion needed every fourth or fifth play of a series. Ten of those calls will occur in the open field, with two to four happening in the red zone. When faced with a 7+ call, offenses have only a 20- to 25-percent success rate. Winning third-and-long is the cornerstone of good defense. Even novice football observers can readily see how successful or unsuccessful a team is offensively or defensively on third down. Offensive failure usually brings out the punt team, while defensive failure causes the chains to move. Good calls and execution by the defense allows the defensive team to get off the field. Confidence levels soar as well as physically allowing defensive players to catch a respite.

Third-and-long is usually a substitution down for most offenses. Substitutions often tip off the type of play to be run. Substitutes often limit or restrict the scope of plays to be used. However, teams who do not substitute retain all their options. The whole playbook is available. Most offenses treat this situation as a passing down and may substitute to get more receivers on the field. Some coaches may choose to pass underneath or hand the ball off to give the player a chance to pick up the distance needed in the open field. Screens and draws are always possibilities. However, the defensive coach cannot expect a lineman to pressure the quarterback and play screen and draw. Unless a particular player has screen or draw responsibilities, he should rush the quarterback and react to screen or draw. Many offensive teams will trap or use some other type of run to pick up a first down when facing a nickel or dime package. Screens, draws, or runs are acceptable ways to get out of a series and safely punt the ball. Many conservative coaches feel any positive gain on third-and-long is better than taking a sack or throwing an interception. Teams that subscribe to this conservative approach usually have a strong defense or variables such as the score, field position, time left, or personnel situation and may call for a wary approach.

Basically, three schools of thought on how to defend third-and-long tend to predominate. Defensive teams may choose to approach this situation in a conservative manner. A second approach would take a much more aggressive course and the third alternative, which is the most popular, would be a mix of both conservative and aggressive tactics. Whatever approach is used, matching personnel is paramount to third-and-long success.

Conservative Approach

Teams who use the conservative approach play a lot of soft zone where the ball is kept in front of defenders who drive forward to make the tackle short of the first-down marker. Conservative coaches don't mind giving up yards as long as the ball doesn't get to the first-down stick. Characteristically, these defenses use a three- or four-man rush with emphasis on containment of the quarterback. Using individual linemen match-ups is the preferred way to apply pressure. This approach allows a seven- or eight-man coverage theme. Lane exchanges is a good way to apply pressure with a minimal rush ratio. Teams who use this approach will consistently be superior to their opponent, personnel-wise. Obviously, the best situation is to be able to exert pressure with the line only. Doing so would allow more defenders to drop and still get an effective pass rush. However, not many teams will out-personnel all of their opponents. As a result, not many teams use this approach exclusively.

Aggressive Approach

The antithesis of the conservative and cautious approach is a total-pressure philosophy. This school of thought seeks to attack the quarterback with numbers and play some sort of man or combination coverage behind it. Aggressive defenses try to force receivers to break off their routes or force the quarterback to throw hot and tackle the receiver short of the line to gain. Assertive defenses put their corners on an island a lot of times. Care should be taken that an inferior defensive back not get caught too many times with one-on-one match-ups without help. Many teams currently use a zone-blitz scheme, which inserts a linebacker or defensive back and covers up with a lineman who drops into coverage. This approach is a great way to apply pressure and play zone behind it.

Mixed Approach

Most defensive coaches have a philosophy somewhere in the middle of these two extremes. Unless a defense is vastly superior, the sustained use of a conservative approach might put the defense at a disadvantage. Conversely, the use of an all-out attacking style on every third-and-long play isn't very judicious. The prudent thing to do would be to use a well-thought-out mix of both conservative and attack philosophies. This course of action would serve to keep the offense off balance, and through the use of effective disguises, keep them guessing about defensive intentions. The opponent should not be given the luxury of knowing which approach the defense will take on any given third and long situation. Sun Tzu in *The Art of War* summed it up best when he wrote, "All warfare is based on deception. When we are near, we must make the enemy believe we are far away; when far away, we must make him believe we are near." To paraphrase: when blitzing (near), make the quarterback think we are dropping (far away); when not blitzing (far away), make him think we are coming (near).

Draw and Screen

Draw and screen plays are designed to take advantage of an aggressive pass-rush. Obviously, an aggressive pass-rush is more prevalent on long-yardage plays—especially third-and-long. Defensive concepts vary from team to team on how they approach this situation. Some defensive schemes teach their linemen to rush the passer and react to the draw or screen. This approach is well and good for teams that have good team speed, but maybe not as effective for teams that are not as quick. Teams that are speed-deficient may have to assign draw and screen responsibility to particular players or positions. Care should be taken, however, that the best rushers are not tied down with this responsibility. A sound move might be to assign the responsibility of spying to a 2i tackle in a 4-3 front, because he will usually be doubled by the center and guard on passes. He is in a prime position to eat up two blocks and "mush" rush versus pass.

Third-and-Medium (3 to 6 yards)

Third-and-medium conversions are crucial to the psyche of the offense. Success rates average 45 to 50 percent. Success in third-and-medium directly affects the proposed calls on first and second down. If the offense is successful with this down-and-distance call, it can be more aggressive and freewheeling with its early down calls. Conversely, should the offense not be comfortable in third-and-medium, it would negatively affect first- and second-down calls. Play callers might abandon running plays on second down and thus lose balance in their play calling. Runs in this situation may consist of misdirection, draws, or trap-type plays. Play-action passes are a possibility, especially if the action mirrors draw or misdirection-type runs. Offenses have the advantage with this call because a first down is reachable by either run or pass. Since the offense can be balanced, the defense in turn must balance up. Defensive success hinges on what it does on earlier downs. Third-and-medium calls need to be minimized. If the offense is in fourth-down territory, care should be taken that the defense not be torched by a play-action pass.

Third-and-Short (1 to 2 yards)

Obviously, offenses have the upper hand on third-and-short situations. Success rates range from 75 to 85 percent in this area. Offensively, two basic philosophies exist in this situation. Conservative or orthodox teams have the goal of simply gaining a first down. Teams that follow this line of thought will usually hand off the ball to their best back behind their best blocker. Another conservative and safe call would be a quarterback sneak, especially if the quarterback has some size and strength. A sneak is the simplest and safest offensive call that can be made. Provisions should be made to defeat this play. Other coaches may have a more aggressive mindset and see this as a big-play opportunity. Play-action passes from jumbo or power sets can be a back breaker.

Offensive attempts may originate from three separate personnel groupings. Offenses may choose to use standard personnel, power formations, or spread-type configurations, which include three or four wideouts. A common offensive tactic on third-and-short is to flood the field with spread sets to thin the defense and run the ball up inside or sneak it for a first down. Stacking the box may be desirable if the offense has this tendency, but coverage can be compromised if the offense chooses to throw the ball. Obviously, many factors (such as the score, time remaining, and field zone) enter into this decision.

Defensive tactics on third-and-short might include putting eight or nine men in the box, calling an inside charge by a lineman, or firing a linebacker to disrupt the inside-run game. Inside pressure can spill a run and force it laterally so it can be run down. The defense's best run front should be used. Personnel-wise, the coach should match strength with strength. Two-deep coverage with hard corners can take away quick routes, but at the expense of only having seven men in the box. Defensive teams should understand that a commonly-used offensive tactic in this situation is the hard count. The defense must be disciplined and sufficiently drilled not to jump offside.

Fourth Down

Fourth-and-Long/Medium (4+ yards)

Many factors are involved in the crucial decision on whether to go for it on fourth down. The offensive coach's philosophy about fourth-down plays is probably the most important ingredient. Some coaches are naturally more aggressive than others. Weather is another crucial factor, along with variables such as score, time remaining, field zone, and so forth. One important consideration that is sometimes overlooked is how effective is your offense. If your offense is below average, the opponent may not feel threatened if they fail to make a first down. On the other hand, if your offense is highly proficient, the opponent may go for it on fourth down to keep the ball away from your offense. Even though fourth-down failures can be disastrous for an offense, success rates on fourth down are fairly high on fourth-and-one plays.

Many times fourth-down plays may decide the outcome of a game. The offensive package on the field should serve as a tip-off on the offense's intentions. 21 personnel usually means they have kept all their options viable. Runs or passes are both possible with this grouping. A more diversified offense is available with standard personnel. Jumbo personnel might indicate more of a run-thought process. However, play-action passes are a distinct possibility when power sets are used. Substitutions that take out tight ends or running backs should be matched with additional defensive backs. Care, however, should be taken that the defense does not become so diluted that traps or other types of inside runs get the first down. Common sense should indicate to the defensive coordinator that if the upcoming play is a run, it will be a play with their best back running behind their best lineman. If the offense decides to throw the ball, it will probably be designed to go to their best receiver. It might be good practice to load up at the anticipated point of attack (over the best lineman) and double cover the best receiver.

Fourth-and-Short (1 to 2 yards)

Time remaining, field zone, and score are all important considerations for fourth-and-short. Care should be taken with this defensive call. Play-action passes or runs that break the line of scrimmage when the defense is pressing the issue could result in a big gain or touchdown. Most signal callers would undoubtedly give the ball to their best runner over the best blocker if they decide to run. The offense might dial up a play that has been effective throughout the game or their signature play. If the third-down spot is close to the marker, the quarterback should ask for a measurement. Doing so allows them to talk over the fourth-down call.

On fourth-and-short, most offenses will avoid shifts or motion. Line splits will be narrowed down to one foot. Offensive linemen may be in four-point stances. Linemen will be coached to block low to high. Most quarterbacks will avoid complicated snap counts for fear of an illegal-procedure infraction. Most offenses will snap the ball on one. Depending on the game situation, a defensive coach might choose not to unduly press the issue. However, if the situation warrants, press the line of scrimmage but be sound structurally, and be alert to the possibility of a play-action pass. Force and secondary-support personnel should be on high alert.

Three indicators can give the defensive coordinator a feel for his opponent's propensity to gamble on fourth-down calls. First, teams with an average field-goal team may elect to go for a first down when they reach that gray area where the kicker's range is an issue. Another decision is whether to punt the ball and take the chance of having the ball go into the end zone (and as a result, net a handful of yards), or to go for it on fourth down. Obviously, if this situation is the case, the offensive coordinator's third-down call is colored. He may decide that he is in fourth-down territory. Secondly, how successful is the opponent's third-and-short game? If the opponent is highly successful on third-and-short, it would stand to reason that they will be successful more times than not on fourth-and-short. Lastly, how effective is their defense? Teams that play solid defense tend to take more chances such as going for it on fourth down because they know they will get the ball back in short order.

6

Field-Zone Breakdowns

Field zones can be divided many different ways. One common way is to divide the field into five distinct areas:

- Goal line to -10—Backed-up zone
- -10 to -20—Coming-out zone
- 20 to 20—Free-wheeling zone
- +20 to +10—Going-in zone
- +10 to goal line—Goal-line zone

Offensive teams will usually have a package of plays for each area. This package will also be influenced by other factors, such as down-and-distance, score, time remaining, offensive strengths and weaknesses, and so forth.

Backed Up (Goal to -10)

Psychologically, this zone is one of the most important parts of the field. If the offense moves the ball out of this area, psychological damage can be inflicted on a defense and the mental outlook of the offense would be buoyed. Most offenses' primary goal in this area is to gain at least one first down. Benefits of accomplishing this goal are twofold. Strategically, it is important because it better facilitates a punt. Moving the ball out of this zone allows the punt to be launched on the fieldside of the goal line and not out of the end zone. Secondly, the mental goal of gaining a first down isn't as difficult as driving 90 to 95 yards for a touchdown. Quarterback sneaks are common in this situation—especially if the ball is backed up against the goal line. A sneak with wedge blocking is a safe play. The offense should run a play that gives the ball to sure-handed players. Plays should not involve difficult ball handling. Most runs will attack A gap or C gap. Attacking C gap is best versus multiple-front defenses. Blocking adjustments are easier in C gap than interior gaps. Play selection may result in a short-yardage-type play with wedge blocking. Offensive coordinators may select closed-type formations. In some cases, a wing may be used to add another gap to the defensive front and stop pressure off the corner. Complicated blocking schemes with pulling linemen should be avoided. Passes using max protection should be of a low and outside nature. Passes over the middle should be avoided because of the possibility of a big hit or a tipped pass. However, this point is a prime time to throw long outside. Some offenses see this time as great to take a shot because the defense has to defend 90-plus yards of grass. A long pass that is intercepted might be considered as good as a punt.

Defensive thinking and strategy should limit the opponent to no more than one first down. The defense's prime objective should be to force a three-and-out series. Effective defensive tactics in this area would include incorporating inside line changes, which might come clean and result in a minus-yardage tackle or an offensive holding call. Schemes to take away the sneak, or at least make the quarterback slide out to B gap if a sneak is called, should be implemented. Corners should be drilled to expect a double move (i.e., quick-and-go, out-and-up, slant-and-up). The defensive huddle call should incorporate the use of a deep-middle or hole player to ensure over-the-top help and be in an advantageous position to field a possible quick kick or tipped pass. Care should be taken when applying pressure on the offense not to sacrifice defensive in-depth alignments. When crowding the line of scrimmage, the threat of a gap responsibility bust or loss of gap integrity might allow a big play. Pressure should be used judiciously.

Coming Out (-10 to -20)

Some coaches refer to this as the green zone. It is just as important to the outcome of the game as the well-known red zone. Even the most novice fan understands how important the red-zone area is, but astute observers realize that the green zone is just as important. In many ways, the green zone can be considered an extension of the backed-up zone. The offensive thought process, for the most part, is usually the same here as it was in the backed-up area. As in the backed-up area, the cardinal rule here is to get first downs. Slight differences may occur, however. For example, the offense can open it up a little more than it could when it was deeper in it's own end. Quarterback sneaks are less prevalent in the coming-out zone. Another difference is a penalty in this zone will not result in a safety. Ball security is still a must. Trick plays such as reverses or double passes are minimally used. However, it is still a great time to attack vertically with a long pass. Also likely to be seen are quick passes for short gains. The quarterback's reads will probably be quick and well-defined with him avoiding holding the ball for any length of time. Passes should be thrown on time. Pass protection is highly important. Backs who check release will ensure extra blockers if the defense brings pressure. Motion may be used to help with pre-snap reads. Play-action passes are possible. The running game will probably consist of base-type runs with power or man blocking. Handoffs will probably be preferable to toss or pitch-type plays. Counters are risky and quick-tempo-type plays will probably be more common. Plays with yardage-loss potential should be avoided. The offense wants to stay on schedule and not be faced with a long-yardage play.

Defensive strategy in this area should be to get a stop and be in position to receive a punt around the 50-yard line. Defenders should be taught to think turnovers. Zone coverages are safer than man coverages. A five-under, two-deep scheme that disrupts routes would be effective in this zone. Be aware, however, that a cover-2 look would result in only having seven defenders in the box.

Free Wheeling (-20 to +20)

The free-wheeling area is where the offense and defense will execute its basic game plan. Most offensive snaps will happen in this zone. Defensively, the basic down-and-distance game plan should be executed. If the offense reaches the 50-yard line, field position will be compromised. A punt from the 50 would put the receiving team in a coming-out mode with all its attendant problems. If the offense breaks the 50-yard-line barrier, the defense should turn it up a notch, especially if the offense has put together several first downs to reach this point. The defense must stop the drive though a sack, tackle for a loss, or a turnover. More aggressive calls may be needed to stop offensive momentum. Continued offensive advancement will put them in scoring position, or at least they will punt the ball and pin the offense near its goal line. As the ball nears the +30 area, the strength of the opponent's field-goal team should be taken into account. Weather-related elements such as wind and rain may affect any field-goal attempt. Field conditions are paramount to any field-goal decision. Conservative offensive calls may be prevalent if the opponent has a capable kicker. If the opponent has a poor or mediocre kicker, or weather conditions are negative, the opponent may consider this area as four-down territory, which would affect their play calling and the defense's response. Once across the 50, a typical offense will run plays they are comfortable with and plays that have a good success rate. Care will be taken to stay on schedule. Some teams will avoid high-risk plays such as reverses that would take them out of field-goal range.

Going In (+20 to +10)

This zone is commonly referred to as the red zone. Even the most novice football fans understand this term. On the average, most defensive teams will face this situation at least three times a game. Different coaches have varying philosophies about this zone. Some offensive coaches consider this to be an extension of the free-wheeling zone, some feel this zone starts at the +30 and extends to the +10, and some consider the going-in area to end at the +seven- or even the +three-yard line. Before defensive coaches can begin to formulate strategy in this zone, they should study and analyze the opponent's kicking game. Offensive strategy in this area should take into account the quality of the field-goal kicker and field-goal team.

The opponent's play-calling approach is tied proportionally to the effectiveness of the field-goal team. Teams that have a poor or mediocre kicking game may consider the going-in zone to be four-down territory. Obviously, this assumption would affect offensive play calling, which in turn would impact the defensive response. Basic offensive philosophy in this zone is colored by the fact that the offense is working with a short field. As has been stated, the field will expand or contract depending upon the ability of the field-goal specialist. Offensive goals include coming away with some points while avoiding turnovers and penalties. Many conservative signal callers will avoid plays that are considered high risk. Play selection may be limited to avoid plays that have potential for a loss while other offensive teams make a conscious effort to play up-tempo. They try to attack the defense while it is tired and reeling from a series of offensive first downs. Most offenses try to run the ball in this area. They will usually feature their best runs—especially if they have had success earlier in the game with these plays. However, this zone is a great place for the offense to run different plays from formations shown in the free-wheeling zone. Many teams will feature their option package in the red zone, especially if the defensive team likes to stunt between the tackles. The defense should be sound against the option. Formations tend to include more tight ends or running backs from the +20. Many teams prefer closed formations with wings to expand the defensive front. Two-tight-end sets are to be expected and planned for. Motion is used to get a desired match-up, disrupt, or confuse force. The quarterback, if he is an athletic type, should be accounted for on any keeps out the back door. Quarterback keeps (or nakeds) should be expected and schemed to be contained.

The opponent's pass game may include rollouts or sprints to take advantage of the quarterback's mobility. The scrambling ability of the quarterback is an important factor when defending the +20 pass game. Spy responsibilities may have to be assigned. Personnel considerations should include the receiving ability of running backs and the tight end. Care should be taken not to allow mismatches. Pass plays in this zone will highlight or feature tall receivers against shorter defensive backs. If man coverage is the staple for the defense, a common offensive tactic would be a throwback to the quarterback. Not many defenses account for the quarterback as a pass receiver. Teams may be reluctant to take deep drops for fear of a sack. As a result, the quick game may be utilized more. The closer to the goal line, the more confined the field becomes. As a result, some offensive coaches may consider a throw into the end zone while they still have a little operating room. If the ball is thrown vertically, most teams prefer corner or fade routes. These routes are harder to intercept since they are thrown high and outside. Most teams who throw the fade adjust to good coverage by throwing the ball to the receiver's backside shoulder and letting the receiver adjust to the ball. As the vertical area becomes more compressed, many teams will resort to crossing or pick-type routes—especially against man-to-man coverages. Many offenses will resort to multiple receivers who align within close proximity to each other. Bunch-style formations are highly effective. Original alignment or motion to the bunch are both sound. Run-force assignments should be clear and precise since play-action passes can be devastating to undisciplined secondaries.

Common defensive actions include loading the box to shut down the run game. If your team is in control of the game, it might be best to stay in base fronts and coverages. The goal is to not give up a quick score. If the defense decides to make something happen with pressure packages to gain control of the down-and-distance situation, it should be aware that crossing and pick-type routes are a distinct possibility. For this reason, some teams take a more conservative approach and play zone to nullify those pick- or rub-type routes. Some teams may choose to play a loose four-across zone in the red zone. On first or second down, force a no-gain or a loss by taking away their favorite runs and force them to throw. Passing situations require alternate aggressive and conservative calls. Don't allow the offense to get locked in. Disguise is a must. Defensive calls should be interchangeable. Mix in aggressive calls, which pressure the quarterback and take away possession-type passes with toughness on short routes, with more conservative measures which keep the ball in front with crossing routes being picked up by zone defenders. Five-under, two-deep zone is good in this zone. Pass defenders, no matter the coverage, should always play "low" shoulder on the receiver as they enter the five-yard-line area. Other red-zone-coverage principles include: middle-of-the-field defenders should never enter the end zone until receivers do, and if the quarterback scrambles, defenders should defend the end line under the goal post.

Goal Line (+10 to Goal)

The goal line is one of the most psychologically important areas on the field. A successful defensive stand here will do immeasurable harm to the opponent. On the average, the defense will be faced with this situation two times per game. One of the most basic questions a defensive coach should ask is: when does the opponent consider itself to be in a goal-line situation? Some offensive coaches consider the +10 to be the magical line of embarkation, while other coaches consider varying yard lines as the start of goal line offense. Some popular designations are the +seven, +five, or even the +three. Film study will reveal the opponent's line of thought as to where their goal-line mentality starts. A very important question to ask here is whether the opponent will run their basic offense or do they narrow their attack to a handful of plays? Although no universal red-zone philosophy is agreed upon, some guidelines exist that most offenses follow. All offenses seek to work for positive gains with no penalties or turnovers. Mental errors and bad plays are poison to red-zone offenses. Some goal-line defensive packages are ineffective versus offenses that use multiple formations or personnel groupings. The defensive scheme employed should be able to adjust to a myriad of offensive formations and personnel packages. Modern offensive football forces defenses to have the flexibility to align in anything from a nine- to 10-man press-the-line-of-scrimmage scheme to a nickel package versus one-back philosophies. Matching personnel is a must in goal-line defense.

Many goal-line offenses will run the ball by giving it to their best back behind their best blocker. Defenders should be assigned to all aspects of the option game. Dive, keep, pitch, and play-action-pass responsibilities should be understood. However, some teams may not like to pitch the ball in this zone. If this situation is the case, consider overloading or overplaying other aspects of the option game. Another pivotal question is whether or not the quarterback is a run threat. A good running quarterback can be very effective in a goal-line offense. If he is in an option system, the defensive coaches may have to assign more than one man to the quarterback. Other plays such as nakeds, throwbacks to the quarterback, draws, and pass-run options should be planned for and defended. A quarterback who can scramble, either by design or when the play breaks down, can be very frustrating for the defense. Spy responsibilities may have to be assigned for this eventuality. Many offenses include, in their goal-line run package, trap-type plays to take advantage of penetration. In addition, quick hitters with base or wedge blocking have little chance of being a minus-yardage play. Line splits should be closely observed. Do they widen splits to run inside or trap? Tighter splits might indicate an outside play or a wedge-type blocking scheme. Tight splits might also indicate some type of pass play. Does the opponent go to a no-huddle mode on the goal line? If so, personnel changes may be difficult.

Bill Walsh advises offenses to throw on awkward goal-line situations. For example, first-and-goal from the nine, or second-and-goal from the seven are good times to throw the ball. Conventional wisdom in this zone seems to be that shorter drops (three or five steps) are more preferable than seven-step drops. Slants, fades, picks, and crossing routes are passing staples in this area. Many defensive teams will play a four-across coverage in the end zone. This serves to clutter up the end zone. As a result, many offenses decide to throw short or drop the ball off to an athletic receiver or back and let them run it in. Play-action passes with the tight end on crossing or submarine routes are very popular. Close receivers may involve banjo or combo coverage.

Defensive backs should be cautioned that the offense will have play-action passes off their favorite runs. How does the offense use their backs in the pass game? Will they screen or leak out the backs? Pass rush may suffer in goal-line situations if the defense subs larger and less mobile linemen. Linemen who are using a goal-line charge are obviously in no position to apply pressure to the quarterback, thus be careful with a predetermined tough or goal-line charges. It might not apply to each down-and-distance situation in the goal-line area.

As mentioned previously, a favorite goal-line route is the fade. It is a high-yield/low-risk play. It will either be a touchdown or an incompletion. It is a staple versus man-to-man coverages, which many teams use on the goal line. Scouting reports should reveal the favorite down and formation the opponent likes to use for this play. Does the offense check to this play? Do they throw it in obvious blitz situations? Is the receiver's split a tip-off? A tight split might indicate a fade and a wider split might signal a slant or quick route. Does the opponent run the fade out? This play looks like the fade until the last second when suddenly the receiver turns it into an out route. Motion is to be expected in goal-line situations. Offenses motion to get a desired match-up, confuse force, overload, or get a read on coverage.

The defense should not allow the opponent to get comfortable in their goal-line offense. An offense's goal-line package is usually the most detailed part of the offensive game plan. They have gone to great pains to scheme the defense in this area. Mundane and predictable defensive reactions serve to give the offense a decided advantage. Most defensive teams change very little from week to week. It is to the defense's advantage to add a wrinkle or curve for each opponent. The wrinkle doesn't have to be complicated or major. The inclusion of a simple run blitz that the opponent hasn't seen before could be effective and easily included. Don't be predictable.

As a basic rule, consider the goal line as beginning at the -10-yard line. However, offensive personnel, down-and-distance, score, and other considerations enter into the equation.

Goal-Line Scouting Checklist

- What yard line does the offense consider a goal-line situation?
- Personnel groups and substitution patterns
- Receiver/defensive back mismatches –(Where is the height disadvantage?)
- Formation Tendencies
  - ✓ Power
  - ✓ Bunch

- ✓ Wing
- ✓ Spread
- ✓ Balanced
- ✓ Overloaded
- Down-and-Distance Tendencies
- Hash Tendencies
- Split Tendencies (Line, Receivers)
- Option (What type(s)?)
- Running Game
  - ✓ Base runs
  - ✓ Special red-zone runs
  - ✓ Draws
- Pass Actions
  - ✓ Protections (Move the pocket.)
  - ✓ Screens
  - ✓ Sprints
  - ✓ Routes
    - ☐ Fades
    - ☐ Fade Out
    - ☐ Slant
    - ☐ Picks
- Running-Back Routes
- Delays
- Gadget Plays
- Snap-Count Tendencies
  - ✓ Quick
  - ✓ Long
  - ✓ Rhythmic
  - ✓ Non-Rhythmic
  - ✓ Hard
- Motions/Shifts
- No Huddle

7

Bad-Weather Planning

It is hard enough to game plan things you can control, but it is doubly frustrating to try to game plan things that are beyond your control. Obviously, the weather is beyond the governance of mortal man. Defensive coaches should not only adjust to foul-weather conditions, but should seek to use it to their advantage. Psychologically, the defense should feel that bad weather benefits the defense. It is the coach's job to indoctrinate the players that bad weather will work to their advantage. Players should be focused on the game, not the weather.

Defensive coaches should use psychology to prepare the players for bad weather by preaching that bad weather is to their advantage. One thing that makes this sell-job easier is that defense is easier to play in bad weather. Offenses are burdened with having to protect the football. Cold or very rainy conditions make it very hard to exchange the ball from player to player. Quarterbacks have problems receiving the ball from the center. For these reasons it would be advantageous, whether an odd- or even-spaced defense is preferred, to cover the center to compound his problems. Running backs sometimes have problems with handoffs from the quarterback, and receivers have problems receiving passes from the quarterback. Cold and rain make it difficult to grip the ball. It is hard to tuck away, and the defense usually thrives on raking the ball. The perception that offenses have the advantage in the passing game when conditions are soggy and wet has merit because receivers know when and where to make cuts, whereas defensive players have to react with reduced traction. However, during cold, fog, and driving rain, the advantage reverts to the defense.

As with other aspects of game planning, the defensive coach should first understand the offensive coordinator's mindset, goals, and objectives before he can ready a defensive response. A previous foul-weather game film from the opponent will help the defense surmise how a particular opponent has previously dealt with inclement weather. Obviously, weather affects some offenses more than others. Power-type offenses are more immune to poor weather than finesse offenses. If an offensive coach knows that the weather is going to get very bad during the game, he might take his shots downfield while he can. A prudent defensive coordinator will know within what framework his opponent will dial up an explosive play. The proposed explosive play might be called to a particular player or a particular play. For example, run-oriented teams may go with a play-action pass. If bad weather is rolling in with all its attendant problems of ball security, teams will try to get the lead so they can play conservatively when the really bad weather arrives.

The coin toss takes on added importance when the game is being played in inclement weather. The initial coin toss usually affects which team gets the early momentum, which is magnified when weather conditions, especially wind, are a factor. Coin-toss strategy should have been discussed and ironed out beforehand. It may be advisable to defer to get the choice later in the game. When deferring, make sure you end up with either the ball or wind. Don't give both away. If weather conditions are especially adverse, it might be desirable to kickoff both halves. Be cautious, however, not to kickoff into the wind to start a half. Most teams want the wind in the fourth quarter.

Coin-Toss Chart (Wind as a Deciding Factor)

You Win the Toss

Your Choice	Opponent's Choice	First-Half Result	Second-Half Result
Defer	The ball	You get the wind.	You get the ball.
Defer	The wind	You get the ball.	You get the ball.
Receive	The wind	You get the ball.	You get the wind.
Kick off	The ball	You get the wind.	You get the wind.

You Lose the Toss

Opponent's Choice	Your Choice	First-Half Result	Second-Half Result
Defer	The ball	You get the ball.	You get the wind.
Defer	The wind	You get the wind.	You get the wind.
Receive	The wind	You get the wind.	You get the ball.
Kick off	The ball	You get the ball.	You get the ball.

8

Planning for Time-Related Situations

During any game, defenses will be confronted by elements that are time-affiliated. During these situations, offensive and defensive strategy will be affected by time considerations. In many cases, victory or defeat will be the direct result of how effectively defenses plan for and react to these time-sensitive issues. Included in this chapter will be four-minute defense, prevent defense, two-minute defense, Big Ben play, no-huddle defense, and overtime procedure. Also covered will be time-out protocol, quarter-change protocol between the first and second quarter (as well as between the third and fourth quarter), and fourth-quarter defense. Offenses can go no huddle at any time, but most offenses choose to use no huddle in a two-minute scenario. No-huddle concerns will be discussed in both a two-minute offense and pre-two-minute situations.

Four-Minute Defense

When the opponent is ahead near the end of the game, they will try to run time off the clock. They will allow the play clock to run down 20 or more seconds before snapping the ball. They will use all the time possible and call plays that keep the clock running. Passes (if any) will probably consist of play-action or rollouts, which allow the quarterback a run or pass option. Quarterbacks will be coached to take a sack or loss of yardage instead of throwing the ball away or taking a chance on an interception. Runs will usually be conservative in nature with no high-risk exchanges. Double handoffs, reverses, and tosses will probably not be used. Runs will normally be basic runs that have been successful throughout the game. Wide runs, which eat up the clock, will be used. Runners will be coached to stay inbounds and secure the ball. Runners are traditionally taught not to fight for extra yardage in an effort to avoid fumbles in a four-minute scenario. Formationally, offenses will use tight formations, which add extra gaps to protect against outside blitzes and penetrations. Quarterbacks will use short snap counts and avoid hard counts. The offense will probably keep the same personnel grouping on the field to avoid illegal-substitution penalties or confusion.

Defensive Tactics

Each week's defensive game plan should have provisions in place to function in the four-minute window. In a four-minute situation, the defense should:

- Save time-outs for just this situation. When calling a time-out, do it aggressively. Do it as the runner is going down. Know where officials are located on the play.

- Force turnovers. Strip the ball. First man ensures the tackle while others strip the ball.

- Force three-and-out. Prevent first downs.

- Force runners out of bounds.

- Treat each down like a short-yardage play.

- Use aggressive fronts. Minus-yardage plays are desirable.

- Scheme solid run support.

- Use run blitzes.

- Unpile quickly. Get off the runner and let officials spot the ball.

- Practice "clock-time-out" situations. Players must be aware of what stops the clock. Defenses can't waste time-outs on plays that stop the clock. When the clock starts and stops are covered fully in the two-minute section of this chapter.

- Have a defense for the kneel-down or victory snap. Miracles do happen. Diagram 8-1 illustrates an Armageddon call for the kneel-down play.

Prevent Defense

Prevent defenses are typically used during the last four minutes of the half or game when your team has the lead. The prevailing philosophy of prevent defense is to contain the opponent while eating up the clock. Objectives include slowing down the offense when ahead, and forcing the opponent to use a lot of time moving the ball.

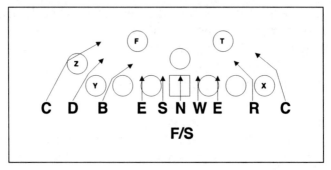

Diagram 8-1. Armageddon call for the kneel-down play

The defense wants to bleed slowly and keep the opponent from executing big plays. Yards will be traded for time.

A distinction should be made between the usage of a prevent defense at the end of the first half and the end of the second half. As a basic rule, prevent defenses are used with two minutes or less left in the first half of the game. A prevent situation during the second half of the game usually occurs with four minutes left in regulation. Another major difference between first- and second-half prevent scenarios is that a field goal isn't usually disastrous when it occurs just before halftime. A field goal at the end of the game could decide the game. Prevent situations should be included in any well-grounded defensive game plan. Anticipate using a prevent defense every game. All too often, the outcome of the game rides on the success or failure during this timeframe. Effective prevent defenses should allow the defense to:

- Adjust prevent calls to match the style of the opponent.
- Mix up the defensive calls. Don't allow the offense the luxury of knowing what to expect. Blend pressure with bend-but-don't-break looks.
- Use defensive back-loaded coverages (five or six defensive backs).
- Have availability of overloaded or double-team coverages.
- Avoid coverages where defensive backs are placed in one-on-one situations with no deep help.
- Allow sufficient quality practice time. Some coaches believe that prevent defense is the most poorly coached defensive category in football.
- Coordinate rush-lane integrity.
- Gang tackle. Keep the ballcarrier inbounds.
- Foster an "I'll make the play" attitude.
- Be aware of double moves (i.e., quick-and-go, out-and-up, etc.).
- Coach the players on the critical circumstances (i.e., what stops the clock, what starts the clock, time, score, what the offense needs, etc.).

Two-Minute Situation

The most important time interval in many games is the last two minutes of the game. Many games are decided in this short interval. The two-minute framework is only 1/24th of a high school game or 1/30th of a college or pro game, but in many cases this timeframe decides who wins and who loses the game. Two-minute offenses put stress on the defense by changing the tempo of the game through the use of an up-tempo pace, which limits defensive substitution and adjustments.

A crucial question to ask when game planning is: how will the defense approach the two-minute period? The age-old debate of how best to approach the two-minute period puts added pressure on the coaches. Coaches who bring pressure are grilled if they get torched. By the same token, coaches who go soft are criticized if the offense scores for *not* bringing pressure. Defenses have to find a happy median. A flexible defensive package allows for a variety of rushers mixed with zone, man, or combination coverages. Some teams zone-blitz the quarterback while dropping in a safe deep zone.

Tactical Situation

Not all two-minute situations are alike. Numerous variables affect offensive and defensive play calls. Following are some of the most important.

Time

Are there two full minutes or something less in the half or game? Offensive play calling will be influenced by the time left when the offense gets the ball. The offense will begin using its time-outs to conserve time and get as many plays executed as possible. The offense can chance a throw down the field if they have one time-out available. With one minute remaining, it is advisable to throw downfield in the sideline area. Ballcarriers will try to run out of bounds to stop the clock. Spiking the ball is an effective way to stop the clock. A spike will typically take 10 to 12 seconds to execute.

Offensive Time-Outs Left

Does the offense have its full complement of three time-outs? If so, they can mix their calls and not have to throw every play. With time-outs, the offense can use the middle of the field and can incorporate running plays. With one or no time-outs, the offense will be forced to work the sidelines and avoid running plays that can eat up time.

Effectiveness of the Opponent's Field-Goal Game

This factor comes into play should a field goal be necessary to win. What yard line is needed to attempt a make-able field goal?

Offense's Base Philosophy

Is the offense known as a passing team, running team, or is it balanced? Obviously, a balanced run-pass attack or a passing team has a better chance to succeed than a one-dimensional run team that has to rely on play-action passes.

Weather

What are the weather conditions? If conditions are horrid, the offense might try to run draws, screens, or short passes instead of down-the-field throws.

Down-and-Distance

Down-and-distance considerations are very important. On possession downs (such as third and fourth down), the offense should focus on plays that will get them first downs instead of trying to break big plays. Also, teams that need a touchdown will look at strategy through a "this is four-down territory" mentality. Third-down calls will obviously be adjusted in this situation, as opposed to a situation where a field goal is needed.

Field Zone

How far does the offense have to go to score? Distance affects offensive play calling. For example, with less than a minute to go before the half with the ball on the offense's end, some offensive coaches will call a draw play to see what happens. Does the defense have the luxury of making them go the long way, or does it have its back to the wall? Certainly, variables such as score, time, and so forth, in conjunction with field placement, will help decide defensive calls.

Score

What does the offense need? Do they need a field goal, a touchdown and extra point, a touchdown and a two-point play, or do they need two scores? The score differential influences strategy.

Offense Needs a Touchdown

- The offense is in a four-down mode no matter where they are on the field.
- The offense will avoid sacks. The quarterback will throw the ball away.
- On fourth down, the offense will throw the ball up for grabs.
- On the last play, ballcarriers will keep the ball alive by laterals or fumbles.
- Big Ben or desperation passes are usually reserved for the last play of a half or game. The offense tries to create a jump-ball situation and hopes for defensive interference or a tipped or batted ball for a touchdown.

Offense Needs a Field Goal

- The offense will avoid loss-of-yardage plays.
- Plays will be run to the middle of the field.
- The offense will avoid the hashes.
- When in field-goal range, the offense will call conservative plays.
- In an overtime situation or in an easy winning field-goal position, they may decide to kick on an early down. It is recommended that if the offense needs a field goal to tie, they should try to get within reasonable field-goal range (+20-yard line) before they try to take a shot to the end zone for the winning score. On the other hand, if a field goal is needed to win, the offense should simply work to get as close as possible for the field-goal attempt.
- The offense will seek to run down the clock as far as possible before kicking. Offenses will seek to save one time-out for the field-goal attempt. An offense should allow 15 seconds for a field goal when the clock cannot be stopped. The defense may be forced to use its time-outs to save time for its offense.

Base Two-Minute Defensive Strategy

In order to effectively combat an offense in a two-minute situation, the defense should know how variables such as time, score, offensive time-outs, the offense's field-goal game, and offensive philosophy will affect the offense's play calling. The main objective for a two-minute defense is to keep the clock running while keeping the offense from scoring. Important factors that coaches and players should know include:

- Gang tackle.
- Unpile slowly, but be onside for the next play. Get the defensive call quickly.
- Protect the sidelines. Turn the ballcarrier inside.
- Keep the ballcarrier in bounds.
- Commit no penalties. Don't stop the clock. The game can't end on a defensive penalty.
- Call time-out only when instructed from the sideline.
- Know the offense's formation rules.
- Distinguish their code words, especially if they use them more than once.
- Understand that the offense will usually go on quick counts if the clock is running. The defense should get an edge on get off. Be careful, however, that the offense may go on longer counts if the clock is stopped.

- Know the down-and-distance and time left.

- Be careful of gambles.

- Be aware that the offense may be in a four-down mode.

- Force the offense to go the long way.

- Mix attack and conservative calls.

- Do not scoop and score on fumbles. Possession is the issue. Fall on the ball.

- Avoid time-outs.

- Be aware that short-yardage plays may be a quarterback sneak from a spread formation.

- Allow no one behind the defense. Don't allow the top of the coverage to be blown off. Keep the ball in front and inside.

- Have the defensive call ready for the officials ready for play signal after an injury or measurement. The clock will start on the referee's signal.

- Align correctly and use correct technique.

- Do not bite on double moves (i.e., out-and-up and quick-and-go).

- Have the field-goal-block team alerted, especially if the offense doesn't have a time-out left.

- Be alert for the "watch" play, where the quarterback feigns a spike and throws a forward pass.

- Fall on a blocked field goal. Treat it as a fumble. Possession is the objective.

- If the opponent lines up in punt formation, the defense should expect to use a "safe" call. Expect a fake. It may be wise to not field the punt if it is kicked.

Game Plan for Big Ben

The climax to a two-minute defense may be defending the Hail Mary or Big Ben play. It is a disaster to lose on the last play of a game. Miracles do happen. Practice defending the Big Ben play each week. During that time, discuss the following defensive responsibilities:

- Play the ball.

- Intercept the ball if possible. At the very least, knock it down.

- Don't tip the ball.

Big Ben Schematics

- Use front and back defenders who look for tipped or batted balls.

- Use two-on-one ratio on the one-receiver side.

- Use the best jumpers to jump for the ball.

- Bunch sets should be defended by two jumpers in front and two defenders in back looking for a tip.

- Provide solid contain on opponents who like to roll out the quarterback.

- Line games for level-three drops by the quarterback

As a point of reference, Diagram 8-2 shows a defense for the Big Ben play if the line of scrimmage is on the offense's side of the 40-yard line. Big Ben is the call. If the goal line is within reach of the quarterback's arm, a more appropriate defense is illustrated in Diagram 8-3, called Big Ben roll.

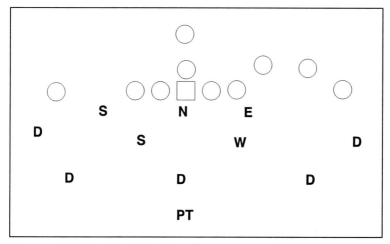

Diagram 8-2. Big Ben defensive alignment

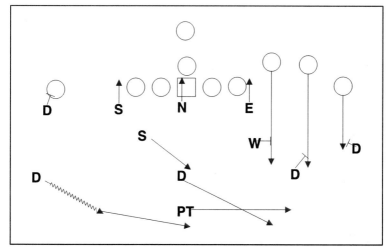

Diagram 8-3. Big Ben roll defensive alignment

To be proficient in the two-minute situation, players should be drilled on what to expect and how they should respond. These crucial situations can be covered in a classroom setting as well as on the field. Two- and four-minute defenses need to be installed early in the season and reviewed weekly. These scenarios can be practiced in shorts or shells. Variables such as time remaining, score, down-and-distance, and field-zone variables should be included. Once the basic package is installed, it can be refined and tweaked for that week's opponent.

Time Considerations

It is crucial for the defense to understand the rules concerning starting and stopping of the game clock. This education makes players more informed and effective in two-minute or four-minute situations. Following are rules that govern clock management. Included are NFL, college, and high school rules.

Actions That Stop the Clock

- The down ends following a foul.
- Official's time-out.
- Called time-out.
- Television/radio time-out [NFHS: 1:00, NCAA: 1:30 (really 1:05), NFL: 1:50]. NFHS and NCAA rules allow consecutive time-outs by the same team.
- The period ends.
- The ball goes out of bounds.
- A legal or illegal forward pass is incomplete.
- A score or touchback occurs.
- Fair catch is made or the ball is illegally touched.
- An inadvertent whistle.
- Measurement for a possible first down.
- When a first down is declared.
- Following a change of team possession.
- When coaches are notified of time remaining if the game clock dies. Two minutes in each half (NCAA). Four minutes in each half (NFHS). Two-minute warning (NFL).
- Player injury.
- Equipment repair.
- Dry or change game ball (NFHS).

- Undue pileups on the runner, or determining possession after a fumble.
- Undue delay by officials in spotting the ball for the next snap.
- Any time the player who originally takes the snap is tackled behind the line of scrimmage (NFL).
- Sideline warning.
- Coach/referee conference.
- If the clock is running and a dead-ball foul occurs.
- When an official suspends or stops play for any reason.
- When a runner's helmet comes off (NCAA). No such rule in NFHS.
- When a legal kick down ends (NCAA).

Clock Starts on the Ready-for-Play Signal (if the Clock Was Already Running)

- After an official's time-out, except when team B is awarded a new series, or when either team is awarded a new series following a legal kick (NFHS).
- If the clock was stopped following a foul and no time-out has been charged during a dead-ball interval, or the action that caused the down to end did not cause the clock to be stopped.
- Because of an inadvertent whistle.
- Injury if no time-outs are left (NFL).
- Team A is awarded a first down (except after a legal kick).
- At the referee's discretion (team trying to manipulate the clock).
- Official's conference.
- Sideline warning.
- For an illegal pass to conserve time (NCAA).
- For a measurement.
- After measurement for first down.
- After undue pileup or delayed unpiling, and no change of possession occurs.
- After removal of an injured player. If no time-out is available, 10 seconds is run off clock (NFL).
- After administration of a penalty following a foul, whether the penalty is accepted or declined.
- After a fumble goes out of bounds forward and officials reposition the ball (NFL).
- Lateral pass out of bounds (NFL).

Clock Starts on the Snap

- Change of possession (NFHS).
- Expiration of a charged team time-out.
- Incomplete pass.
- Out-of-bounds play.
- Start of the two-minute period (NFL).
- Media time-out.
- Ball goes out of bounds (carried or kicked) (NFHS).
- After a fair catch.
- After a touchback.
- Penalty for delay of the game is accepted.

A good rule of thumb concerning when the clock starts is "what stops the clock, starts the clock." If an official stops play, he will start the clock with a ready-for-play signal. If the ball stops the play (incomplete pass, out of bounds), the snap of the next play starts the clock. Another good rule of thumb deals with starting the clock after a penalty is enforced. When considering if the clock will start on the ready or the snap, ask, "What would the clock status be if the penalty had not occurred?" If the clock would usually be running and it was only stopped to enforce a penalty, it will restart on the ready. If the clock would be stopped anyway, such as for pass interference or an incomplete pass, the clock will restart on the snap. Some exceptions exist; however, this method is good to use in situations where clock management is essential.

No Huddle

An effective offensive change-up is the no huddle. Most offenses have a no-huddle package in their system. It can be used in a variety of ways. Some teams use it as a predetermined part of the offensive game plan, while others use it only during time-related segments of the game. No-huddle execution is usually triggered by a code word such as "jet" or "red." A no-huddle mindset is a great way to offset blitzing defenses or defenses that are using unexpected tactics, in the hopes of forcing the defense to check into base looks. The reasons for using the no huddle include:

- Allows the offense to play uptempo.
- Limits defensive substitution.
- Wears down defenses.
- Keeps defenses off balance.

- Defenses who have a structured huddle are forced out of their comfort zone.

- Hampers defensive communication.

- Allows offenses to slow down defensive blitzing or defenses that have surprised the offense with its game plan.

No-huddle offenses can function at various speeds. When most coaches think about no-huddle offense, they conjure up an image of a hurry-up and uptempo pace—which is not always the case. Some offenses do use a fast pace when they go no huddle, especially if it is used in a two-minute situation. Other no-huddle teams may use it in a more deliberate manner. A lot of the same advantages are possible no matter what pace the no-huddle offense uses. Some no-huddle offenses will come to the line of scrimmage, set the defense by giving the appearance the snap was imminent, and then look to the sideline for the play call. This procedure allows coaches in the box and on the sideline to signal in the play after they see the defensive alignment. The defense needs to do a great job of disguising what defense it is in. If it is a two-safety look, they are going to run. If it is a one-safety look, they are going to throw. The defense should have a procedure in place to combat no-huddle situations. Defensive response to no-huddle situations should be put in place during pre-season practice and schooled periodically throughout the year.

Defensive Responses to No Huddle

- Hanging huddles are more conducive to combating a hurry-up mode as opposed to more rigid and structured huddles. The offense can't force players out of their comfort zone as easily.

- Clear and concise communication should be stressed.

- Use of wrist bands with defensive calls is highly efficient.

- The offensive personnel on the field stays on the field. The defense has a good idea of offensive personnel.

- If the offense is freezing the defense so they can match a call with the defense shown, be able to change the defensive call. Show *them* something different. Change the front and/or coverage. If they have time, you have time.

- Use "mill-around" alignments. Use a "mixer" or "radar" scheme where the front moves around in a two-point stance and then strikes a particular gap on the snap. The radar scheme has several advantages. Offenses can't discern what front the defense is in and your defensive linemen don't have to hold in place in a three-point stance.

- Have code words for defensive calls. For example, to repeat the previous defensive call, signal "Mayday." To line up in a base front and coverage, signal "bingo." To run a programmed stunt, yell: "Bonzai."

Overtime Procedure

Coaches should prepare not only for the four quarters of the game, but also for the possibility of overtime. The team that prepares for and understands overtime procedure has a better chance of success if overtime becomes necessary. Coaches should condition their players for a game plus overtime, and also prepare themselves and their players for overtime. Familiarity of overtime procedures will help players and coaches avoid panic and mistakes if that eventuality arises. Following are overtime procedures for high school, college, and the NFL.

High School: National Federation of State High Schools Association (NFHS)

An overtime period is untimed. The play clock is in use, but the game clock is turned off. This period is used when the regulation game has ended in a tie. During overtime, each team will be given the opportunity of an offensive series of downs. However, the game can end after only one series of downs if the defense scores a touchdown or a safety. This situation is very, very rare since the ball is dead when B gets possession. The defense must gain possession while the ball is in the offense's end zone.

At the end of regulation, the referee will instruct both teams to return to their respective team box. At this point, both teams have a three-minute interval to confer with their coaches. During this interval, the officials confer at midfield and review the overtime procedure among themselves. Unused second-half time-outs are carried over to the overtime period. Regulation penalties are in effect (dead-ball foul). At the end of the three-minute intermission, officials will inform both benches of any carryover penalties and the number of time-outs they have. Each team receives an additional time-out for each overtime period. The visiting team calls the coin toss at midfield. The winner has the choice of offense or defense or the end of the field to defend. The loser of the toss has the choice of the other options. The offensive team puts the ball in play at the +10, or succeeding spot if a carryover penalty is administered. The offense has a series of four downs. The series is terminated if the offense scores or the defense secures possession. After a score, the offense can choose to go for one or two points. A field goal can be attempted at any time. The team with the most points at the end of the overtime period is the winner. If the score is tied after the first overtime period, a two-minute intermission will occur before the second overtime period. The loser of the first coin toss will be given first choice of options. During play the offensive team can be awarded a new set of downs if:

- Defensive pass interference occurs.
- The offensive team recovers a blocked field goal that has crossed the line of scrimmage but hasn't broken the plane of the goal line, and was touched by a defensive player beyond the neutral zone.
- The defensive team roughs the kicker, holder, snapper, or passer.

Summary of NFHS Overtime Rules

- Unused second-half time-outs carry over.
- Each team will receive one additional time-out for each overtime period.
- Some penalties from regulation can carry over. These penalties will be assessed to start the overtime procedure.
- Visiting team calls coin toss.
- Winner of coin toss can choose offense or defense, or the end of the field to play.
- Ball put in play at the +10, or succeeding spot if a carryover penalty is administered.
- Line to gain is always the goal line.
- Offense has a series of four downs (first-and-goal).
- Series is over if the offense scores or the defense secures possession.
- Try after touchdown can be for one or two points.
- The offense can kick a field goal at any time.
- If additional overtime periods are needed, first options will be alternated without a coin toss.

NCAA Overtime Rule

Overtime procedure is very similar to NFHS rules in some respects and different in others. Possession starts on the 25-yard line with 10 yards to go for a first down. College rules allow the possibility of one or more first downs. Each team retains possession of the ball during a series until it scores, turns over the ball, or fails to make a first down. The ball remains live after a change of team possession until it becomes (or is declared) dead. However, team A may not have a first-and-10 again if it regains possession of the ball after a turnover. Besides starting on the 25-yard line, another major difference between NCAA and NFHS rules is that college teams must go for two points starting in the third overtime period. Unlike NFHS rules, college rules do not allow for a carryover of unused time-outs from regulation. Each team will be allowed one time-out for each extra period. Unused extra-period time-outs may not be carried over to other extra periods.

Summary of NCAA Overtime Rules

- Possession starts on the 25-yard line.
- Ten-yard line to gain mark.
- Offenses must go for two points starting with the third overtime period.
- No carryover of unused regulation time-outs.
- One time-out allowed per overtime period.

NFL Overtime Rules

NFL rules on determining the winner when the score is tied at the end of regulation is drastically different from high school and college. Under the sudden-death system used by the NFL, the first team to score is the winner and the game is automatically ended upon any score (including a safety) or when a score is awarded by the referee for a palpably unfair act.

Summary of NFL Overtime Rules

- At end of regulation, the referee will immediately conduct the coin toss in accordance with rules pertaining to a usual pre-game toss.
- Three-minute intermission after coin toss.
- Play for a 15-minute period, or until either team scores (whichever comes first).
- Each team in a pre-season or regular season game receives two time-outs. Playoff games allow teams three time-outs.
- Team that scores first wins.

Defensive Mindset During Overtime (NFHS)

Defenses should have an understanding of how the rules affect them in an overtime situation. Goals and objectives should be spelled out so that players have no confusion and a clear and concise understanding of what they should do in each situation.

The guidelines to be presented to the defense are as follows:

- Avoid penalties. Don't give the offense more than four downs.
- If on defense first, hold the offense to a field-goal attempt.
- If on defense second, hold the offense to one point less than your offense scored.
- If on defense second and your offense didn't score, think turnover. You cannot allow *any* score.
- If a field goal will win it, force a bad kick or block the kick. The defense may have to think of a "sell-the-farm" scheme and sell out on the block—especially if the field-goal kicker is an effective kicker. A sellout might be risky against a poor kicker because a fake might be a possibility.
- If a field goal for the win is attempted on an early down, block or force a bad kick, but cover eligibles for a fake. If the offense doesn't score on the fake, they still have another down to kick the winner.
- Should the offense fumble, fall on the ball. The series ends on a change of possession. If the kick is blocked or tipped, call "Peter" and get away.

Time-Out Protocol

A structured time-out procedure should be planned for every game. The system should teach players how and when to call time-outs. The defense shouldn't waste time-outs that may be needed later, but by the same token don't be short on personnel or have too many people on the field. Time-out protocol should be taught early in the season. Periodically, the system needs to be reviewed. Following is a blueprint for time-outs:

- Time-outs will be called from the sideline or as instructed by the defensive coordinator (i.e., clock time-out).
- Sam or the free safety will call time-out if the defense doesn't have the proper number or right combination of players on the field. Sam controls the front and linebackers while the free safety regulates the defensive backs.
- On all time-outs, Sam and the free safety will come to the sideline for instruction. In some situations, the entire defense may go to the sideline.
- On official time-outs, when the teams have to stay on the field, the defense should look to the sideline for instructions. NFHS rules allow players to come to the hash.
- Players should be taught the positioning of the various officials. This knowledge will allow the defense to get time-outs called quickly without having to look for officials.

Quarter Change

While the defensive unit jogs to the other side of the field, players should work down the hash closest to the defensive bench and look to the sideline for instructions from position coaches.

- Sam will come to the sideline for any instructions and to get the next call.
- Coaches can call the entire defense or selected players to the sideline.

Fourth-Quarter Defense

At the interval between the third and fourth quarters, players on one or both teams will raise four fingers into the air and/or raise their helmets skyward. This motion is the universal symbol that the fourth quarter is here. It is time to turn it on and win the game. In most cases, this quarter is the most important quarter in the game, and many games are won or lost during this interval. Conditioning and good habits will usually mean the difference between winning and losing. Conditioning and good habits are crucial in the fourth quarter when players get tired.

Components of a Solid Fourth-Quarter Defense

- Pride.
- Picking up the tempo.
- Being mentally tougher than the opponent.
- Being better conditioned than the opponent.
- Keeping pressure on the offense every play. Think three-and-out.
- Play each play as if it were the last.
- Playing error-free. No penalties to prolong a drive.

9

Game Planning
Base-Defensive Systems

This chapter will compartmentalize various aspects of a team's base defensive system and tweak them for a particular opponent. The variables explored here should be in place, no matter the upcoming opponent. To apply them to a specific opponent, the defensive coach simply fashions and molds them to meet current conditions. Included are the following variables:

- Defending gadget plays
- Defending two-point plays
- Incorporating defensive substitution packages
- Formulating the stunt-game plan
- Game planning turnovers and how to deal with sudden change
- Safe calls
- Pre-snap game planning
- Alerts

Defending Gadget Plays

Most offensive playbooks have a collection of gadget or trick plays. These plays—sometimes called "specials"—serve to develop and take advantage of defensive conflicts. Many offensive teams practice selected trick plays on a weekly basis in anticipation of using them that particular week. Offenses will try to take advantage of unsound technique by a player (or players). For example, backside defenders on running plays may be susceptible to a reverse.

Film study may reveal the opponent's philosophy of exotic plays. Do they view gadget plays as a basic part of their offense, or do they use those plays sparingly and for shock value only? How do variables such as field zone, score, time, personnel, and so forth affect how and when the offense dials up an exotic play? Most teams will avoid high-risk plays near their own goal line as well as close to the opponent's end zone. Game planning for trick plays might be the most difficult segment for defensive coaches to deal with because they may have to prepare for plays not seen before. Most offenses have one or more of the following gadget plays:

- Hitch-and-pitch, or hook-and-ladder
- Flea flicker
- Statue of Liberty
- Halfback pass
- Throwback to the quarterback (especially in the going-in and goal-line areas)
- Fumblerooski-type plays
- Reverse-family plays (reverse, fake reverse, reverse pass, double reverse, double reverse pass)

Playing disciplined defense is the best way to combat trick plays. Well-schooled defenses are not as likely to bite on plays such as halfback passes. Fundamentally sound defenses are hard to trick or fool. Also, pressure-type defenses will defeat a lot of trick plays, as well as make the opposing coach leery of calling them. Defenses should be coached to call time-out if the offense shows a completely off-the-wall formation that it isn't prepared to defend. Basic trick plays should be run during the week as you implement your weekly game plan.

All offenses have reverse-type plays in their playbook. It is a very important part of any offensive attack. Reverses seek to take advantage of undisciplined defenses. Most reverses come off a base running play. Reverses are easily run out of a wide variety of formations. A lot of teams are running plays off Zarc motion. The threat of a reverse is present every time this motion is used. Diagram 9-1 illustrates this concept—an offshoot of the wing-T buck-sweep series.

Defenses should have reverse responsibilities assigned on every call and situation. In addition to reverse responsibilities, fake reverses and reverse passes should also be covered. Minus-splits and certain types of motion may be tip-offs to reverses. Reverses, while presenting a big play potential for offenses, can also be a liability if defended effectively. Big losses or fumbles are possible because of the extra ballhandling. Outside blitzes or the threat of an outside blitz can discourage reverses.

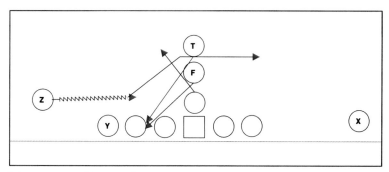

Diagram 9-1. Zarc motion

Two-Point Play

One commonly overlooked part of game planning is defensive reaction to a two-point play. This oversight can be fatal since, in many cases, when the offense goes for two, the game is on the line. Admittedly, two-point plays are few and far between. College and high school ratios are higher than NFL attempts. NCAA rules state that teams must go for two points after the second overtime period. To put it into perspective, if a team only faces two attempts per year, it could equate to two wins or losses on the schedule. In high school, that is one-fifth of the schedule.

The offense usually has one of three goals in mind in a two-point situation: a successful two-point attempt will tie the game, a two-point play puts the offense in the lead, or the offense is seeking to make up for an earlier missed extra-point attempt. No offensive play list would be complete without a pre-conceived plan for a two-point play. How many defensive coordinators have similar preparation? Two-point plays are similar to fourth-down plays in that film study of the opponent may not offer any clues as to how they will approach the play call. If the defensive coaches are lucky enough to see the opponent run on a two-point play, it will help them plan for this situation.

Basic Questions To Ask About the Offense in a Two-Point Scenario

- How athletic is the quarterback? Could they sprint him to the corner with a run/pass option?

- How do their receivers match up height-wise with your defensive backs?
- Do they like picks or crossing routes?
- What personnel package do they prefer?
- What is their best running play?
- What is their best play-action pass?
- Will they use motion to pick or flood?
- Do they move the ball to a hash? In high school, with the ball on the hash, the offense will have two-thirds of the field to work with to the wideside.
- Do they use their base goal-line package here?
- Do they load up with receivers, which removes defenders from the box? With an empty backfield, quarterback draws are always a distinct possibility.

Basic Questions About Defensive Reaction to a Two-Point Play

- Should the defense play zone or man? You only have to defend twelve yards of the field.
- Should the defense use man coverages that are susceptible to picks, rubs, and crossing routes?
- Should the defense bring pressure with a pass or run blitz, or should you play a base look?
- How does the defense adjust to wide formations? Should you remove defenders from the box, or should you adjust with the secondary only?
- What kind of charge does the defense want from its linemen? Should the defense be in run or pass-rush stances?
- Should the defense tighten down on line shades, or should you get on the edge?
- Is it advisable to bring defenders off the edge of the formation to get quick force, contain on the quarterback, or offset any quarterback naked keep?
- Will linebacker stunts inside be productive?

Another aspect of a two-point defense that should be addressed is what to do after the offense scores a touchdown and their extra-point team comes onto the field in a swinging-gate or water-bucket alignment. Some coaches see this situation as a way to "make hay" (score two points) while the defense is in disarray or mentally affected by the touchdown. Some coaches see this situation as an easier way to score two points than going against a forewarned defense that has time to make a two-point call. Diagram 9-2 is an adjustment to a swinging gate. A two-point chart is shown in Diagram 9-3. Some coaches follow this chart religiously throughout the game, while others consult it only in the fourth quarter.

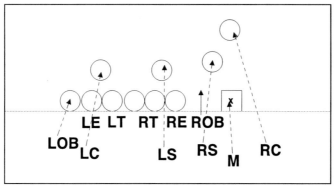

Diagram 9-2. Swinging-gate defense

Two-Point Chart
When To Go for Two

Ahead By	Behind By
+1 point - Go for two	-1 point - Decision
+2 points - Kick PAT	-2 points - Go for two
+3 points - Kick PAT	-3 points - Kick PAT
+4 points - Go for two	-4 points - Decision
+5 points - Go for two	-5 points - Go for two
+6 points - Kick PAT	-6 points - Kick PAT
+7 points - Kick PAT	-7 points - Kick PAT
+8 points - Kick PAT	-8 points - Kick PAT
+9 points - Kick PAT	-9 points - Go for two
+10 points - Kick PAT	-10 points - Kick PAT
+11 points - Kick PAT	-11 points - Go for two
+12 points - Go for two	-12 points - Go for two
+13 points - Kick PAT	-13 points - Kick PAT
+14 points - Kick PAT	-14 points - Kick PAT
+15 points - Go for two	-15 points - Kick PAT
+16 points - Kick PAT	-16 points - Go for two
+17 points - Kick PAT	-17 points - Kick PAT
+18 points - Kick PAT	
+19 points - Go for two	
+20 points - Kick PAT	

Diagram 9-3. Two-point chart

Substitution Defenses

During the season practices, the coaches should install and fine tune a variety of personnel packages for use in the upcoming season. A study of the season's schedule should provide an idea of the various offensive philosophies to be faced throughout the year. Game planning doesn't start anew each week, but should start in the off-season and be a continuous process. Development of substitution defenses should follow these basic principles:

- Clearly define the purpose of a particular package. Ask the following pertinent questions: Why do we need this package? What are its goals and objectives?
- Substitution defenses should be a continuation of base fronts and coverages (for example, substituting a nickelback for the strong or weak outside linebacker). A dime package would sub two defensive backs for both outside linebackers. A quarter scheme, in a 4-3 configuration, would involve subbing three defensive backs for all three linebackers. The same defense can be called with either base personnel or substitution personnel in the game.
- Be flexible enough to sub up or down in size. Be able to sub in size by incorporating more linebackers and linemen in a goal-line or short-yardage situation, or down in size but more quickness by inserting more defensive backs to defend during passing downs.
- Sufficient practice time should be allocated to develop these different packages.
- Decide how injuries would affect the use of substitute defenses. Will a package need to be scrapped because of injury or if a particular defender is incapacitated? For example, are there eight capable pass defenders in a quarter package? If one of the seven defenders in this package were injured, can the eighth man be trusted?
- Substitutes, situational or otherwise, need to stay near the signal caller.
- Substitutes should be aware of the situation.
- The substitution package should be all-encompassing as well as week-to-week specific.
- Packages shouldn't be stereotyped. Keep the quarterback off balance. Make him guess as to what coverage will be called, who will be doubled, who will stunt, and who will drop.
- The scheme should allow the defense to match offensive personnel and be field-zone sound.
- Disguise is paramount.
- The defense should be run sound no matter the defensive personnel on the field. Run force shouldn't be sacrificed with defensive-back-loaded coverages. Also, it is

not advisable to have a defensive back responsible for C gap versus runs. A prudent defensive coach will place his strong end in C gap. Not only does this move place a bigger body in the power gap, but a 7 technique will give the defense a quick pass/run read.

- Substitution packages should be flexible enough to give the offense both even and odd spacing. A good rule of thumb to follow is: if you are a base even-front team use an odd look as a change-up. By the same token, if you base out of an odd front, make use of an even front as a change of pace.

- Tailor substitutions to different contingency factors such as down-and-distance, field zone, and so forth.

Formulating the Stunt-Game Plan

An integral part of any defensive game plan is drafting that particular week's stunt game. An effective stunt game is a must for any defense to be successful. Stunts should be an integral part of any defensive game plan. All defenses have a basic stunt game, but the defensive coach should tailor and refine his stunt game to fit that week's opponent. He should decide what aspects of his stunt package will be viable and which part will be ineffective against a particular opponent. This section will explore various aspects of a well-prepared stunt package, such as the benefits and drawbacks of implementing a particular stunt package, how to study the opponent's run and pass game, and basic offensive counter-measures against defensive stunting. Line games conclude this section.

Benefits of Stunting

- Stunting gives you a chance if you are outmanned. Stunting gives smaller, quicker players a chance.

- Produces big plays (i.e., minus-yardage tackles, sacks, fumbles, interceptions, forced passes).

- Helps to regain and hold momentum.

- Can stop a long drive.

- Forces turnovers.

- Pressures the run game.

- Pressures the pass game.

- The offense has to be patient.

- Confuses blocking schemes.

- Offenses have to cut down their play selection. Pressure negates some gadget plays and some slow-developing plays.

- Offenses must spend time preparing for stunts.
- Speeds up slower players and makes fast players faster.
- Limits double-moves by receivers. The ball must come out quickly.
- Forces backs and Y to protect instead of getting into pass pattern. Forces the offense to get only two or three receivers in the pattern.
- Fun to play.

Drawbacks of Stunting

- Mobile quarterbacks can hurt stunts because defenders have their backs to the ball.
- Leaves the defense open to giving up big plays.
- Defenses must play a lot of man coverage with all its inherent drawbacks.

Run Blitz

It is wise to game plan blitzes to use in run situations, especially if the opponent is physically superior or stunting is necessary to stop a drive. Blitzes, which are designed to disrupt a play or at least redirect the running lane, are needed no matter the physical match-ups. Run blitzes are designed to get straight-line penetration instead of delayed changes or loops, which are more effective versus pass plays. Run blitzes can be designed to include a sudden inside change by a lineman, a coordinated front slant, or a linebacker fire or a combination of all. If a linebacker is sent and zone coverage is desired, the void can be filled by a lineman (zone blitz) or by vacating a zone. Game plans may include five-, six-, seven-, or even eight-man stunt packages. These packages should be tailored to meet that particular week's offensive philosophy. Good scouting techniques can narrow possible attack areas by such variables as down-and-distance and field zone. A line stunt or linebacker insertion in that area can be effective. Run blitzes can be planned to attack all along the front or can be tailored to attack either the strongside or weakside, depending upon tendencies.

Run-Game Breakdown

A breakdown and study of the opponent's run game should include:

- Runs by formation
- Runs by down-and-distance
- Runs by field zones

- Strongside runs
- Weakside runs
- Runs after motion or shifts
- Blocking schemes to strongside
- Blocking schemes to weakside
- Runs by hash

Studying these variables will allow the defensive coordinator to formulate an intelligent and effective run-stunt package and not have to depend upon random and haphazard schemes.

Pass Blitz

The coach should design stunts for the type (or types) of pass actions used by the opponent's offense. Stunts for one particular type of pass style may not work for others. Stunt packages should be designed for dropback (three-, five-, seven-step), play-action, sprint, bootleg, and so forth. Not only should the coach plan for various passing styles, he should also game plan for passes by formations, down-and-distance, field zone, and the like. Stunts should also be designed or adjusted to attack various types of pass protections. Stunts should be tailored to attack cup, man, fan, and turn-back protections, just to name a few. Provisions should also be made to counteract the offenses max protecting and running one-man routes when the defense gets pressure on the quarterback.

Pass-Game Breakdown

A breakdown and study of the opponent's pass game should include:

- Passes by formation
- Passes by down-and-distance
- Passes by field zones
- Pass-protection schemes by pass action
- How the opponent uses backs in the pass game
- Hot scheme

Offensive Countermeasures Versus Defensive Stunt Game

As in other aspects of defensive game planning, it is a good idea to understand how the offense seeks to counteract defensive designs.

- Most teams scout the defense as to defensive stunt tendencies by down-and-distance, field zone, personnel, variables, and so on.
- Offenses will carry two or three blitz-beaters into each game. For example, some teams have automatic checks when they see a Bears (or 46) look.
- Throw "hot."
- Max protect.
- Attack certain personnel. Offenses scheme to find a mismatch.
- Use of spread formations make the defense declare the blitz quicker. It is harder to disguise the blitz.

Line Games

By strict definition, line games are not true blitzes or stunts. However, lane exchanges can be effective versus pass and certain types of runs. Lane exchanges can disrupt runs and pass-blocking schemes. Also, defenders stunting into draw lanes are highly effective.

A variety of ways to run line games exist. They are effective in even- or odd-front spacings. They can be run to one side only, or both sides if desirable. Exchanges can be executed on the snap or after several steps (delayed). Read exchanges can be run only if linemen read pass. Defensive coordinators should determine if the opponent pass protects using man or zone principles. Snap stunts are effective versus man schemes. Snap exchanges are also desirable versus offensive linemen who set up on different planes. Adjoining offensive linemen cannot switch off if they are on different

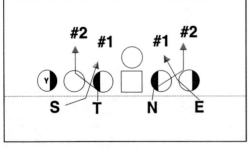

Diagram 9-4. Double pick

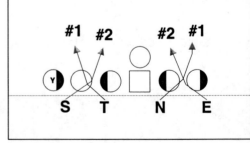

Diagram 9-5. Double pop

levels. Against offensive linemen that stay on the same level, an effective defensive counter would be to fake line exchanges. Delayed stunts are better versus zone protection. Effective scouting will help to determine which side has man and which side has zone responsibilities and tailor exchanges to take advantage. Diagrams 9-4 through 9-7 illustrate some basic lane exchanges.

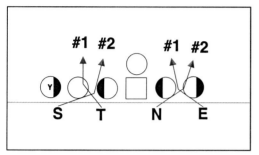

Diagram 9-6. Change

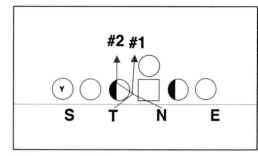

Diagram 9-7. Twist

Game Planning Turnovers

Most defensive coordinators teach their players how to produce turnovers. An age-old truth in football is that the team that doesn't turn the ball over has an advantage over teams that are error prone. Statistics prove this universal truth. Teams that win the turnover battle will usually win the game. Coaches should teach their players what to do with fumbles and interceptions as it pertains to the game situation. Only two defensive reactions to a fumble exist. Either scoop and run with the ball or fall on the loose ball. The same principle applies to interceptions. Either catch and run the ball or get down with the ball after the interception. A well-schooled defensive unit will understand how to react to turnovers based on the game situation. This reaction should be a segment of the total game plan. Each game plan should have an organized methodology on how to treat interceptions and fumbles. Following are guidelines to use for interceptions and fumbles.

Interceptions

Defenders should be taught when and when not to intercept a pass. In some cases, it would be advisable to knock down a fourth-down pass instead of intercepting it. A clear distinction should be made between when to run back a pick and when to get down and not take a hit (victory interception). A game could be lost by a player who intercepts the ball, runs it back, and then fumbles on a hit. If the offense recovers the ball, they may score to win the game.

Base Interception Return

- Yell, "Oskie!" to alert the defense.
- If two defenders have a chance, communicate with "you-me" calls. Don't knock each other off.
- Return to the nearest numbers. Start upfield to draw tacklers to the middle.
- Put the ball in the outside arm.
- The nearest defender to the interception should block the intended receiver. He is the guy who usually makes the tackle.
- Defensive linemen should block the quarterback.
- Other defenders should work to the nearest numbers.
- Blocks should be in front and above the waist.
- Don't block unnecessarily behind the ball.

Fumbles

- As a basic rule, scoop and score unless in a scrum situation.
- Defenders are to fall on the ball if they don't get it cleanly on the first attempt.
- In a late-game situation with your team in the lead, fall on the ball (victory fumble).
- In a late-game situation with the defense behind on the scoreboard, scoop and score unless in a crowd.

Sudden Change

Defensive players should be coached on how to react when the offense turns the ball over. If the offense has just thrown an interception (or the opponent has just blocked a punt), how the defense reacts may decide the outcome of the game. The opponent may be thinking:

- What a great break.
- Let's get them while they are down.
- Their defense is tired.

    Your defense's thoughts might be:

- You've got to be kidding me.
- We just left the field.
- I'm tired.

- I hope they don't come my way.
- Who is going to make the play?
- If they score it won't be my fault.

Coaches should not allow these negative attitudes to happen. Instead, install an aggressive and opportunistic mindset when faced with a sudden-change situation. The players should see this as both a challenge and an opportunity. A defensive stop here while their offense is fired up will send a message. It is good to have a blueprint on how to react to a turnover. Following is an example of a sudden-change procedure:

- Players huddle up on the sideline with the defensive coaches before they go back out.
- As a basic rule, starters will enter the game unless it is a blowout.
- Players yell "sudden change" as they enter the game.
- Players should want to be the one who makes the play.
- Players must be in control.
- Players should accept the challenge.

Sudden-change situations should be practiced weekly during the season. Script turnovers into practice scrimmages. A good way to do this is insert the second unit for one play after the starters have worked up a good sweat and script in a make-believe turnover on that one play. The starters who have just taken a knee or just put a water bottle to their mouth have to strap back up and go right back in.

After the base sudden-change procedure is in place, it should be molded to meet that week's opponent. Film study will help reveal how the opponent approaches a sudden-change scenario. Some offensive coaches take this opportunity to go up top for an easy score. Some offensive coaches may attack by throwing play-action or running double-move routes. Sudden-change breakdowns should be an integral part of the scouting report. Film breakdown should include first-down plays after a turnover.

Safe Calls

Within each game plan, a well-prepared defense should have provisions in place to defend possible kick fakes. Previous behavior by the opponent will uncover a propensity toward faking punts, field goals, or extra points. Some offensive coaches will play very conservatively in those situations, while other coaches may prefer a more risk-taking high-yield mentality. Understand, however, that all coaches have fake kicks in their system. It takes courage to run a fake punt, but it can be a high-yield play. The game can turn on a well-executed fake kick or a well-defended kick fake. Most coaches feel it is best to keep the defense on the field whenever the probability of a fake is high. Some teams prefer to defend possible fakes with their special team designed for that phase of the kicking game. For example, some coaches place their punt-return team on the field to return/block a punt, as well as to execute the safe call. However, it is best to prepare only the defense for a safe call rather than both, because the defense will have its best defenders on the field in these situations. Diagram 9-8 is a safe call used versus punt formations.

The linemen penetrate and go full speed to the depth of the personal protector. If a fumbled or errant snap occurs, they continue and play football. If the punter has it clean, they should pull up. This call can also be used when your team is ahead or you are content just to get the ball and don't want to take a chance on running into or roughing the kicker. If the offensive team is within five yards of a first down, an ultra-conservative "cushion" call can be used. This call tells the linemen to back off the ball a good yard and play from that point. Diagram 9-9 illustrates a safe call versus a field-goal formation. With this call, the linemen are trying to block the kick while B and W slam the wings, then explode upfield for contain. The other defenders play man on assigned receivers.

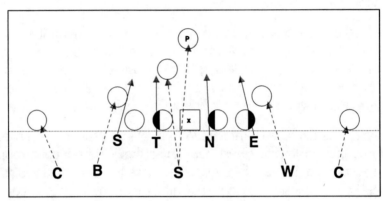

Diagram 9-8. Safe call versus punt formation

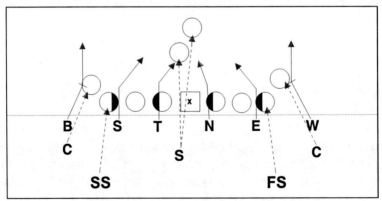

Diagram 9-9. Safe call versus field-goal formation

Pre-Snap Game Planning

Astute pre-snap observation can go a long way in securing success after the ball has been snapped. Observation of pre-snap tendencies of the offense starts with film study and continues throughout the game. According to Buddy Ryan, the secret to great defense is to play the run when the offense is going to run and play pass when the offense intends to throw the ball. This scenario is an ideal one, but it can be accomplished somewhat through shrewd pre-snap game planning. Pre-snap reads can be divided into four separate entities: the huddle, how the offense gets the play call in, at-the-line-of-scrimmage reads, and the offense's cadence.

Huddle Protocol

Knowing huddle protocol can give the defense advance intelligence of the upcoming play. Knowing how they function in the huddle can give the defense some important advantages:

- Can give clues to an unbalanced line or tackle-over formations.
- Identifying receivers is easier if you are in match coverage.
- Knowing where Y is helps alignment calls. The defense can determine strength more quickly.
- Long huddles might mean passes or trick plays.
- Short huddles might indicate base runs.
- If the quarterback talks to a particular player, it might serve as a tip off.

Play-Call Procedure

How the opponent gets play calls into the game should be understood to see if an edge can be gained. Do they signal the plays in? If so, the possibility of stealing signals exists. Do they use runners to get the play to the quarterback? Tip-offs may be offered by who the messenger is. Some coaches communicate with the quarterback by having him come to the hash. If this situation is the case, it gives the defense the opportunity to eavesdrop. The defensive coach may decide not to allow the opposition to bring their quarterback near the sideline for play calls or on the field coaching. He can decide to have a cornerback, whenever legally possible, go with the quarterback and stand beside him as the coach tries to talk to him.

Line-of-Scrimmage Tip-Offs

Close observation of the offense at the line of scrimmage can give the defense advance warning as to the type of play to be executed. Film observation may give the defense clues on who and what to observe for tipsters. The section on personnel in this book covers in detail how to scout personnel.

Pass-Play Tip-Offs

Certain clues or tip-offs may alert a well-schooled defense to the possibility of a pass play. Attentive defenses should expect pass plays after a time-out, long time in the huddle, delay-of-game penalty, first and last play of the quarter, substitutions, sudden change, or an explosive run. Also well-scouted offenses can give the defense pass clues through observation of certain personnel. Close observation of offensive stances often give advance notice of pass plays. Following are some pass tip-offs:

- Long huddle
- Linemen sitting back in their stance with little weight on their fingers
- Tight splits by the line
- Quarterback nervous habits (i.e., licking fingers, toweling hands, etc.)
- Running backs in wider alignments

A code word for pass would place the defense in an advantageous position. For example, experienced defenders can make a "bird" or any other buzz word for pass when they expect pass. This use of a code word would allow quicker drops by pass defenders and would heat up the pass rush by the defensive linemen.

Run Tip-Offs

- Short huddle.
- Big splits (inside run)
- Line digging in, or line in heavy stances
- Guards off the line (pulling)
- Running backs leaning or pointing

A "rabbit" call preceding a running play could serve as a tip-off for linemen to thicken their alignment on their assigned offensive lineman and linebackers to tighten down on their alignment in anticipation of a run.

Cadence

Try to determine the opponent's cadence procedure. Cadence can be studied several different ways. The question of how and when the ball is snapped is readily discerned by the timing of the snap. Long and short snaps are obvious through film study. Observation of the quarterback's mannerisms is necessary to note hard and silent counts. In some shotgun situations, the center will give the cadence especially if there is a lot of crowd noise and adjoining linemen can't see the ball on a silent snap. Chances are the offense won't go on two in a no-huddle shotgun situation. This tip-off should allow defensive linemen to get a great jump on the snap. Knowing the opponent's cadence ritual is highly beneficial. It allows the scout offense to use their cadence during the week's practice. Doing so will help the defense get into a comfort zone if they are familiar with the opponent's cadence. It will also allow the defense to better time up stunts.

Most offense's snap system has four variations:

- First sound
- On one
- On two
- On three

Usually, if a particular team uses a non-rhythmic count, voice inflection will be greatest on the next-to-last sound. For example, if the snap count is on three, the cadence would be "Go *go* go." The emphasis would be on the second "go."

Close study will reveal that most offenses are predictable on how and when they snap the ball. If the defense picks up on these tendencies, it will give the defense an advantage. Most offenses will go with a quick count during two-minute offense (if the clock is running), goal-line offense, and quarterback sneaks. Most offenses will be leery of a complicated snap count on the goal line. Short yardage is a good time for the offense to go with a hard count. Long cadences may force the defense to show their hand on fronts, stunts, and coverages. Defensive advantage can be gained when it can anticipate the snap. The defense can stem or incorporate "move-to" defenses. Linebackers can better time up stunts and defensive linemen can beat the offensive linemen to the "punch." Does the offense employ a "molasses" snap count where the quarterback goes through the cadence twice in an effort to get the defense to tip its hand on a potential stunt? If so, disguise will be more difficult.

The last cadence to be explored is the "freeze" count. In this case, the offense may have no intention of snapping the ball. They are trying to draw the defense offside to get a cheap first down. This strategy is used mainly on third- or fourth-and-less-than-five-yards, and with the ball near midfield. If the defense gets antsy, takes the bait, and crosses the line of scrimmage, the center will snap the ball and the quarterback will take a knee. In high school, the defense needs to only break the plane to be offside. If the defense doesn't jump, the offense has a wide range of options. They can take a delay-of-game penalty and punt the ball, drop the quarterback back as a punter and kick the ball, or run a predetermined play after the defense has relaxed or celebrated what they thought was a no-snap situation.

Audibles

Offenses audible for a variety of reasons. Some common reasons for audibles are:

- To get out of a particular play versus an unblockable front or blitz.
- As a pressure check.
- "Check with me" where the quarterback calls the play at the line using a set of parameters given by the coach.
- To gain an advantage by calling a better play at the line of scrimmage than the huddle call as a result of seeing the defensive structure after the huddle break.
- Some offenses audible to a particular category of plays versus a Bears (or 46) defense.

No matter the reason for the check and the previous snap count, most offenses will go on "one" when they audible. If the defense can discover the offense's live color, an advantage can be gained by anticipating the snap. An "easy" call followed by colors and numbers is usually an audible to get out of a particular play that was called with a quick snap count. Again, chances are the ball will be snapped on "one." "Opposite" calls usually mean a running play was called. The play will have the basic concept as the huddle call except the play will be run to the other side. For example, if 45 was called in the huddle, the quarterback may opposite to the other side and run 46. Opposite calls are usually triggered by a code word that starts with "O." Some teams use an "Otto" call, for example. Again, the defensive advantage to be gained here is that most teams *do not* opposite a pass play. Chances are great that a run has been called.

If you can discern your opponent's audible system, you can obviously use this to your advantage. When the offense checks, you can check your defense to give them a different look. If the offense checks to particular routes, the defense can overplay and jump them. Care must be taken however, that the offense isn't feeding you a dose of dummy audibles.

Alerts

Effective game planning includes well-established defensive-back communication. Defensive backs can use the following alerts in communicating with each other.

- "Pass": when anyone recognizes that the play is a pass. This alert is especially needed in man coverage.
- "Run": when anyone recognizes the play is a run. This alert is crucial in man coverage.
- "Crack": when wideouts block inside.

- "In" or "out": calls to alert linebackers that receivers are entering or leaving their area.
- "Reverse": whenever a receiver is going against the grain on a running play.
- "Stay": when the quarterback scrambles.

10

Film Analysis

Once a working nomenclature has been established to describe an opponent's offense, a coach is ready to put the tape on and dissect the opponent. The recommended tool to use in film breakdown is the play-breakdown sheet (Diagram 10-1). The sheet contains two boxes per play. The box to the left is the information box, where all the pertinent information on the play is recorded. The box on the right is the formation box, where personnel are cataloged and the play is diagrammed.

Information Box

Play Number

Insert the play number. This number allows the coach to chart offensive drives and a reference to a particular play should the need arise.

How

This box reflects how the offense obtained possession of the ball. This information is valuable because some teams have tendencies in their play selection depending upon how they obtained the ball. For example, after a turnover, some teams will try to hit the defense with an explosive-type play. Was it through a fumble recovery, interception, punt, or kickoff?

Film Break Down Sheet   OPPONENT:

Play #_____   Strong_____ Weak_____

How_____

Down_____   Distance_____

Personnel_____

Hash_____

Field Zone_____

Two Minute_____   Motion_____

Formation_____Play_____

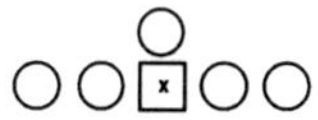

Play #_____   Strong_____ Weak_____

How_____

Down_____   Distance_____

Personnel_____

Hash_____

Field Zone_____

Two Minute_____   Motion_____

Formation_____Play_____

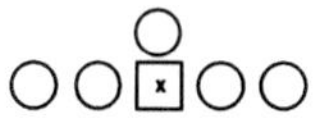

Play #_____   Strong_____Weak_____

How_____

Down_____   Distance_____

Personnel_____

Hash_____

Field Zone_____

Two Minute_____   Motion_____

Formation_____Play_____

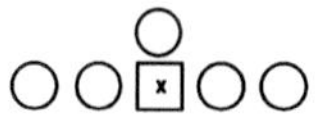

Diagram 10-1. Film-breakdown sheet

Down-and-Distance

These boxes contain down-and-distance information.

Personnel

This blank reflects the personnel grouping the offense employs on that particular play. Do they have 21 personnel (two backs and one tight end) or a 12 grouping (one back and two tight ends)? Player jersey numbers should be recorded in the formation box.

Hash

Does the play originate on the right hash, left hash, or in the middle? This information is recorded in the hash blank. The hash should be indicated from the defensive side. For example, a play originating on the offense's right hash will be on the defense's left hash. Consider the play to have started from the left hash. Use the same thought process on formations also. A pro-right set to the offense would be a pro-left formation to the defense. It is best to communicate variables from the view of the defense. See the play through player's eyes.

Field Zone

In what zone was the ball snapped?

- Backed up; goal line to -10
- Coming out; -10 to -20
- Free wheel; -20 to +20
- Going in; +20 to +10
- Goal line; +10 to goal line

On the first play of the drive, it is advisable to put the yard line. Doing so allows the coach to plot drives and know the inception point of the series.

Two Minute

This box is checked whenever two or less minutes are remaining in the half or game. This information gives the coach an insight on the opponent's two-minute thought process.

Formation

This box describes the offensive formation on the play being charted. Using the terminology from Chapter 2, the coach can describe the formation using standardized terminology. For example, a 34 pro-left formation describes a straight I backfield set with the tight end and Z to the defense's left and the X-receiver to the right of the defense. A 24 twins-right set would describe a formation with an offset I with the fullback set behind the offensive tackle, and tight end to the left with X and Z aligned to the defense's right.

Motion

Motion is described in this box. As an example, Z-motion from left to right from a pro-left set is referred to as zac to twins right.

Play

The play should be designated using an established vocabulary. The descriptive terms used in earlier chapters are preferred.

Strong-Weak Designation

These boxes are placed so each play can be broken down as to whether the running play was executed to the closed (or tight-end) side or to the open (or weak) side. If no tight end exists, the strongside would be the side with the most receivers. Pass plays to the side with the most receivers would be marked as occurring to the strongside, and passes to the side with fewer receivers would be to the weakside.

Formation Box

The box to the right already contains the interior offensive line. For the most part, these players will stay consistent. The following information should be included:

- Formation
- Skill players' numbers
- Receiver splits
- Motion
- Blocking scheme (line, backs, receivers)
- Pass protections
- Receiver routes
- Defensive alignment
- Note any abnormal line splits

Listing player numbers gives a running account of the various players in the game and the plays they participated in. This information may give an idea on personnel groupings. Receiver splits should be noted using the previously-covered system of using plus or minus designations to reflect the width of their alignment. For example, a receiver who aligns three yards outside the hash is referred to as a "hash +3 receiver." If a receiver aligns three yards inside the hash, he is tagged as a "hash -3 receiver." Receiver splits may offer important insights on play calls.

Blocking schemes should be charted, especially if the defense is similar to the one your team uses. It is an advantage to obtain a film on the opponent versus a similar defensive philosophy to your own. Doing so will give insight on how they will block your base front. Even if the game film is against a team that runs a different defense than the one you run, it still may offer insights on their blocking philosophy. The same holds true for pass protections.

11

Personnel Analysis

Personnel considerations are paramount in game planning. Study of individual players allows the defensive coach to minimize their strengths and maximize their weaknesses. Understanding the opponent's idiosyncrasies can provide a decided advantage in game planning. The opponent's personnel should be broken down into five major positions or divisions. A simple system would involve breaking down the opponent's personnel into offensive line, back, receiver, tight end, and quarterback categories. Most of the information on a particular player will be gleaned from game film. Additional information can be obtained from media sources (television, radio, newspapers, magazines). With the explosion of information on the Internet, in-depth knowledge of the opponent may be found online. Websites can supply vital information or statistics on a particular team.

Offensive Line

The breakdown of an opponent's line starts with the physical characteristics of each player. How much does each player weigh? How tall is each player? What grade is each player in? This information is readily available from the opponent's program. However, be wary because some teams embellish physical measurements, while some coaches tend to underreport.

Understanding characteristics and habits of offensive linemen can lead to a basic understanding of the upcoming play. A pre-snap read can tip off the defense as to the type of play to be run and, in some cases, direction or the point of attack. Valuable parts of the game plan can be implemented from these tip-offs.

A lineman's stance speaks volumes about his intentions. Linemen who are high in their stance with little weight on their down hand usually indicates pass, while a lineman who wiggles or digs in with his cleats and has a lot of weight on his down hand probably indicates a run. Linemen who lean in their stance might indicate a pull scheme—for example, if the guard is light and the ball is snapped with no motion and the play is a pass to a particular wideout. If motion originates away from the guard and he is in a light stance, the play is a counter with the guard and tackle pulling. If the guard is heavy and motion started away from him, the play is an option to the left. If the guard is heavy and motion left from his side, the play is a counter back to his side. These were actual keys the author used in a particular game. These types of keys give the defense the opportunity to slow down the offense and to compete with teams that are more talented. One word of caution, however: care should be taken to not place too much emphasis on game planning according to a particular stance because the intended tipster may show up at the game in street clothes or crutches. However, time spent studying personnel is highly beneficial when it can be used to diagnose the play before the snap. Identification of tipsters goes a long way in diagnosing the upcoming play. Tipsters are more readily identified through tight-angle films. Following are basic run, pass, and line split indicators.

Run Cues

- Feet staggered
- Heavy stance—Lots of weight on down hand (white knuckles)
- Leaning—Must pair up with adjacent linemen. Leaners could also indicate bootlegs or play-action-type passes.
- Wiggling cleats
- High heel on back foot

Pass Cues

- Feet more square
- High in stance
- Little weight on down hand
- Low heel on back foot

Line Split Cues

- Wide splits—Inside runs
- Tight splits—Outside runs or pass

Game Planning Pass-Rush Maneuvers

A common theory of pass rush states that defenders should power rush finesse blockers and finesse rush power blockers. Film study helps to tailor pass-rush moves that give defensive personnel a chance to be successful.

Rip Move

Rips should be a tactic to use on blockers who play too upright or who are much taller than the rusher. The defender should attempt to sink the top of his shoulder underneath the armpit of the blocker. Rips should be avoided on an aggressive pass blocker who has his shoulders low or his head forward too much. Defenders should not try to rip if the blocker retreats too quickly. A better move on a retreating pass protector might be a power rush.

Swim Move

Swims should be used when the rusher has a height advantage, or against a blocker who leans forward or lowers his shoulders. Defenders should never swim versus a blocker who is still retreating.

Power Rush

Defensive coaches should game plan to power rush if the rusher is physically stronger than the blocker or the offensive man retreats too quickly. Power rushers should stay out of the middle of the blocker. When power rushing, the defender should get his hands inside and force the blocker back to the quarterback. If the blocker scotches or sets his feet, he is open to a pull and swim.

Discus Spin

Spin moves should be used when blockers place too much weight outside and lean too heavily into the block. The spin is also effective when the blocker overextends with his inside hand. A pass rusher should pivot on his inside leg and throw his outside arm 360 degrees. He should spin tight and get north. He should also sink his tail to lower his center of gravity.

When studying the opponent's line, it is advisable to break down personnel into three parts. Start with the center because each play starts with him possessing the ball.

Can he identify and communicate line-blocking schemes? Can he block if covered, or does he require help? Can he pull? Guards are examined next. Most offenses play to the strength of their guards. Decide each guard's strong suit. Usually one guard will be a better puller than the other. Decide which guard is the best pass protector and attack the other. Since guards set the pocket, attack the weak link and don't allow the quarterback to step up. Collapse the pocket. Tackles should be studied for agility, girth, and foot quickness. Observe their arm length. Tackles with long arms have an advantage over short-armed tackles in pass protection. Can the tackles be beaten off the edge? Following are film checklists that can be used during personnel breakdown from the game film. Included will be a generic offensive-line breakdown sheet, which is followed by a position-specific breakdown sheet.

Offensive-Line Film Checklist

Each lineman should be examined for:

- Size
- Weight
- Splits
- Stance
- Vertical alignment
- Leaner
- Post-snap giveaway screen
- Post-snap giveaway draw
- Blocks linebackers low to high
- Pass-set style

Individual-Lineman Film Checklist

Center

- Strength
- Mobility
- Athleticism
- Initial quickness
- Can the lineman handle being covered?
- Can the lineman block level 2 (work in space)?

- Is the lineman able to block one-on-one?
- Can he pull?
- Shotgun snapping ability
- Does lineman need help with pass-protection ability?

Guard

- Strength
- Mobility
- Athleticism
- Initial quickness
- Can the guard handle being covered?
- Can the guard block level 2 (work in space)?
- Is the guard able to block one-on-one?
- Can he pull?
- Pass-protection ability
- Can he be collapsed (bull rush)?
- Can he pick up twists and lane exchanges?
- Overextender
- Can he pull on screens?

Tackle

- Strength
- Mobility
- Athleticism
- Initial quickness
- Girth
- Footwork
- Long/short arms
- Can the guard get to the second level?
- Pass-protection ability
- Can he be bull rushed?
- Can he be beaten inside?

- Can he pick up twists and lane exchanges?
- Overextender
- Can he pull on screens?

Running Backs

The fullback position closely parallels the tight-end position. Is the fullback classified as a runner/blocker, blocker/runner, or does he do it all? Is he a halfback-type masquerading as a fullback? What type of pass receiver is he? Is he a legitimate receiving threat, or is he limited to outlet or checkdown routes? How effective is he in pass protection? If he is smallish, he can outmuscled with more physical rushers.

The tailback is usually the featured back. Most offensive packages revolve around the tailback. Is the tailback durable? Can he carry the ball thirty-plus times in a game? Stamina is a trait of an effective tailback. Does he get stronger as the game goes on? Is he effective in the fourth quarter? How are his blocking skills? Most standout tailbacks are not very effective blockers, thus find a way to take advantage of him. Is he a receiving threat? If so, how far downfield is he effective? Following are film checklists, which can be used during personnel breakdown. Included will be a generic running-back breakdown followed by a position-specific breakdown sheet.

Running-Back Film Checklist

Notes on the following details should be specific to each running back:

- Size
- Weight
- Pre-snap habits: lick fingers, wipe hands, foot placement
- Depth keys
- Lean in stance
- Cheat alignments
- Post-snap giveaway screens
- Post-snap giveaway draws
- How well does the running back fake?
- Does he juke or bull in the open field?
- Does he block high or cut on run blocks?
- Does he block high or cut in pass protection?
- How effective is he chipping on defensive linemen?

- Hands
- Inside-running ability
- Outside-running ability
- Favorite routes
- Blitz pickup
- Blocking ability

Fullback Checklist

- Speed
- Runner/blocker
- Blocker/runner
- Effective in space
- Effective blocker (dominant lead blocker)
- Running style: high/low
- Gains yards after contact
- Effective in short-yardage situations
- Durability
- Inside-running ability
    - ✓ Moves piles/falls forward
    - ✓ Cutback ability
    - ✓ Explosiveness
- Outside-running ability
    - ✓ Speed
    - ✓ Acceleration
    - ✓ Can he turn the corner?
- Pass game
    - ✓ Effective receiver
    - ✓ What routes does he run?
    - ✓ Best routes
    - ✓ Can he gain a mismatch?
    - ✓ Blitz pickup ability
    - ✓ Does he sell play-action?

Tailback Checklist

- Speed
- Vision
- Effective blocker
- Running style: high/low
- Gains yards after contact
- Effective in short-yardage situations
- Durability
- Inside-running ability
  - ✓ Moves piles/falls forward
  - ✓ Cutback ability
  - ✓ Explosiveness
- Outside-running ability
  - ✓ Speed
  - ✓ Acceleration
  - ✓ Can he turn the corner?
  - ✓ Home-run threat
- Pass Game
  - ✓ Effective receiver
  - ✓ What routes does he run?
  - ✓ Best routes
  - ✓ Can he gain a mismatch?
  - ✓ Blitz pickup ability
  - ✓ Does he sell play-action?

Receivers

As has been previously observed, how the defense matches up coverage-wise with the opponent's receivers dictates how effective the defense is in stopping the opponent's running game. One of the most important aspects of the study of opposing receivers is their speed. Break down each receiver's running ability. What type of explosion does he have? Does he have run away or elite speed? How well does he accelerate? Does he possess track speed? Agility allows receivers to evade defenders near the line of scrimmage. Agility also means possessing the ability to change body position in order to receive the ball. Jumping ability is also a concern, especially near the goal line. What measure of strength does each receiver have? Which receivers have strength enough to maintain their balance after the catch and break tackles? Who can gain yards after the catch? Can he catch the ball in a crowd? How durable are the receivers? Do nicks and injuries affect them mentally as well as physically? These receivers can be intimidated. Following is a film checklist, which can be used during personnel breakdowns from the game film.

Receiver Checklist

Notes on the following checklist should be specific to each receiver:

- Size
- Weight
- Speed (home-run/elite speed)
- Stance (different for run-pass)
- Splits (ball in middle/hash)
- Pre-snap habits
- Alignments (Does he show run-pass?)
- How competitive is the receiver?
- Durability (Can he be intimidated?)
- Hands
  - ✓ Go-to receiver (game breaker) or possession receiver
  - ✓ Catches ball well on the run
  - ✓ Has over-the-shoulder catching ability
  - ✓ Catches the ball away from his body
  - ✓ Effective catching the ball outside the body frame
  - ✓ Leaping ability (downfield or red-zone threat)
- Routes
  - ✓ Most effective routes (in, out, short, medium, deep)
  - ✓ Over the middle receiver or sideline preference
  - ✓ Type of stem used on various routes
  - ✓ Cut tip-offs on routes
  - ✓ Does he lose speed on cuts?
  - ✓ Effective in traffic

- ✓ Effective versus zone–Can he find holes or seams?
- ✓ Effective versus man-to-man coverage
- ✓ Tips off screens
- Run after catch
  - ✓ First move after catch
  - ✓ Tackle breaker
  - ✓ Makes tacklers miss
  - ✓ Across the grain runner
- Release
  - ✓ Can he beat press coverage?
  - ✓ Escape moves–rip/swim/size/quickness
  - ✓ How quickly does he reach top speed?
  - ✓ Can he separate?
- Blocking ability
  - ✓ Motivated to be a blocker
  - ✓ Block technique (position/aggressive)
  - ✓ Tip off cracks (eyes/split/release)

Tight End

How the defense matches up against the opponent's tight end greatly influences how to game plan. If the tight end can be handled with a safety or linebacker, the defense is in a good position. If it cannot favorably match up with the tight end, a major problem exists. Basically, tight ends fit into one of three categories:

- He is a blocker first and a receiver second.
- He is a receiver first and blocker second.
- He is a great all around player. He can do it all.

What types of routes does the tight end run? Does he run short, intermediate, or deep routes? Which routes does he run most effectively? Following is a film checklist for the tight end.

Tight-End Checklist

- Size

- Weight
- Blocker/receiver
- Receiver/blocker
- Does it all
- Split tip-offs
- Stance tip-offs
- Can he handle a 7 technique?
- Can he be held up?
- What is his favorite route?
- Does he tip off routes by his release?
- Does he have speed to get deep?
- What is his first move after the catch?
- Can a linebacker or safety cover him one-on-one?
- What is his running ability after the catch?
- How well does he pass protect?

Quarterback

Head

Does the quarterback look at the pre-snap defense, then devise a plan with eye fixes and execute the play, or does he get the snap, watch what the defense does, and then decide what to do? Defensively speaking, the hope is that he does the latter. Can he read coverages, or is he easily confused? How is his concentration? Is he conservative and will he throw the ball away when necessary, or is he a risk-taker, gambler, or gunslinger? Is he subject to impulse throws? Is his cadence rhythmic or non-rhythmic? Can the quarterback improvise or ad-lib? Can he create plays, or is he a grinder? Can he exploit man coverage if the defense gets eight in the box? How well does he check off? Does the offense get to the line quickly enough to allow for check-offs?

Eyes

Does the quarterback scan pre-snap the same way each time? Does he scan right to left or left to right? Does he scan the same way on run or pass plays, or does he offer tip-offs? How well does he play in the shotgun? Is he able to lock onto the snap as well as scan downfield? Is he a "stare-down-his-receiver" quarterback, or does he move the defense with his eyes?

Arm

Can he execute a complete inventory of passes (i.e., screens, timing routes, short-middle-deep, and play-action)? Is he a true quarterback, an athlete playing quarterback, or is he a caretaker whose main job is not screw things up? Just how strong is the quarterback's arm? Is he a deep threat with the ball? Does he have a quick release? If so, he would nullify some blitzes and it might be advisable to put the accent on containment and coverage. Short quarterbacks or quarterbacks that overstride are subject to having passes knocked down. Also, quarterbacks who throw sidearm are not only sometimes horizontally inaccurate, their passes are more subject to tips and knockdowns by defensive linemen. A defensive option when facing a short quarterback might be to keep the quarterback in the pocket and make him throw through the trees. How is his touch? Can he hit receivers in stride? What is his reaction time? How quickly does he deliver the ball to an open receiver?

Feet

Does he give pass or run away with his foot placement under center? Some quarterbacks tip off the play with their feet. Some quarterbacks stagger their feet on pass and square up on runs. Some quarterbacks jab step just prior to the snap, which gives the defense a get-off point on the snap. This move allows the defense to beat the offensive line to the punch. In the pocket, does the quarterback have patient or happy feet? Can he be flushed from the pocket easily? Does he throw off his back foot? Do you cage (contain) first and foremost? If he scrambles, does he juke, bull, or slide? Do you have to count the quarterback as a running back? If so, in actuality, a one-back set might have to be played as a two-back set. Is the quarterback in the mold of a classic dropback passer who runs as a last resort, or is he mobile and athletic and doesn't mind pulling the ball down and running? Does the defense need to take him away on option plays, or is he the one you want to carry the ball? Is it advisable to assign a "spy" on him on pass plays? Is he a running threat on the goal line? Does he have to be accounted for in pass coverage?

Ballhandling

Does the quarterback set the defense by getting his hands under center early, or does he allow prowls and "move-to" defenses by placing his hands under center late? Does he give a tip-off by opening his hands a split second before the snap? How effective is he in carrying out fakes? Can the defense tell when the quarterback hands the ball off or keeps the ball after a fake to a running back? Poor fakers sabotage their team's play-action game. What he does after a handoff can serve as a tip-off for quarterback nakeds, reverses, or throwback to the quarterback.

Toughness

Just how tough is the quarterback? Is he a fighter and battler, or is he all fluff? How does mental and physical pressure affect him? Will he stay in the pocket and take a hit, or will he bail when pressured? Following is a quarterback film checklist.

Quarterback Checklist

- Height
- Weight
- How does he scan pre-snap?
- Conservative/risk-taker
- Rhythmic/non-rhythmic cadence
- Check-off ability
- Stare down/eyes move defense
- Arm strength
- Release
- Contain/pressure
- Foot placement pre-snap
- What moves first (quarterback's feet, hands, or butt serves as tip-off on snap)?
- Does he set the defense?
- Hand mechanics
- Pocket presence (stays in the pocket, or pulls down the ball and runs)
- Carries out fakes
- Pocket passer/scrambler
- Take him away on options/make him keep on options
- Need spy on him
- Leader or caretaker
- Toughness

Defending an Athletic Quarterback

Some coaches envision the perfect quarterback as a tall guy who can stand in the pocket and deliver the ball. Some coaches do not like quarterbacks with happy feet.

Versus athletic defensive players and/or loaded defenses, offensive coaches look for quarterbacks who can dance around pressure and make plays. Athletic and mobile quarterbacks are the perfect antidote for pressure defenses. Double-threat quarterbacks serve to add pressure to defenses. Special defensive preparations may have to be factored in when game planning for this type quarterback. Against mobile quarterbacks, rushers have to be more disciplined than if they were playing a classic dropback type. Defenses should maintain lane integrity with a more balanced rush that is easier for the offense to identify and block. Listed are some defensive considerations that may be included to reduce damage done by an athletic quarterback.

- Be selective when blitzing. The defense may have to zone blitz and play zone behind it.
- Man-coverage principles with defenders turning their backs to the ball is a highly dangerous proposition.
- Zone coverages solidify the defense's ability to play quarterback scrambles.
- Defenses may have to assign a spy on the quarterback. If a spy is used, he should be an athlete and not a slug. Be aware, however, that if a spy is used, it will water down either the coverage or rush.
- Lane exchange games are beneficial if rushers keep good lane integrity.
- The pass rush should be balanced. Defenses can't have overloaded rushes to one side and have their pants down to the other side.
- Scramble rules for defenders should be in place.
- Versus option plays, make the quarterback give up the ball quickly. Make him pitch. Don't allow him to carry the ball. Approach this situation as a golden opportunity to hammer him.
- Make the quarterback pay as he comes off fakes. This moment is another opportune time to lay some wood on their best player.

Non-Film Study of Opponents

In addition to firsthand study of the opponent through live scouting or film study, other avenues are available for fostering familiarity of the next opponent. In high school football, coaches may not be able to see all the opponent's games on film unless played early in the season and film exchange involves all the games played. You can size up the opponent in other ways. It is advisable to subscribe to the local newspapers covering all opponents. Through the use of these papers, the coach has access to the box scores of all opponent's games. As a result, insight is gained on personnel, philosophies, and priorities. Have they been a pass, run, or balanced attack? Statistical study will reveal the following scouting nuggets.

Points per Game

What is their scoring average and how are they scoring? Who is doing the scoring?

Passing Statistics

How effective is their quarterback? Who else has thrown the ball? These statistics are a good way to find out if a back or receiver has thrown a pass. This statistic would provide a tip-off of halfback passes, double passes, or reverse passes. Statistics would also serve to highlight their best receiver(s). Who is their go-to-guy in the red zone?

Rushing Statistics

Do they have a workhorse running back, or do they rush by committee? Do they have a back they prefer in a goal-line situation? Is the quarterback a major figure in their running game? These factors, many times, will determine how to defend the quarterback. Is he considered another running back, or does he run only when necessary?

Turnovers

How well do they protect the ball? How many times have they fumbled the ball or thrown interceptions? If they are turning the ball, overemphasis should be placed more so than usual on turnovers during practice sessions. The game could hinge on a turnover.

Special Teams

Game statistics will provide a good idea of the effectiveness of the opponent's kicking game. Statistics will divulge the range of their field-goal kicker. Statistics will clue you in on the effectiveness of their extra-point game. Another benefit of statistical study is the competency of their punter. This information will help you set the depth of the punt-return man. When statistical breakdown is dovetailed with film study, a real sense of the opponent's mindset is revealed. Philosophical changes will be readily noticeable. Is the statistical breakdown reflected in the film watched? A change in offensive philosophy may result from a variety of reasons. One reason may be the need to focus more on the run in the playoffs to be successful in the post-season. Another reason for change may be that defenses forced an offense to run the ball. If defenses load up on coverage, offensive coaches should be smart enough to take what the defense gives them. Another factor that may steer an offense toward the running game is weather. On the other hand, a defense might focus inordinately on the run game. Thus, because of the defensive scheme and personnel, the offense may need to rely more on the passing game.

Another avenue in sizing up the opponent is the study of websites. Many teams and conferences have websites. These websites can be gleaned for information on players, coaches, and previous games. Many of these sites give pertinent information on injuries, line-up changes, and changes in philosophy and many give useful insight on your opponent's mindset. These sites provide a chance to find a quote or statement that can be used as a motivational tool.

12

Designing and Implementing a Defensive Practice Plan

Effectively breaking down the opponent's offense and interpreting the data collected will not equate to success if the coach is unable to impart the knowledge gained to his players or properly prepare them on the practice field. This chapter is an attempt to design and implement a defensive practice plan. Three areas of focus exist, including principles of effective practice, basic defensive practice organization, and game-specific defensive practice.

Principles of Effective Practice

Principles and fundamentals should be followed when establishing a foundationally-sound practice organization. This section will explore four aspects of effective practice, which include four teaching and learning variables that are controllable by the coach, and other selected practice axioms.

Goals

As in any endeavor, goals should be established and objectives laid out to reach a specific target or result. Goals should be established for individuals, groups, and the defensive team as a whole. Drills and progressions should be effectively tailored to best install and perfect the proposed defense or game plan. Only game-specific drills should be incorporated. Practice only movements that players will actually use in the game. Following is a recommended defensive practice progression. The use of this list will allow the coach to be more organized and time effective. A proposed drill should fit into one of the categories. If it doesn't, it should be eliminated from consideration.

- Stance/initial step(s)
- Alignment
- Assignment
- Technique
- Keys
- Reads
- Block protection
- Block escape
- Pursuit angles
- Tackling
- Forcing turnovers

Time Frames

Time frames should be interrelated to goals. Questions to be asked include:

- What skills need to be taught?
- How best to use available time? Prioritize skills needed and spend the most time on the most crucial skills.
- How is time divided between individual, group, and team segments?
- How much practice time is available? Longer isn't necessarily better, especially during in-season practice. Long practices may reflect poor planning and have many negative effects, such as physical and mental fatigue. Long, drawn-out practices lead to mental errors, raise chance of injury, and are less productive.

Tempo

Three types of practice or drill speed exist. Those include walk-through, half speed (thud), or game speed. The slower speeds (i.e., walk-through and thud) are more conducive to learning than full (or game) speed. Care should be taken that instructional drills don't deteriorate into competitive situations, which is especially true in combo or group work. Another crucial issue concerning speed is service personnel. Service people should fully understand their role in the drill. Practice attire is closely related to practice speed. The three major modes of dress include full pads, shells, and shorts. Care should be taken that the manner of dress is compatible with the practice speed desired.

Progression

The progression of skill development is crucial to a successful practice. For example, individual work should occur at the beginning of practice. Individual work should progress to group work and then on to team practice. Individual and group work lays the ground work for team periods. One method of teaching technique is called the alphabet method. This method believes that in order to effectively teach a technique, the coach should break down the technique or skill into steps or a progression. Each step of the skill is taught separately. The first step in the progression is step A. When step A is mastered, move on to step B. When step B is grasped, go back to step A and then B before moving to step C. This system of breaking down a scheme or technique into segments or parts, and then beginning with the simplest movement first and progressing, allows players to build on prior knowledge and skills as they seek mastery of the particular skill.

Teaching and Learning Variables

Many variables exist that are out of the realm of the coach's control. Players come from many different backgrounds and possess different characteristics, which affect their ability to learn. These backgrounds and personalities are beyond the control of the coach. However, some variables that affect learning the coach can control. Those include:

Reinforcement

Rewards can be intrinsic or extrinsic. They can be positive, negative, or neutral. The coach can decide which type of reinforcement he prefers and which one suits his personality. Coaches should also realize that the timing of the reward is as important as the type.

Motivation

Motivation is the desire of individual players to perform a task or tasks required by the coach. The old saying goes that "Motivation is getting someone to do something they don't want to do or wouldn't do on their own." You can motivate in many ways. Effective motivation will differ from player to player. One of the coach's primary jobs is to find the motivation button for each player. Care should be taken that the required task is both attainable and interesting to the player.

Retention

Research has shown that 80 percent of new learning is lost in the first 24 hours after its introduction. Coaches should plan for this learning curve in practice construction. Coaches should provide for as many repetitions at the first practice as possible with review of the skill occurring over a long period of time to ensure maximum retention.

Transfer

Transfer occurs when players use the technique or skill learned and apply it to a game situation. The old adage that practice makes perfect is misleading. A more accurate statement would be "Perfect practice makes perfect." Practice makes things permanent, whether it is positive or negative.

Practice Axioms

Following are some practice axioms, which serve to foster effective practice sessions.

- Inform players the tempo you desire.
- Make it fun. Each drill needs an element of fun.
- Limit standing-around time. Avoid idle time. Don't allow a number of players to idly wait while you coach one player. Practices should be well organized, fast-paced, and interactive.
- Encourage players to work the drill at the desired tempo. The coach shouldn't be the center of attention or dominate the drill.
- Drills should be short in duration. Don't allow drills to become tedious and drawn out. Fifteen to twenty minutes is the maximum time to spend on a particular drill.
- Don't use up all the players' energies on one particular drill per practice.
- Don't use consecutive physically draining drill periods.
- Emphasize fundamentals. Build a sound foundation by teaching the basics.
- Yell encouragement. Whisper constructive criticism. Make corrections in a positive manner. Coach enthusiastically.
- Start selected contact drills against dummies or sleds. Stationary objects offer no resistance, they don't move, and they don't present a competitive situation like a one-on-one match-up between individuals. Teaching contact drills against stationary objects serves to build confidence.

Basic Defensive Practice Organization

The most important element in any practice is drill work. To keep from falling into the trap of drilling just for the sake of drilling, coaches should be careful that the proposed drill falls into one of the following kinds of drills for it to be considered productive.

Skill Drills

These drills are used to teach the tools of the trade. Skill drills should assist players in mastering the basic and necessary techniques to play the game and improve play at their chosen position. These drills train motor skills and are tailored for individuals.

Conditioning Drills

These drills prepare players' bodies to withstand the physical activity necessary to play the game. It is best to tie in conditioning with prescribed movements needed to play football. A carryover effect should result from conditioning drills, which would serve to make players more effective. Care should be taken, however, that skill drills do not turn into conditioning skills.

Situation Drills

Some coaches believe these drills are the most important in football. These particular drills teach players how to play the game. These drills teach the nuances of the game. Situation drills place players in game situations. Situation drills are tailored for group and team personnel. Coaches whose teams are considered well-coached excel in planning situation drills.

Interaction Drills

These drills teach individual defenders how to function as a member of a group or unit. For example, linebackers working with secondary members on a particular coverage is an interaction drill.

Team Drills

Team drills are where all the disparate parts of the defense are put together. Teamwork is vital, especially in fostering timing and familiarity. However, a common mistake some coaches make is to spend too much time on team drills. Care should be taken that the groundwork is laid before all 11 defenders come together.

Auxiliary Drills

These drills serve to help or aid defensive effectiveness. This particular type of drill includes warm-up, mental, morale, and agility drills. Following is a laundry list of drills that may be used year round. These drills would be applicable during spring practice, fall camp, and in-season. These drills include practice buildup activities, individual, group/combo, team circuits, and situation-specific drills.

Practice Buildup

- Skull

Skull meetings are a good way to start the day. Mental preparation for practice begins in a classroom setting. At this time, players are given background information on the day's practice. Vital information such as goals and objectives, time frames, and installation schedule are disseminated.

- Pre-Practice

It is good policy to start on the filed practice by implementing a short period for position coaches to put their charges through a light warm-up routine to get the blood flowing. The routine should include skills and techniques, which are basic and inherent to the position. These drills should be simple and easy to perform. Coaches should not look for perfection in these drills. Drills should not be slowed or stopped for corrections. Players should spend the allotted time moving. The drill should be specific to the position. Linemen could participate in take-off drills, for example. Linebackers can work on stance, starts, and gap fits. Ball drills also would be appropriate. Defensive backs can perform backpedal, breaks, and ball drills.

- Flex

The short pre-practice can then progress to a full-scale team stretch period. This period should be led by a trainer or the strength-and-conditioning coach. Stretching, as a team, provides an opportunity to develop the team concept. Team flex places emphasis on listening skills, concentrating to follow a command, and working together. The team, at this point, is focused on working together to accomplish a shared goal or objective.

Individual Drills

Many coaches call this interval a daily must, or fundamentals period. Individual-drills period is the time to teach fundamentals relative to a position. Also, these drills are typically practiced by position. For example, defensive linemen work on stance and starts, hand placement, and line changes to name a few. Linebackers need to develop stance and start inherent to the position, work on run or gap fits and pass drops. Defensive backs need backpedal, turn-and-run, and head-whip drills. Individual periods should be upbeat and time-sensitive. Coaches should do a good job of motivation by using different ways to teach the same skill because doing the same moves and fundamentals day after day can become boring. Creative coaches are always searching for new and interesting ways to teach the same skills or fundamentals. Coaches should be very demanding and force players to strive for perfection. The tempo of the drill can be enhanced by injecting competition or a time factor into the drill.

One of the most difficult balancing acts a football coach must perform is in the area of individual, or daily must, work during game week. Individual drills in the spring or fall camp are paramount in installing the necessary techniques needed to execute the desired defensive scheme. The scheme to be installed is usually spoken of in generalities. However, individual work during game week is a delicate matter. Drills during game week should focus on specific skills that have direct application to the demands of the upcoming game. Linemen may need a lot of trap work. Linebackers may need to refine their counter skills, while defensive backs may have to spend a lot of time on crack replacement skills. During game week, time becomes even more of a factor. Much individual work can occur in one-on-one drills. These drills can pit defenders against offensive personnel. Care should be taken that these drills aren't expected to be half-speed or teaching drills. This type of drill will always result in a competitive drill. Some good examples of one-on-one drills would include defensive linemen working against a blocker in a pass-rush drill, linebackers covering backs in a pass-coverage drill or in a blitz-pickup period, or defensive backs covering receivers one-on-one.

Group/Combo Drills

These drills require offensive and defensive segments to service each other. These drills are also called unit drills.

• Seven-on-Seven Drill

The seven-on-seven drill has been called the most commonly used group drill. This drill involves an offense that consists of one quarterback, one center, and five receivers against a defense comprised of linebackers and defensive backs. Effective seven-on-seven sessions should include interjecting game situations into the script. Down, distance, and field zone should be made known before each repetition. Quarterback scrambles can also be added to the drill. A good rule of thumb is for two scrambles to be executed for every 20 plays. This ratio serves to give defenses work on pass plays that have broken down but still have a high degree of danger to an unprepared defense. Parameters of defensive conduct on a thrown ball should be clear. Do you allow defenders to make a full break on the ball and risk injury, or must they use a controlled break to avoid collisions? Many coaches prefer the controlled break during in-season practice. Care should be taken that the seven-on-seven doesn't become a conditioning drill for the defense, especially when the offense is using two groups which are alternating every other play. Try to rotate defenders every four or five reps. Force the defense to sprint to the ball when it is thrown, whether a no-full-speed-break rule is in place or not. This full-speed sprint is crucial in creating good pursuit habits. It also makes players cognizant of where their help is coming from and how all the parts fit together in a particular coverage. Demanding that defenders two-hand touch the receiver below the waist after a catch fosters good tackling position without full-speed contact.

- Three-on-Three Drill

The three-on-three drill can be used in conjunction with (and at the same time as) the seven-on-seven drill. The set-up is simple. The three-on-three drill is run on the same field as the seven-on-seven, just behind the seven-on-seven but facing the opposite direction. Three-on-three personnel has two running backs and a tight end going against three linebackers not involved in the seven-on-seven drill. The set-up includes play-action, dropback, and flow passes. Coverages in which linebackers have man coverage on the backs and/or the tight end are used. Coverages where the tight end is covered by the strong safety may also be incorporated. Also, stunt schemes can be used. The three-on-three drill with stunts would give defenders work on taking on and getting off blocks.

- Underneath Coverage Drill

This drill set-up is closely akin to the three-on-three drill. This particular drill involves players manning the short or underneath areas of the coverage. Players include safeties, inside linebackers, outside linebackers, and cover-2 corners. Zone or man coverage would be drilled.

- Half-Field-Coverage Drill

This pass-coverage drill breaks the offense down into strongside and weakside. Pass plays tailored for the strongside of the formation are executed against the strongside of the coverage and weakside patterns are run against the weakside of the defense. The focus can be on either the strongside or the weakside for the period, or the strongside can be in one area and the weakside nearby in another area, and alternate plays. It is advisable to mix in perimeter runs to keep the defense honest and to check out proper run-support techniques.

- Deep-Pass Drill

This drill is similar to the underneath coverage drill that it focuses on one area of a particular coverage. This drill serves to develop the deep defenders in a selected coverage package. The only defenders are those with deep responsibilities. Those defenders would include corners and the free safety in cover 3, safeties in cover 2, and any defender in man coverage whose assignment will run a deep route.

- Nine-on-Seven Drill

This drill has been referred to by various names. Some coaches call it the middle drill, or inside drill. The nine-on-seven drill involves nine offensive players versus the defensive front. The only offensive players excluded are the two wideouts. The nine-on-seven drill is the most effective way, short of a full-speed scrimmage, to give the defense work on defending run plays. When this practice segment is filmed, it should be done from behind the defense to give a good picture of shades, alignments, stances, line splits, and steps. Defensive backs can be inserted into this drill to perfect run-fit responsibilities. These defenders don't participate in actual contact but work on angles. Nine-on-seven drills can have different degrees of emphasis or speeds. The inside period can be a teaching nine-on-seven or a challenge nine-on-seven. The parameters for teaching nine-on-seven has the offensive line blocking full speed above the waist with the defense getting off blocks full speed and running full speed to the ball. The defense will front up or thud the ballcarrier. Defenders aren't allowed to leave their feet or make full-speed contact on the ballcarrier. This drill can be done in full pads or shells. Challenge nine-on-seven is executed full speed with an element of competition added. Any run over three yards gives the offense one point. Runs held under three yards gives the defense one point. Decide beforehand punishment for the losing side and reward for the winners.

• Perimeter Drill

A perimeter drill can be devised as a run-only drill, or it can incorporate run and pass. Sweeps, off-tackle runs, or option plays can be used. A variety of perimeter-blocking schemes can be used. Crack blocks, stalk blocks, or cross blocks can be implemented. If this drill is used in-season, focus should be on the opponent's favorite outside plays. If passes are to be included, play-action, rolls, sprints, and halfback passes are appropriate. The drill can incorporate selected offensive linemen if they are an integral part of the offensive outside package. Some examples would include using a fullback as the lead blocker on a lead-option play or using both offensive guards with a wing-T offense.

• Half-Line Run Drill

The half-line run drill can be structured one of two ways. The defense can focus on the opponent's running plays in a strongside/weakside breakdown. Drill the defense on the offense's favorite runs and blocking schemes to the tight-end side, and then focus on their favorites to the open (or weak) side. Using the half-line drill to reflect the offense's wideside-shortside running-game tendencies is another set-up. Place the ball on the hash and work the offense's favorite boundary plays, then place the ball on the hash and focus on the offense's favorite wideside runs.

• Team Drills

Since the bulk of plays can be run in group settings (e.g., half-line, seven-on-seven, nine-on-seven, etc.), it is best to focus on other plays (such as play-action passes, boots, waggles, draws, screens, and reverses) during the team period. In some cases, these plays are hard to cover in individual and group settings. Reverses, for example, need to be drilled in a team setting. Team periods are a good time to perfect defensive adjustments to motions, shifts, and unbalanced lines. The double-whistle concept is advisable during the team drill. The double-whistle concept says that defenders should pursue full speed beyond the first whistle. The first whistle occurs when the ballcarrier is fronted up, two-hand touched, or taken to the ground, depending upon the speed desired, but the defenders not in on the hit continue until they get to the ball. In other words, the play isn't over when the ballcarrier is assumed to be down. Once all defenders get to the ball, they keep their feet moving in place while in a good football position. When all 11 defenders reach the ball, the second whistle sounds to end the play. Defenders who don't sprint full speed to the ball cause the entire defense to do grass drills at that point or after practice. The two-whistle concept serves to foster unbridled pursuit. One very important question to be asked, as it relates to the team period, is how to divide reps between the first and second teams.

Circuits

Circuit drills teach basic defensive fundamentals, which need to be stressed and developed year-round. Fundamentals such as pursuit, tackling, creating turnovers, and block protection are crucial to a defense's effectiveness. Circuit work can be done during spring practice, fall camp, and in-season. Circuit work can be started after the warm-up and stretch periods. Circuits help to set the tempo for the rest of practice. Everyone is involved and a lot of electricity is in the air. All this movement and involvement results in a beehive of productive activity. Circuit drills serve to build team unity because the entire defense is practicing the same fundamentals at the same time, and every defender will have contact with all the defensive coaches (not only his position coach). Performing circuits early in practice serves to emphasize its importance. Rotation from station to station relieves the monotony of practice.

The first fundamental to be covered is pursuit. Unlike the other three circuits where all defenders are working at the same time, only 11 players at a time are involved in this drill. Three or four groups will alternate in this drill. The following pursuit drills should be included at some point:

- Wide runs
- Off-tackle runs
- Reverse runs
- Option runs
- Draws
- Quarterback scramble (run)
- Three-, five-, and seven-step passes
- Screens
- Quarterback scramble (pass)

Choose the pursuit drill that is most applicable to the upcoming opponent. For example, if the next opponent is a passing team, use the three-/five-/seven-step pass, screen, and draw pursuit drills. If the opponent is a strong running team, off-tackle and wide-run pursuit drills would be appropriate. A five-minute block of time is sufficient for pursuit drills if the drill has been discussed or run before, so that no on-the-field time is spent explaining the drill. From the pursuit drill, move on to the remaining circuit work. A 10-minute block of time divided evenly between the remaining circuits is satisfactory. Depending upon available time or the coach's preference, players can be put through a series of tackling, turnovers, and block-protection circuits where defenders run through several tackling drills, and then move on to turnover drills. Finish with a variety of block-protection drills, or practice time could include one tackling station, one turnover station, and one block-protection station.

Coaches can choose to refine one skill or may choose to mix and match several skills. Regardless of the chosen set-up, circuits should be high intensity with little transition time. Stations should be in close proximity with each other so travel time is limited. Players should experience a high number of quality repetitions. Station set-up should include having a coach at each station. This coach stays in the same area and repeats his assigned drill for the entire circuit as players rotate through the circuit. Four groups of players is an appropriate number. Each group should have approximately the same amount of players. Players can be of the same general positions or positional crossovers can occur. The use of an automated horn will keep the drill on time. A very quick breakdown before rotation allows the coach to get a buzzword or phrase said in unison. This technique allows coaches to reinforce a coaching point or motivational issue.

- Tackling Circuits

This circuit teaches players the proper and safe way to tackle. This approach not only refines tackling technique but it serves to protect coaches from liability because tackling technique is taught *ad nauseum*. Players are taught proper head placement, use of hands, and hip roll. Drills are executed at various speeds. Some tackling drills are at a very slow pace (such as form tackling), while other drills are performed at thud speed. Very rarely should players do a full-speed tackling drill in circuits. Many of these drills can be performed with the tackler two-hand touching the ballcarrier below the waist. This posture gets the tackler in a good tackling position without full-speed contact. Following are recommended tackling drills:

- ✓ Form
- ✓ Open field
- ✓ Goal line
- ✓ Quarterback strip

- ✓ Roll
- ✓ Last chance
- ✓ Second/third man
- ✓ Angle
- ✓ Eye opener
- ✓ Sideline
- ✓ Quarterback scramble
- ✓ Gauntlet
- ✓ Popsicle sled
- ✓ 747
- ✓ Door

Each type of tackling requires its own inherent points of emphasis, which are offered and reinforced by the coach of the station.

- Turnover Circuit

The turnover circuit focuses on forcing turnovers and how to react to a loose ball. Game-situation scenarios are also added to the drills. Adding game situations teaches defenders that how they react to turnovers is inherently tied to variables such as the score and time remaining. Many creative ways exist to design drills that relate to game-like situations. Drills run the gamut from a simple fumble recovery to a three- or four-man strip drill. Points of emphasis include properly securing the ball and ensuring that all defenders get practice on handling the ball. Ball security is taught as if it were being taught to offensive skill people. Once you get the ball, you don't want to give it back. Turnover drills include:

- ✓ Strip (club-punch)
- ✓ Fall on fumble
- ✓ Scoop-and-score
- ✓ Hockey
- ✓ Blind man's bluff
- ✓ Shuffle through bags—fall on fumble
- ✓ Shuffle through bags—scoop-and-score
- ✓ CPR (club-punch-rip)
- ✓ Interception (catch-and-score—catch-and-get-down)

- Block-Protection Circuit

Block-defense skills are imperative for defenders to be able to finish the play. If defenders get blocked and stay blocked, they will not be able to tackle the ballcarrier or affect a turnover. Coaches should stress to players that everybody gets blocked at some point, but real football players get off the block and make plays. Emphasis should be placed on attacking potential blockers and not catching the block. Desire is an important component players should bring to this drill. Block-protection drills include:

- ✓ Blow delivery
- ✓ Machine gun
- ✓ Door
- ✓ Cut block
- ✓ Blocker has the angle.
- ✓ Crossface wipe release
- ✓ Rip release
- ✓ Snatch release

Situation-Specific Drills

These types of drills are usually more relevant during in-season game preparation. However, some of these drills are appropriate no matter the time of the year.

- Pass skel (seven-on-seven) on the -25-yard line
- Two-minute defense. Plug in important factors such as time left, field zone, score (what does the offense need?), and time-outs.
- Short yardage (third-and-short, fourth-and-short)
- Field zones. Many plays are zone-sensitive.
  - ✓ Backed up
  - ✓ Coming out
  - ✓ Going in
  - ✓ Goal line
- Trick plays. Emory Henry formations, reverses, tackle over, and so forth.

Game-Specific Defensive Practice

Basically, two types or styles of practice exist: pre-season and in-season. Pre-season practice would occur during the spring and fall camp. The basic goal of practice during these timeframes would be the development of skills and techniques needed to run a specific offensive or defensive scheme. Fundamentals such as blocking and tackling would be high on the priority list. Little or no attention is paid to a specific game or opponent. Energies are focused on getting a system in place. The focus is first and foremost on your team. In-season practice is channeled toward game preparation against another team. The coach has to devise a way for his defense to slow or stop the opponent's offense and implement and refine that plan on the practice field during the week leading up to the game. The focal point of this section will be practice organization leading up to a particular game. This section includes preparatory work leading up to the workweek as well as practice set-up. Game and practice planning begins immediately after the last game. From the coach's view, Saturday is the day to put to rest the last game and kickoff preparation for the next opponent. Coaches' Saturday activities include grading Friday night's game and posting player's grades. When this task is completed, film breakdown of the next opponent will begin. Sunday will see the completion of film breakdown of the upcoming opponent.

Analysis of the information garnered from film study is the next step. Hit charts reflecting runs and passes will be developed. Variables such as down-and-distance, field-zone, and hash tendencies will be charted. From the data, develop a master list of plays the opponent runs. This list will be consulted throughout the week in practice organization. Prioritize the plays to defend. It is impossible to practice every player against every play the opponent runs. Decide where to focus the attention. Taking away what they like to do best is a good policy. Next, identify how each defender will be attacked. Discern their favorite blocking schemes versus the front, linebackers, and secondary. This significant material will allow you to plan individual and group work for the week. Discern how individual players or groups of players will be attacked and prepare them to fight back. Player packets with tip sheets should be finalized. This packet will be the players' bible for the next week. The packet should be chock full of information on the opponent as well as personal information on the player (or players) they will personally be engaged with during the upcoming game. The week's overall practice schedule should be planned and scripted at this point.

Game Week

Monday

Classroom

Monday will begin by showing Friday night's game. Discuss the positives and negatives of the last game. Discuss which goals were reached. The last game should be put to rest for everyone at this point. Shift the players' focus to the next opponent. Show the opponent's last game to the players, and at the conclusion of the film, give each player a packet on the opponent. Give the players a feel for the upcoming offense. Let them know the offensive philosophy the opponent uses. Let players know if they are going to face a running team, passing team, balanced, option-oriented, finesse, or such. State what you have to do to win the game. At this time, lay out the basic game plan. What do you have to stop to be successful? Start focusing the players on the big picture.

On the Field

Use a short period to make corrections from the previous week. It is best to break up into units or groups for this correction. Next, give the team an on-the-field scouting report on the week's opponent. Discuss personnel while showing the opponent's favorite formations, runs, and passes. Show basic defensive adjustments to be used versus this opponent. At this point, the defense should break up into groups and each position coach expounds on the information just discussed and how it affects their individual unit or group.

Force Drill

Script this drill using the opponent's run package to refine run force duties. The service team should also mix in play-action passes.

Pass Skel (Seven-on-Seven), Inside Runs (Nine-on-Seven)

Expose the defense to the opponent's favorite pass plays. Use the coverages that have been pre-determined to use that week. While the pass skel is in progress, drill the front on the opponent's favorite inside running plays. At a pre-determined time, switch linebackers from the seven-on-seven to the nine-on-seven so linebackers get a diet of both run and pass. It is advisable to use selected defensive backs not directly involved in the pass skel in the nine-on-seven run period. Doing so allows defensive backs to get a feel for their run fits. As with the linebackers, switch out defensive backs so they too get run and pass work.

Goal-Line Defense

Most teams don't drastically change their goal-line defensive package from week to week, so even on Monday the defensive coach is probably set on what he wants to do in the red zone.

Tuesday

Classroom

Give players tip-off sheets on the opponent's personnel. Talk about tipsters. Follow up with more film on the opponent.

On the Field

Tuesday is a heavy practice day. The bulk of the week's hitting and contact work occurs on Tuesday and Wednesday. Tuesday is a good day for circuit work. Scout plays are packaged by field zone. Focus will be on the opponent's favorite plays in the backed-up, coming-out, and going-in zones. In addition, normal down-and-distance plays are focused on. First- and second-down plays are scripted. Play-action passes make up the bulk of pass plays. It is advisable to have a short-yardage period on Tuesday. Package the opponent's third- and fourth-down short-yardage plays.

Wednesday

Classroom

Practice film from Tuesday is viewed and corrections are made. In addition, more film of the opponent is shown.

On the Field

Wednesday is the last physically hard day of practice for the week. Circuit work is a big part of Wednesday's practice just as it is on Tuesday. Focus on Wednesday includes long-yardage offense. Included will be a red-zone period, which will include two-point-play defense. Focus on the opponent's passing game will include their dropback passing game and pass protection. Wednesday's individual work will include individual pass rush, line games, along with a pass-blitz period.

Thursday

Classroom

Most of the work done on Thursday, on the field and off, is mental. It is good to begin Thursday's workday with film review and corrections from Wednesday's practice. Players take a written test on the game plan before they dress and go to the practice field.

On the Field

Physical work includes a two-minute drill against the first offense. A run-through period includes scripting situations to get a smooth transition from defense to special teams and special teams to defense. Particular care is taken to practice water-bucket situations in order to prevent giving up two points after the opponent scores a touchdown. During Thursday's practice defensive checks, Big Ben defense, and defensive substitution packages are reviewed. The last thing to be covered is an on-the-field alignment and adjustment test. Defenders should align correctly and answer questions about coaching points that were covered during the week's practice. It is good to make this session an intense time-sensitive exercise. Defenders have five seconds to align correctly and make required calls and communications, or they run extra sprints on Monday. This drill is done with the second unit also. The second-teamers seem to pay more attention during the week, are better prepared to play on game night, and for some reason get a great amount of encouragement from the starters because everyone runs extra if a mistake is made by either unit.

Game-Day Organization

How effective the week of game planning has been is revealed on game day. Don't allow an effective week of work to go down the drain because of ineffective game-day organization. Game-day coordination is a crucial part of getting the game plan executed. The following five-man coaching staff guidelines for the game are used. Teams with more or less coaches can tailor this approach to suit their needs. In the five-coach system, the defensive line coach, linebacker coach, and the defensive coordinator are on the sideline. The defensive back coach and chart man work in the press box.

Responsibilities

Defensive Coordinator

- Signals defensive front.
- Relays coverage call to the linebacker coach.
- Communicates with other defensive coaches. Communicates with the head coach on strategic decisions, such as whether to block or return a punt, defensive time-outs, or penalties.

Linebacker Coach

- Receives coverage call from the defensive coordinator and relays it to the free safety.
- Checks for force-call communication.
- Watches linebackers during the play.
- Makes linebacker substitutions.

Defensive Line Coach

- Makes sure sub defenses are ready to go, and is responsible for inserting them into the game based on the defensive call.
- Receives injury reports from trainer.

- Checks front stances, alignments, pass-run recognition.
- Checks pass protections.

Defensive Back Coach

- Relays down-and-distance, yard-line, and hash information to coordinator.
- Identifies offensive personnel grouping in the game with a volunteer who uses binoculars.
- Identifies formations, strengths, alignments, and motion.
- Checks defensive-back alignments.
- Makes substitutions of defensive backs through the defensive line coach.
- Assists the chart man on formations, play name, and defensive calls, if necessary.
- Has a two-point chart.

Halftime Coordination

- Defensive coaches meet outside the dressing room or away from players. They consult the hit chart and discuss needed adjustments.
- The players will take care of personal matters while the coaches meet. Equipment needing repairs should be given to the equipment man.
- Defensive coordinator meets with the entire defensive unit and coaches for adjustments and second-half plan.
- Break up into defensive groups with the position coaches after the defensive coordinator has finished. Position coaches should make sure players understand any adjustments made at halftime and the second-half plan. Any player concerns should be put to rest before going back out.
- Defense gathers with the offense to be addressed by the head coach.
- Defensive line coach meets with the trainer about the injury situation.
- As the team heads back to the field, coaches can talk to specific individuals for further instructions or motivation.

13

Illustrative Game Breakdown

Film-Breakdown Results

Ideally, defensive game planning involves these five steps:

- Film study of the opponent's offense
- How the opponent's offense attacked defensive personnel
- Breakdown of film information
- Film breakdown on opponent's personnel
- Practice plan

This chapter incorporates breakdown of film information and how the offense attacked defensive personnel of the five-step game-plan system. This breakdown involves the use of defensive game planning as discussed in previous chapters. This particular game was broken down using step one, film study. A conclusion section is included after each category. These conclusions give a clear picture of the offense's philosophy and how they attacked the defense. This breakdown reveals a world of information. When this information is combined with an in-depth study of individual personnel, defensive coaches can become very familiar with an upcoming opponent. Remember, this information is for one game only. Just imagine the data that can accumulate on an opponent when multiple games are studied.

Huddle

Study of the huddle gives the defense a head start on the next play. Knowing where the Y is helps determine run strength quickly. Outside linebackers should key the offensive tackles to quickly identify any tackle-over formations. Knowing where X and Z are in the huddle allows defensive backs to match up in coverage. Following X and Z from the huddle allows for quick identification of the formation. As a basic rule in this game, if X and Z split as they left the huddle, defenders knew they were going to be in a pro set. If they traveled together from the huddle, the odds were good that they were going to be in a twins set. T going wide tipped off the defense that they would be facing a one-back set.

Offensive Personnel Groups

The only offensive personnel group used in the game was 21 or regular people. When they went to one back, they would place T wide.

Formations

Twins were used 54 percent of the time. Twins was far and away the favorite offensive set used in this game. 52 percent of twins plays were passes. 48 percent of twins plays involved a run.

Running Game

During this game, the offense called 25 runs, which consisted of 56 percent of all plays. The breakdown on those runs are as follows.

Two-Back Runs

- Off-tackle power (9 times) (45 was run 6 times)
- Isolations (3 times)
- Traps (3 times)
- 33 option with zing motion (2 times)
- 49 toss sweep (2 times)
- Sneak (1 time)
- 45 counter (1 time)

One-Back Runs

- Speed sweep (2 times)
- 4 zone (1 time)
- 42 midline with tarc motion (1 time)

Types of Offensive Blocks Seen

Defensive tackle and end blocks are broken down into two categories: individual and combo blocks.

Tackles

The defensive tackles saw the four basic man-on-man blocks. The offense used the three basic one-on-one run blocks: base, reach, and down. Also used was the fourth man-on-man block, the pass set. Six combo-blocking schemes were employed.

Ends

The ends, like the tackles, saw the four basic one-on-one blocks. They saw a wide variety of combo blocks. They received two types of kickout blocks off their primary alignment's down block. They were kicked out by the off guard on the counter and kicked out by F on power plays. The strong end was doubled by Y and the tackle, while in a 7 technique. They were also doubled in a wing set by the wing (Z) and Y. The most exotic scheme was a tackle reach off Y's outside release.

Linebackers

Blocking schemes against the linebackers were not every effective. The strong outside linebacker had a wider variety of schemes aimed at him than the middle linebacker or the weakside linebacker. As a matter of fact, the weakside linebacker had to deal with only one primary weakside blocking scheme—the crack. Because of a feeble attack on the linebackers, they had a total of 35 hits during this game.

Safeties

Run force during this game was relatively unaffected by blocking schemes. No designed blocks were used on the free safety, while the strong safety had to deal with only arc blocks by Y.

Corners

Defensive corners saw the basic perimeter blocks, such as dig out, stalk, cutoff, and run-off blocks. Crack blocks on Will were executed off of zing motion. This block requires effective crack-replace techniques. Safeties must give a "run-run" call, so run-off schemes won't be effective if the defense is in man coverage. Stalk blocks require good secondary-support technique. Prototypically, 400-series passes (running-back passes) come off stalk and go routes.

Passing Game

The centerpiece of the offense's passing game was level-3 passes. Eighty-five percent of all of their passes involved level-3 action. Out of 17 dropback passes, 11 were of the three-step variety. The other passes involved included screens and one counter boot. The defense did not see any seven-step drops. Both screens were to the defense's right in the 9 area. No 60-, 100-, 200-, 400-, 600-, or 700-series passes were encountered.

Passing Zones

Most of the offense's passing game involved either short passes in the flat areas or deep outside. Sixty-five percent of passes were targeted for short zones or behind the line of scrimmage. Seventy-five percent of all passes were designed to go to the offense's right.

Formations

Thirteen (65 percent) of passes in this game involved twins or invert sets.

Protections

The offense used two major pass protections. The offense preferred big-on-big protection and a turn-back scheme. On the one counter-boot play, they pulled both guards. A variation of the man-on protection was blockers cutting defensive linemen on quick routes, while they used man-on and turn-back schemes on deeper routes.

Routes

Running Back

F was involved in only one route—a flat route on the counter boot. T received a pass on a flare route. These instances were the only times the backs were involved in a route. The offense did not run any checkdowns. Backs had blocking assignments on most pass plays. This information will allow the defense to game plan additional rushers by green-dogging these backs in man coverage.

Y

Y's favorite route was a veer/seam.

Receivers

X's favorite routes were quicks and sidelines. Z's favorite cut was the flat route. The Z ran this route five times. Combination routes were limited to an X and Z combination in twins. No combo routes involving Y and Z in a pro set were utilized.

Motion

In this game, motion had a specific purpose. Motion was definitely not superfluous. The motion man was either the primary ballcarrier or the lead blocker on run plays and the primary target on a pass play.

Hash

With the ball in the middle of the field, 66 percent of plays went to the offense's right. Right hash plays involved 57 percent to the left (or wide) side, 66 percent of pass plays went wideside, and left-hash plays saw a 50/50 breakdown wideside versus shortside.

Most passes occurred near the end of the game when the offense was playing catch up. The favorite run was 45. 45 was used for 40 percent of their run offense on first down.

Down-and-Distance Breakdown

First Down (+10)

- 10 runs (10 strong, zero weak)
- Five passes (four strong, one weak)
- 67 percent runs

Play distribution: T (9 times), Z (3 times), F (2 times), X (1 time)

First-and-Long After an Offensive Penalty

They were faced with 2 first-and-15 situations. Both plays were passes.

- Zero runs
- Two passes (two strong, zero weak)
- 100 percent passes

Play Distribution: Z (2 times)

First Down After a First-Down Rushing

Three runs were 45 while the other two were isolations.

- Five runs (four strong, one weak)
- Three passes (two strong, one weak)
- 63 percent runs

Play Distribution: T (5 times), F (1 times), X (1 time), Z (1 time)

First Down After a First-Down Passing

The runs included one trap and one 45. That makes four times out of 10 that they gained a first down that they ran 45. 45 was the call on 40 percent of first-down calls after they gained a first down.

- Two runs (two strong, zero weak)
- Zero passes
- 100 percent runs

Play Distribution: T (1 time), F (1 time)

First Down After an Opponent's Turnover

After the offense turned the ball over, they ran 46G.

- One run (one strong, zero weak)
- Zero passes
- 100 percent runs

Play Distribution: T (1 time)

First Down After an Offensive Turnover

The next calls after the offense turned the ball over were 4 zone and 831 Z flat.

- One run (one strong, zero weak)

- One pass (one strong, zero weak)
- 50 percent runs

Play Distribution: T (1 time), Z (1 time)

First Down After an Explosive Run

After a +31 run, the offense ran 549 flare screen.

- Zero runs
- One pass (one strong, zero weak)
- 100 percent pass

Play Distribution: T (1 time)

First Down After an Explosive Pass

After a +18 pass play, the offense ran 45.

- One run (one strong, zero weak)
- Zero passes
- 100 percent run

Play Distribution: T (1 time)

First-and-Medium/-Short After a Defensive Penalty (5 yards)

The only play was 45 counter.

- One run (one strong, zero weak)
- Zero passes
- 100 percent run

Play Distribution: T (1 time)

Second-and-Long (7 yards)

Five passes were three-step drops. The other two were five-step drops.

- Four runs (two strong, two weak)
- Seven passes (six strong, one weak)
- 64 percent passes

Play Distribution: T (5 times), Z (4 times), X (1 time)

Second-Down-and-Medium (3 to 6 yards)

Three of these runs were from a two-back set.

- Four runs (four strong, zero weak)
- Zero passes
- 100 percent runs

Play Distribution: T (3 times), F (1 time)

Second-and-Short (1 to 2 yards)

- None

Third-and-Long (7 yards)

Two passes involved the quick game. One screen and one flare to T was used.

- One run (one strong, zero weak)
- Five passes (five strong, zero weak)
- 80 percent passes

Play Distribution: Z (4 times), T (2 times)

Third-and-Medium (3 to 6 yards)

The only play-action pass seen, 346 counter boot, occurred on this down.

- Two runs (two strong, zero weak)
- One pass (zero strong, one weak)
- 67 percent runs

Play Distribution: T (2 times), Y (1 time)

Third-and-Short (1 to 2 yards)

- Two runs (two strong, zero weak)
- Zero passes
- 100 percent runs

Play Distribution: F (1 time), Q (1 time)

Fourth-and-Long (4 yards)

The play was 851 X sideline.

- Zero runs
- One pass (one strong, zero weak)

Play Distribution: X (1 time)

Fourth-and-Medium (3 yards)

- None

Fourth-and-Short (1 to 2 yards)

- None

Field Zone

Backed Up (goal line to -10-yard line)

- Two runs (two strong, zero weak)
- Zero passes
- 100 percent runs

Play Distribution: T (2 times)

Coming Out (-10- to -20-yard line)

- Two runs (two strong, zero weak)
- One pass (one strong, zero weak)
- 66 percent runs

Play Distribution: F (1 time), T (1 time), Z (1 time)

Free Wheel (-20- to +20-yard line)

- 18 runs
- 18 passes
- 50 percent runs

Play Distribution: T (16 times), Z (11 times), X (4 times), F (3 times), Q (1 time), Y (1 time)

Going In (+20- to +10-yard line)

- Three runs (three strong, zero weak)
- One pass (one strong, zero weak)
- 75 percent runs

Play Distribution: T (3 times), Z (1 time)

Goal Line (+10-yard line to goal line)

- None

APPENDIX

Defensive Game Planning Manual

Contents

Step #1: Film Study

Break down each play using the following variables:

- Play number
- How they got the ball
- Down-and-distance
- Personnel (play numbers)
- Hash
- Field zone
- Two minute
- Formation (back set and receiver alignment)
- Receiver split
- Motion
- Play
- Strong/weak designation
- Penalties
- Explosive play
- Game score

Film Breakdown Sheet

Film Break Down Sheet	Opponent:

Play#_____   Strong_____Weak_____

How_____

Down_____Distance_____

Personnel_____

Hash_____

Field Zone_____

Two Minute_____Motion_____

Formation_____Play_____

○ ○ ☒ ○ ○

Play#_____   Strong_____Weak_____

How_____

Down_____Distance_____

Personnel_____

Hash_____

Field Zone_____

Two Minute_____Motion_____

Formation_____Play_____

○ ○ ☒ ○ ○

Play#_____   Strong_____Weak_____

How_____

Down_____Distance_____

Personnel_____

Hash_____

Field Zone_____

Two Minute_____Motion_____

Formation_____Play_____

○ ○ ☒ ○ ○

Numerical Back Alignments

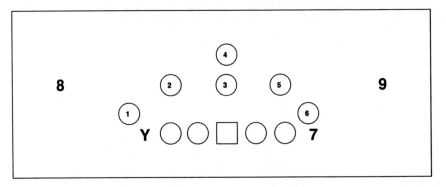

One-Back Designations

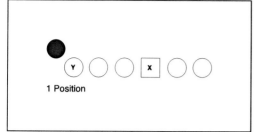

1 Position

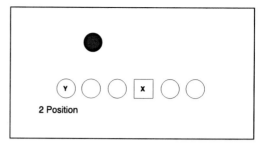

2 Position

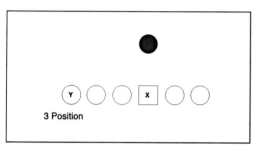

3 Position

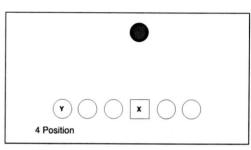

4 Position

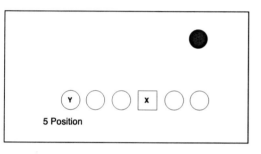

5 Position

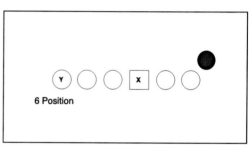

6 Position

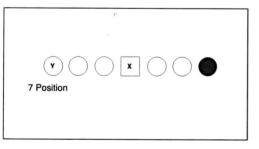

7 Position

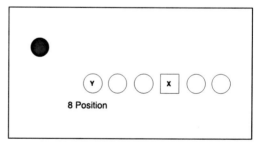

8 Position

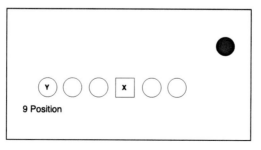

9 Position

Two-Back Designations*

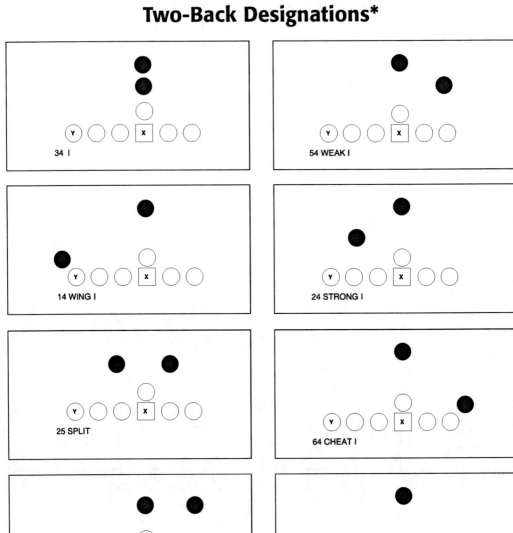

34 I

54 WEAK I

14 WING I

24 STRONG I

25 SPLIT

64 CHEAT I

35 BROWN

74 TWO TIGHT

32 BLUE

25 GUN

*F is tagged first.

Three-Back Designations*

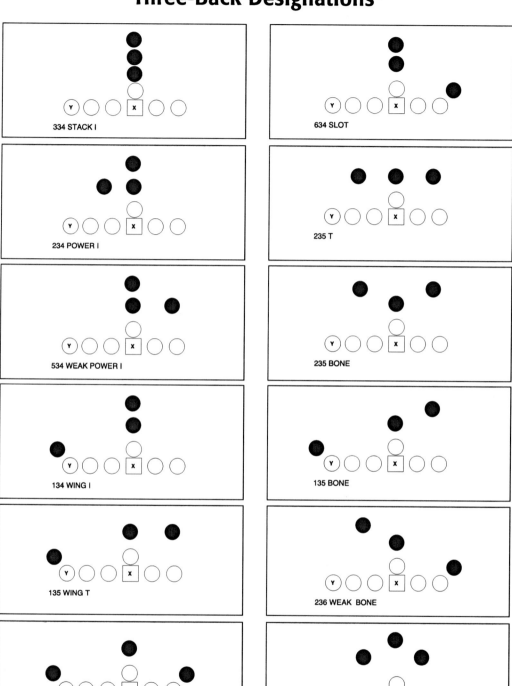

334 STACK I

634 SLOT

234 POWER I

235 T

534 WEAK POWER I

235 BONE

134 WING I

135 BONE

135 WING T

236 WEAK BONE

136 TIGHT MIRROR

245 DIAMOND

*H listed first, F second, T listed third.

Receiver Formations

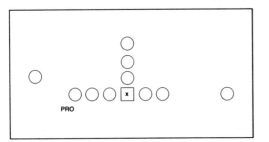

PRO

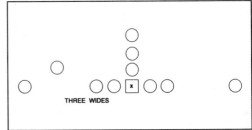

THREE WIDES

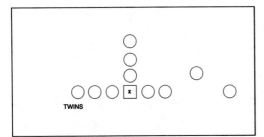

TWINS

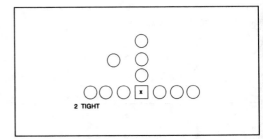

2 TIGHT

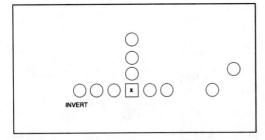

INVERT

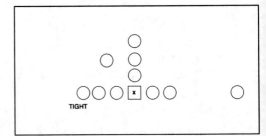

TIGHT

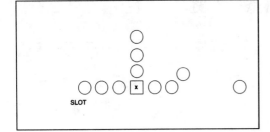

SLOT

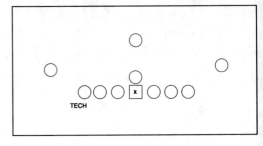

TECH

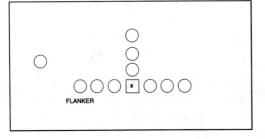

FLANKER

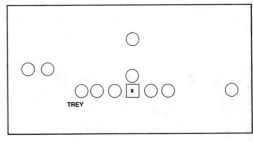

TREY

Receiver Formations

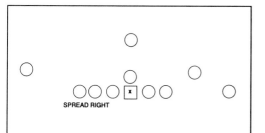

SPREAD RIGHT

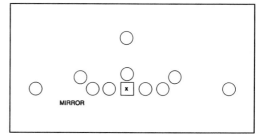

MIRROR

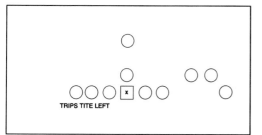

TRIPS TITE LEFT

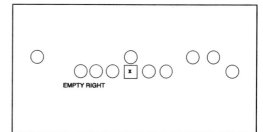

EMPTY RIGHT

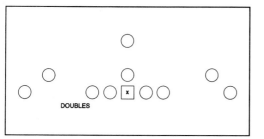

DOUBLES

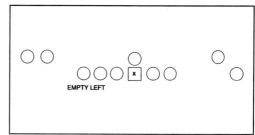

EMPTY LEFT

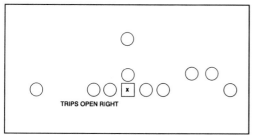

TRIPS OPEN RIGHT

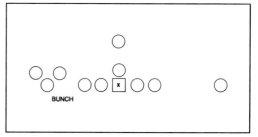

BUNCH

Formation Abbreviations

Bu: Bunch	Rt: Right
Ch: Cheat	Sl: Slot
Do: Doubles	Sp: Spread
Em: Empty	Ta: Tag
Fl: Flanker	Te: Tech
He: Heavy	Th: Thunder
In: Invert	Ti: Tight
Lt: Left	Tre: Trey
Mi: Mirror	Tri: Trips
Ov: Over	Tw: Twins
Op: Open	Un: Unicorn
Pi: Power	Wi: Wing
Pr: Pro	Wk: Weak
Q: Quads	Wd: Wide

Run Reference

Hole Numbers

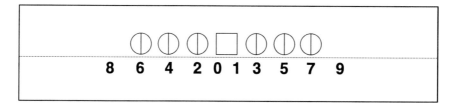

```
8   6   4   2   0   1   3   5   7   9
```

Gaps Lettered

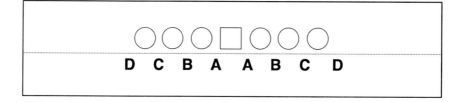

```
D   C   B   A   A   B   C   D
```

Quarterback Run Actions

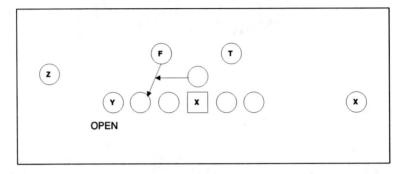

OPEN

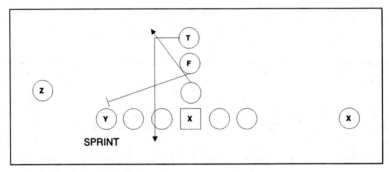

SPRINT

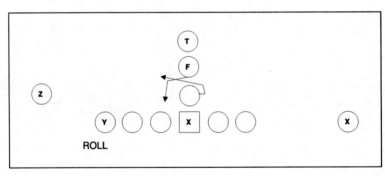

ROLL

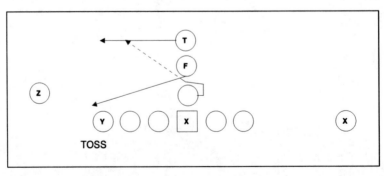

TOSS

Passes Reference

60 Series

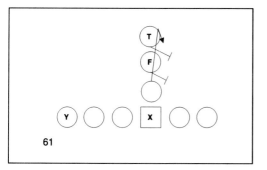

61

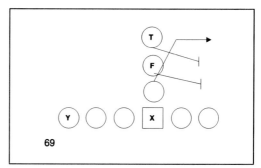

69

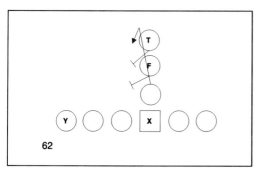

62

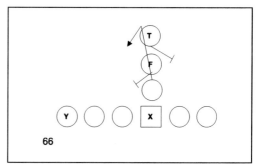

66

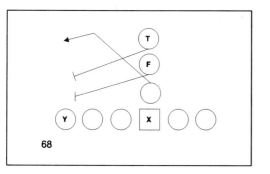

68

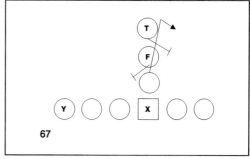

67

100 Series: Play-Action With the Quarterback in the Box

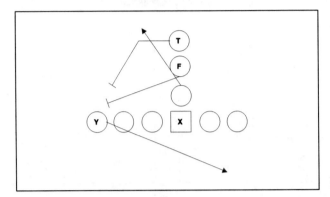

Fire action

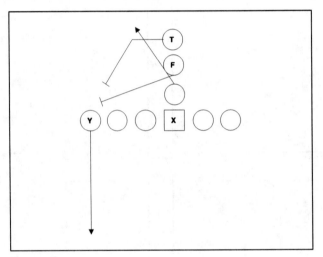

Flow action

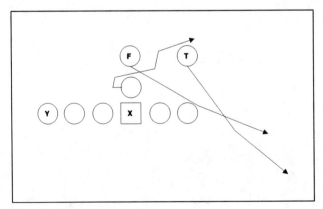

Flood action

200 Series: Play-Action With the Quarterback in the Box

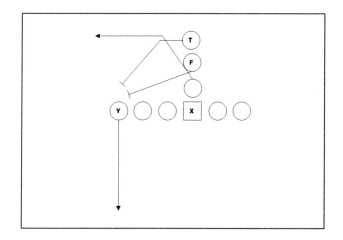

300 Series: Bootleg/Counter Boot

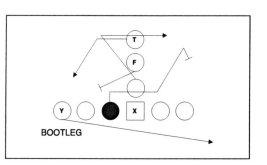

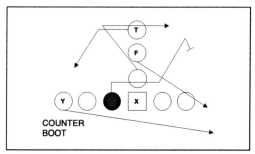

400 Series: Halfback Pass

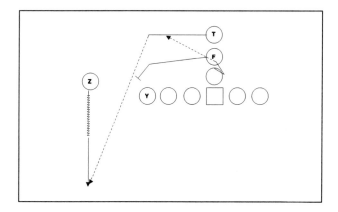

500 Series: Screens Categories

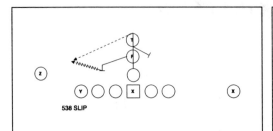

538 SLIP

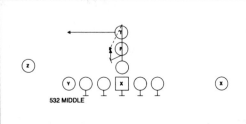

532 MIDDLE

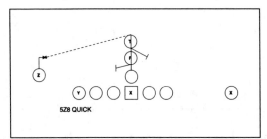

5Z8 QUICK

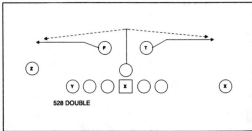

528 DOUBLE

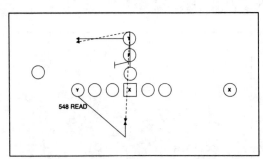

548 READ

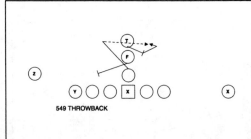

549 THROWBACK

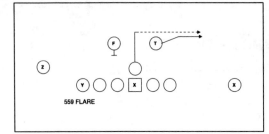

559 FLARE

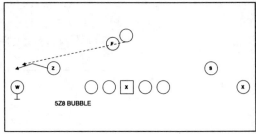

5Z8 BUBBLE

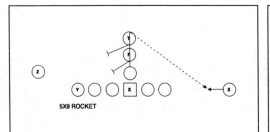

5X9 ROCKET

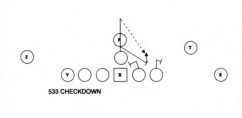

533 CHECKDOWN

600 Series: Dash

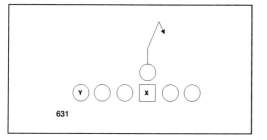

631

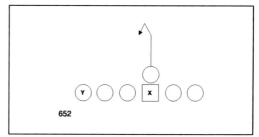

652

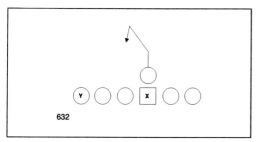

632

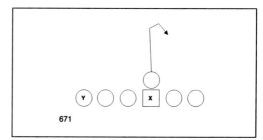

671

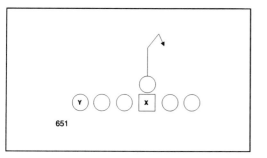

651

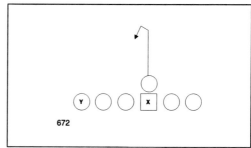

672

700 Series: Quarterback Away From the Flow

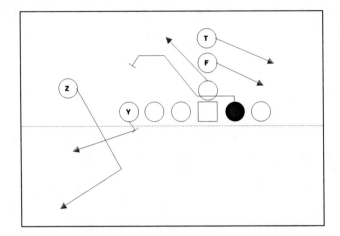

830 Series: Three-Step Level-Three Pass

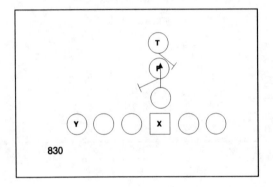

830

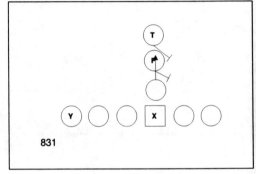

831

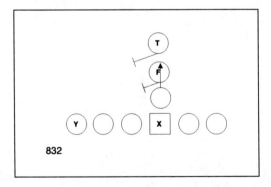

832

850 Series: Five-Step Level-Three Pass

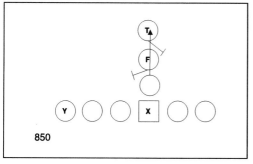

850

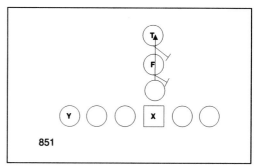

851

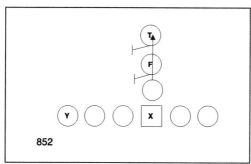

852

870 Series: Seven-Step Level-Three Pass

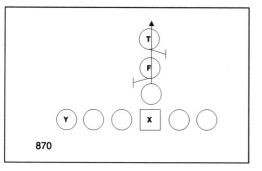

870

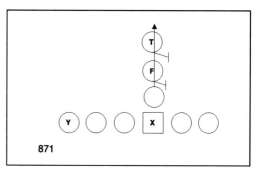

871

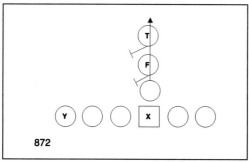

872

Pass Routes

Back Quick Routes

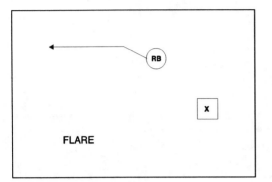

FLARE

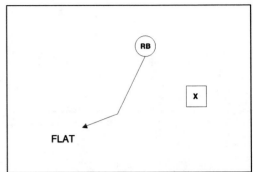

FLAT

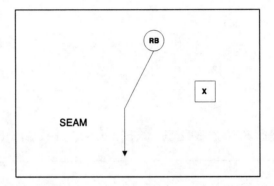

SEAM

Y Quick Routes

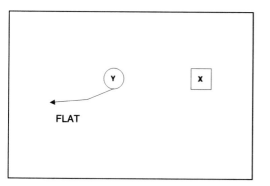

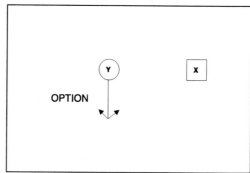

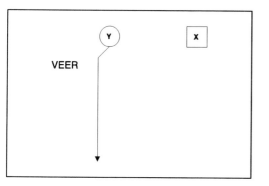

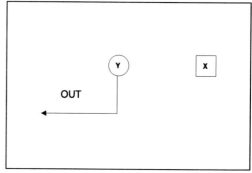

Receiver Quick Routes

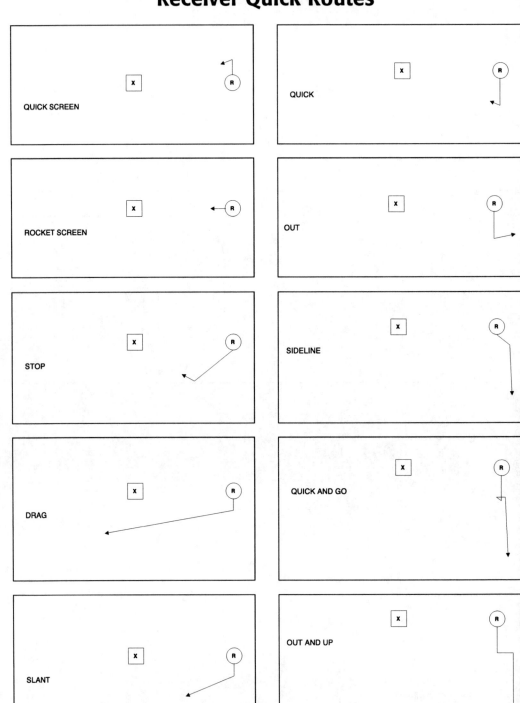

QUICK SCREEN

QUICK

ROCKET SCREEN

OUT

STOP

SIDELINE

DRAG

QUICK AND GO

SLANT

OUT AND UP

Back Intermediate and Deep Routes

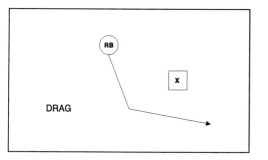

DRAG

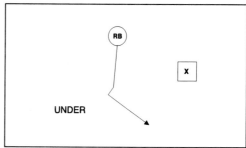

UNDER

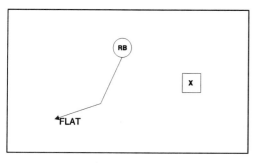

FLAT

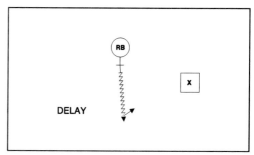

DELAY

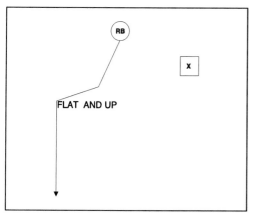

FLAT AND UP

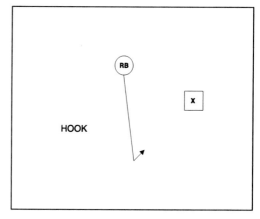

HOOK

Back Intermediate and Deep Routes

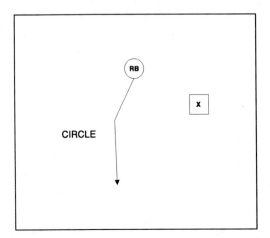

CIRCLE

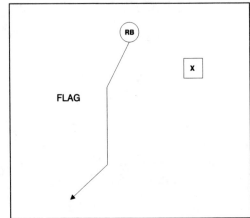

FLAG

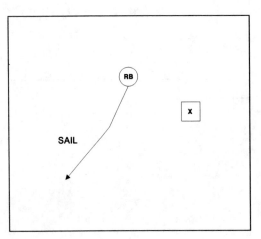

SAIL

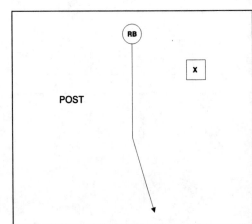

POST

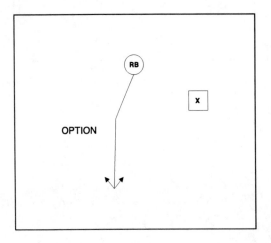

OPTION

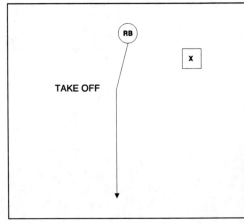

TAKE OFF

Y Intermediate and Deep Routes

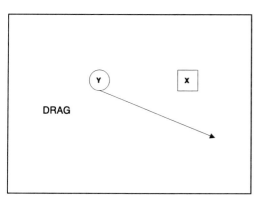

DRAG

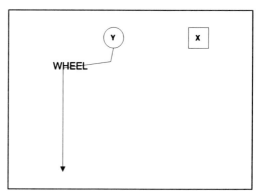

WHEEL

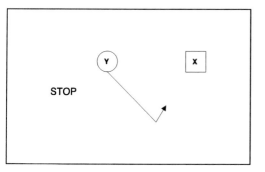

STOP

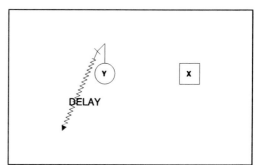

DELAY

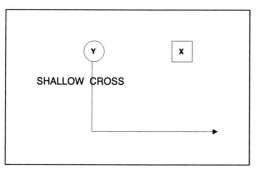

SHALLOW CROSS

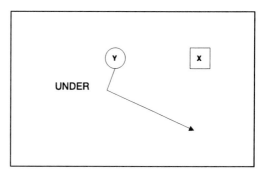

UNDER

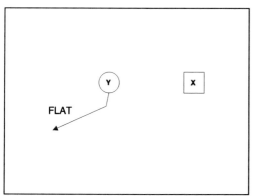

FLAT

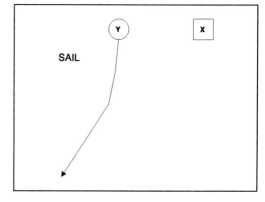

SAIL

Y Intermediate and Deep Routes

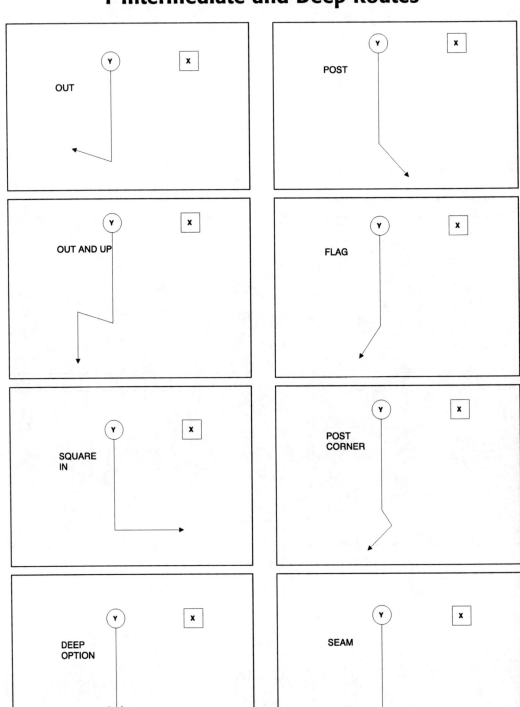

OUT

POST

OUT AND UP

FLAG

SQUARE IN

POST CORNER

DEEP OPTION

SEAM

Receiver Intermediate and Deep Routes

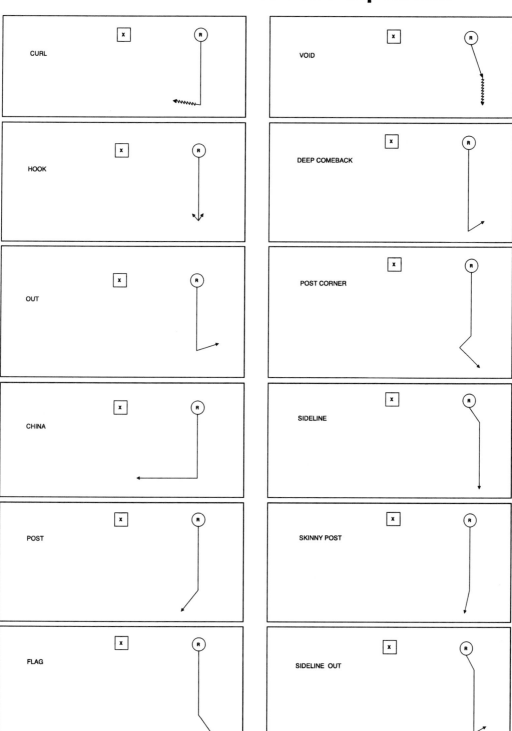

CURL

VOID

HOOK

DEEP COMEBACK

OUT

POST CORNER

CHINA

SIDELINE

POST

SKINNY POST

FLAG

SIDELINE OUT

Position Variations

X Variations

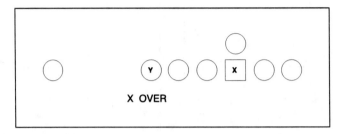

X OVER

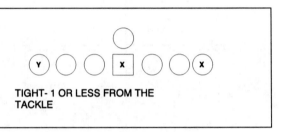

TIGHT- 1 OR LESS FROM THE
TACKLE

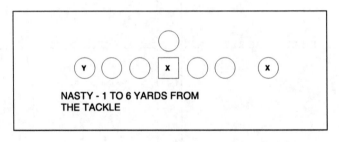

NASTY - 1 TO 6 YARDS FROM
THE TACKLE

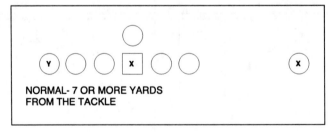

NORMAL- 7 OR MORE YARDS
FROM THE TACKLE

Y Variations

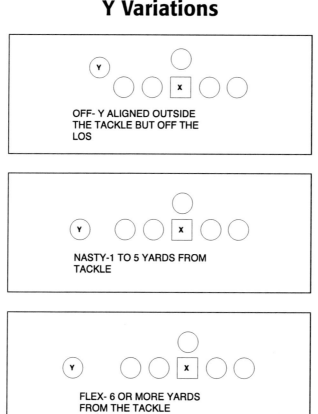

OFF- Y ALIGNED OUTSIDE
THE TACKLE BUT OFF THE
LOS

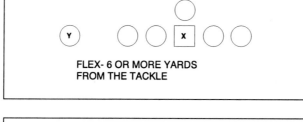

NASTY-1 TO 5 YARDS FROM
TACKLE

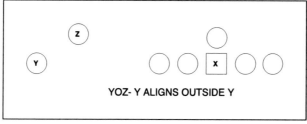

FLEX- 6 OR MORE YARDS
FROM THE TACKLE

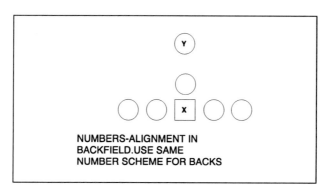

YOZ- Y ALIGNS OUTSIDE Y

NUMBERS-ALIGNMENT IN
BACKFIELD.USE SAME
NUMBER SCHEME FOR BACKS

Z Variations

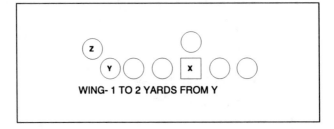

WING- 1 TO 2 YARDS FROM Y

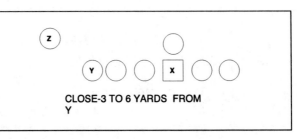

CLOSE-3 TO 6 YARDS FROM Y

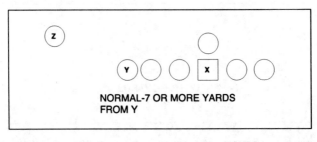

NORMAL-7 OR MORE YARDS FROM Y

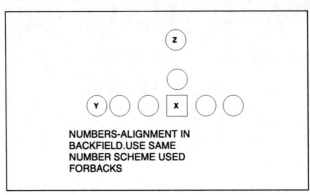

NUMBERS-ALIGNMENT IN BACKFIELD.USE SAME NUMBER SCHEME USED FORBACKS

Motions

F Motions

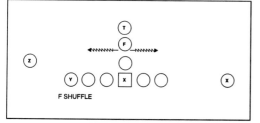

F SHUFFLE

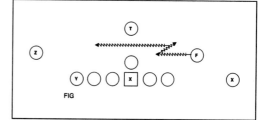

FIG

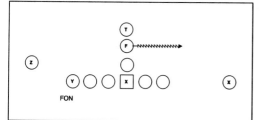

FON

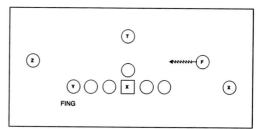

FING

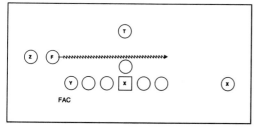

FAC

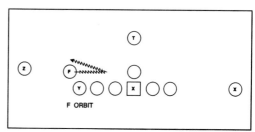

F ORBIT

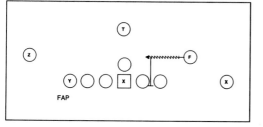

FAP

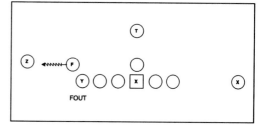

FOUT

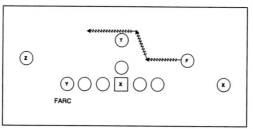

FARC

H Motions

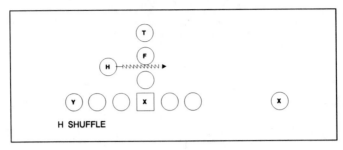

H SHUFFLE

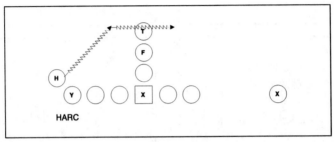

HARC

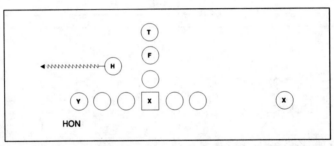

HON

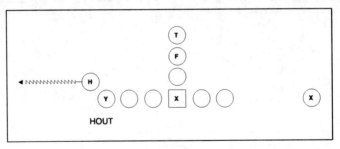

HOUT

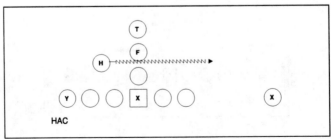

HAC

R Motions

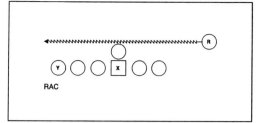

RAC

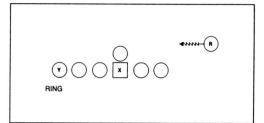

RING

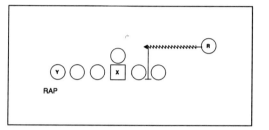

RAP

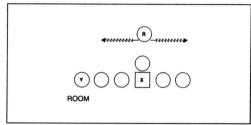

ROOM

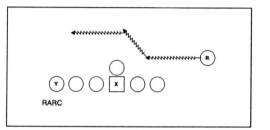

RARC

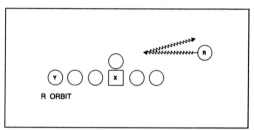

R ORBIT

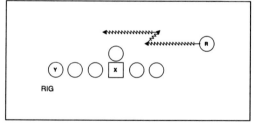

RIG

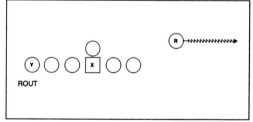

ROUT

S Motions

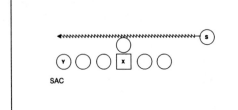

SAC

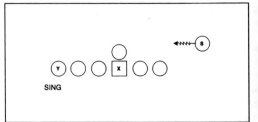

SING

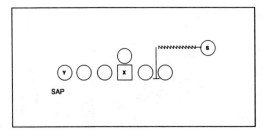

SAP

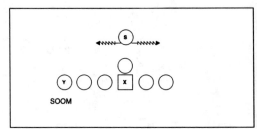

SOOM

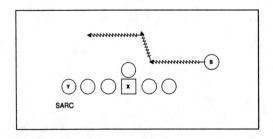

SARC

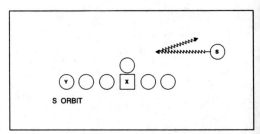

S ORBIT

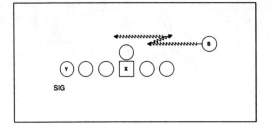

SIG

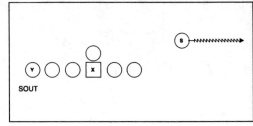

SOUT

T Motions

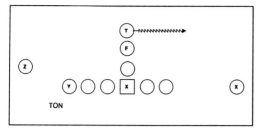

TON

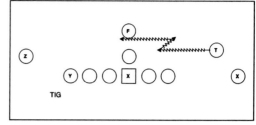

TIG

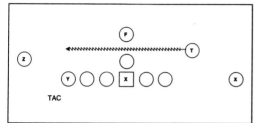

TAC

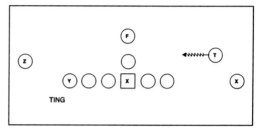

TING

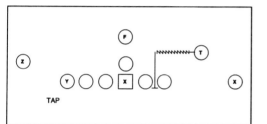

TAP

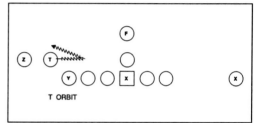

T ORBIT

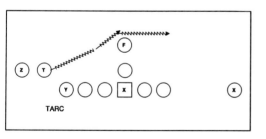

TARC

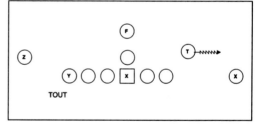

TOUT

U Motions

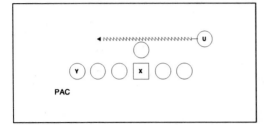

PAC

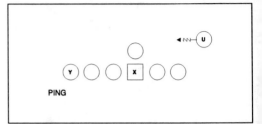

PING

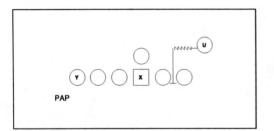

PAP

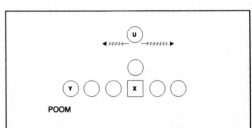

POOM

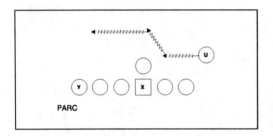

PARC

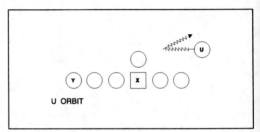

U ORBIT

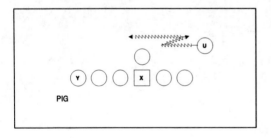

PIG

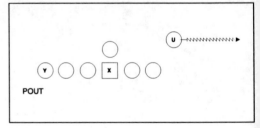

POUT

V Motions

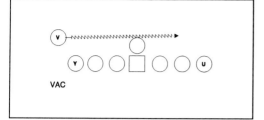

VAC

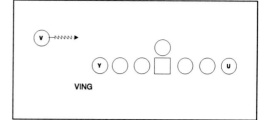

VING

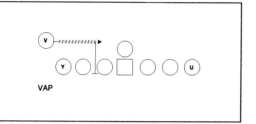

VAP

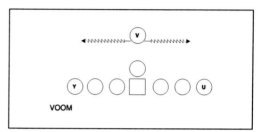

VOOM

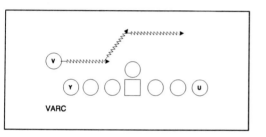

VARC

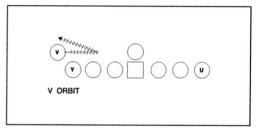

V ORBIT

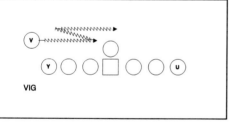

VIG

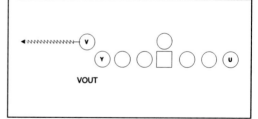

VOUT

X Motions

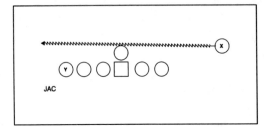

JAC

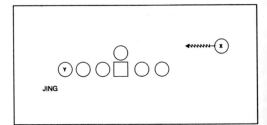

JING

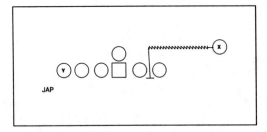

JAP

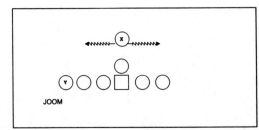

JOOM

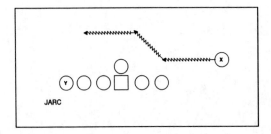

JARC

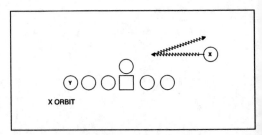

X ORBIT

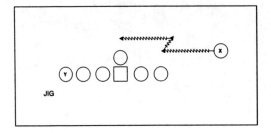

JIG

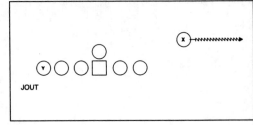

JOUT

Y Motions

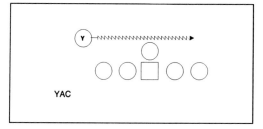

YAC

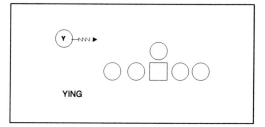

YING

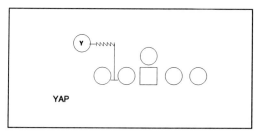

YAP

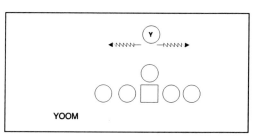

YOOM

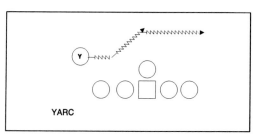

YARC

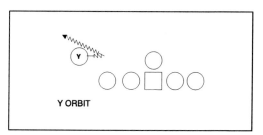

Y ORBIT

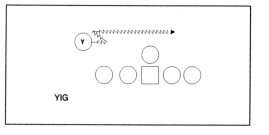

YIG

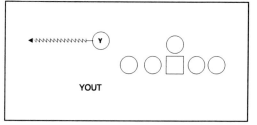

YOUT

Z Motions

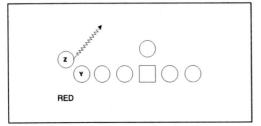

RED

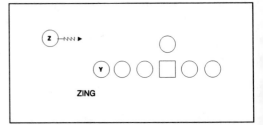

ZING

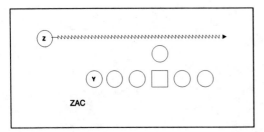

ZAC

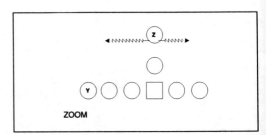

ZOOM

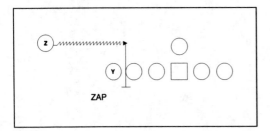

ZAP

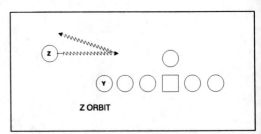

Z ORBIT

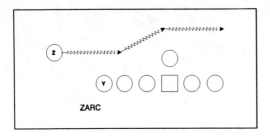

ZARC

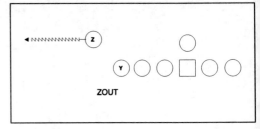

ZOUT

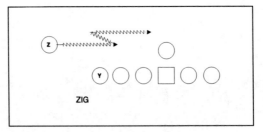

ZIG

Step #2: How the Offense Attacked Defensive Personnel

Catalog blocks. How did the offense attack the three levels:

- Defensive line (tackles/ends)
- Linebackers
- Secondary
  - ✓ Blocks that affect force
  - ✓ Blocks on safeties
  - ✓ Blocks on corners

Blocks on Tackles (Individual/Combo)

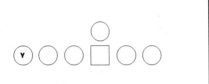

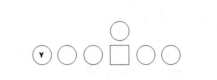

Blocks on Ends (Individual/Combo)

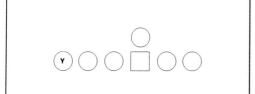

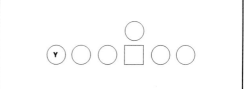

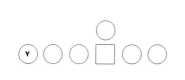

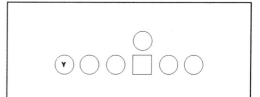

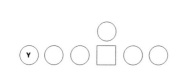

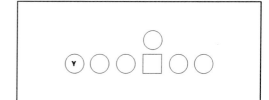

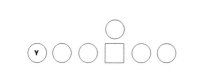

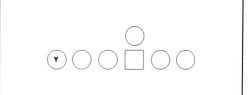

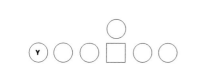

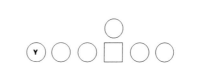

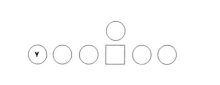

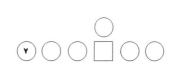

Blocks on Linebackers

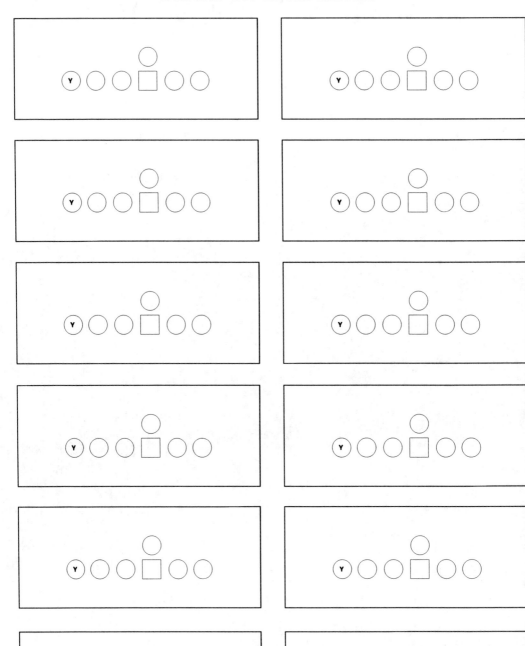

Blocks That Affect Force

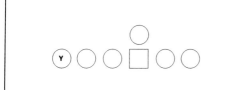

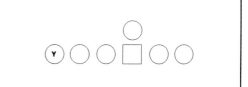

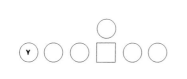

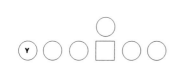

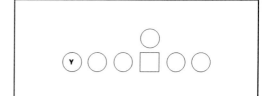

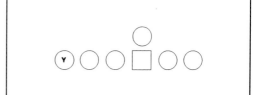

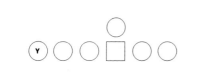

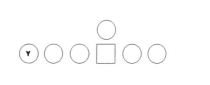

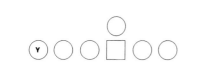

Blocks on Safeties

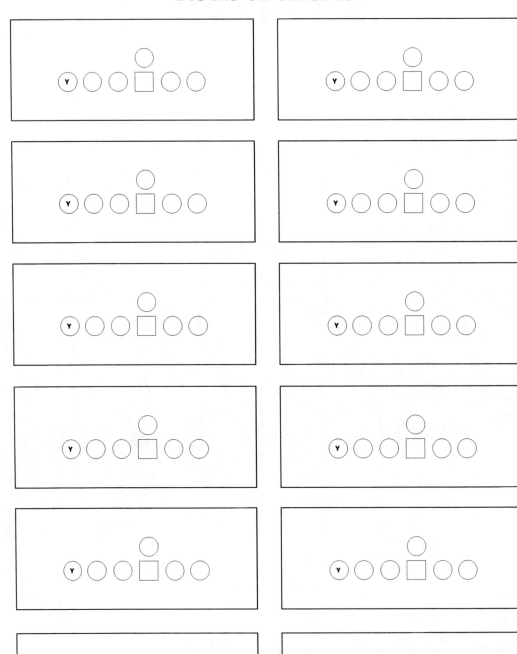

Blocks on Corners

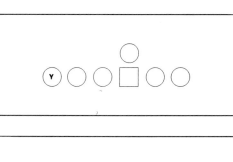

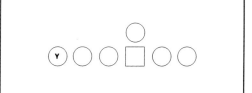

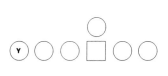

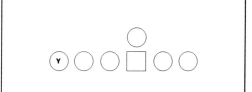

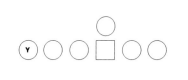

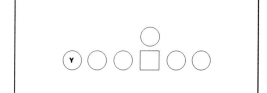

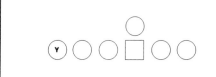

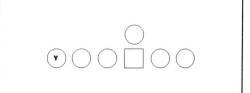

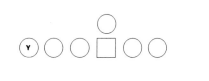

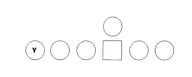

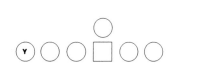

Step #3: Breakdown of Film Information

Huddle

Run Analysis

Type(s) of Offense

- Finesse
- Power
- Option
- Zone
- Gun

Run-Hit Chart (Formations)

Strongside Run-Blocking Schemes

Weakside Run-Blocking Schemes

○○□○○

○○□○○

○○□○○

○○□○○

Pass Analysis

Pass-Hit Chart (Formations)

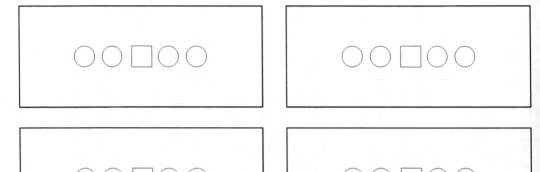

Passes By Areas

DEEP OUTSIDE   DEEP MIDDLE   DEEP OUTSIDE

FLAT   CURL   HOOK   HOOK   CURL   FLAT

Passes Checklist

- 60 Series
- 100 Series
- 200 Series
- 300 Series
- 400 Series
- 500 Series
- 600 Series
- 700 Series
- 830 Series
- 831 Series
- 832 Series
- 850 Series
- 851 Series
- 852 Series
- 870 Series
- 871 Series
- 872 Series

Strongside Pass Routes

Weakside Pass Routes

Running Back Routes

- Flare
- Flat
- Seam
- Under
- Delay
- Flat-and-Up
- Hook
- Circle
- Flag
- Sail
- Post
- Option
- Takeoff
- Others

Y Routes

- Flat
- Veer/Seam
- Option
- Out
- Drag
- Stop
- Shallow Cross
- Wheel
- Delay
- Under
- Sail
- Out-and-Up
- Square-In
- Deep Option
- Post
- Flag
- Post-Corner
- Others

Receiver Routes

- Quick Screen
- Rocket Screen
- Stop
- Drag
- Slant
- Quick
- Out
- Sideline
- Quick-and-Go
- Out-and-Up
- Curl
- Hook
- China
- Post
- Flag
- Void
- Deep Comeback
- Post-Corner
- Sideline
- Skinny Post
- Sideline Out
- Flat
- Others

Pass-Protection Schemes

○ ○ □ ○ ○

○ ○ □ ○ ○

○ ○ □ ○ ○

○ ○ □ ○ ○

Motions/Shifts

Run-Hit Chart

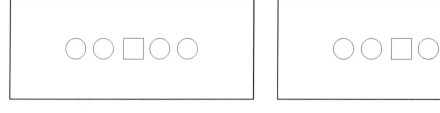

Pass-Hit Chart

Hash Breakdown

LEFT   MIDDLE   RIGHT

ⓧ

WIDE SIDE

ⓧRIGHT HASH

WIDE SIDE

LEFT HASH   ⓧ

Down-and-Distance

First-Down Play Distribution

First-and-Long (+10)

Runs_____%

Passes_____%

Strong Runs_____%

Weak Runs_____%

Strong Passes_____%

Weak Passes_____%

First-and-Long After an Offensive Penalty (10+)

Runs_____%

Passes_____%

Strong Runs_____%

Weak Runs_____%

Strong Passes_____%

Weak Passes_____%

First Down After a First Down Rushing

Runs_____%

Passes_____%

Strong Runs_____%

Weak Runs_____%

Strong Passes_____%

Weak Passes_____%

First Down After a First Down Passing

Runs_____%

Passes_____%

Strong Runs_____%

Weak Runs_____%

Strong Passes_____%

Weak Passes_____%

First Down After an Opponent's Turnover

Runs_____%

Passes_____%

Strong Runs_____%

Weak Runs_____%

Strong Passes_____%

Weak Passes_____%

First Down After an Offensive Turnover

Runs_____%

Passes_____%

Strong Runs_____%

Weak Runs_____%

Strong Passes_____ %

Weak Passes_____%

First Down After an Explosive Run

Runs_____%

Passes_____%

Strong Runs_____%

Weak Runs_____%

Strong Passes_____%

Weak Passes_____%

First Down After an Explosive Pass

Runs_____%

Passes_____%

Strong Runs_____%

Weak Runs_____%

Strong Passes_____%

Weak Passes_____%

First-and-Medium/-Short After a Defensive Penalty

Runs_____%

Passes_____%

Strong Runs_____%

Weak Runs_____%

Strong Passes_____%

Weak Passes_____%

Second-Down Play Distribution

Second-and-Long (7+)

Runs_____%

Passes_____%

Strong Runs_____%

Weak Runs_____%

Strong Passes_____%

Weak Passes_____%

Second-and-Medium (+3/+6)

Runs_____%

Passes_____%

Strong Runs_____%

Weak Runs_____ %

Strong Passes_____%

Weak Passes_____%

Second-and-Short (+1/+2)

Runs_____%

Passes_____%

Strong Runs_____%

Weak Runs_____%

Strong Passes_____%

Weak Passes_____%

Third-Down Play Distribution

Third-and-Long (7+)

Runs_____%

Passes_____%

Strong Runs_____%

Weak Runs_____%

Strong Passes_____%

Weak Passes_____%

Third-and-Medium (+3/+6)

Runs_____%

Passes_____%

Strong Runs_____%

Weak Runs_____%

Strong Passes_____%

Weak Passes_____%

Third-and-Short (+1/+2)

Runs_____%

Passes_____%

Strong Runs_____%

Weak Runs_____%

Strong Passes_____%

Weak Passes_____%

Fourth-Down Play Distribution

Fourth-and-Long (4+)

Runs_____%

Passes_____%

Strong Runs_____%

Weak Runs_____%

Strong Passes_____%

Weak Passes_____%

Fourth-and-Medium (+3)

Runs_____%

Passes_____%

Strong Runs_____%

Weak Runs_____%

Strong Passes_____%

Weak Passes_____%

Fourth-and-Short (+1/+2)

Runs_____%

Passes_____%

Strong Runs_____%

Weak Runs_____%

Strong Passes_____%

Weak Passes_____%

Field-Zone Breakdowns

Backed Up (G to –10)

Runs_____%

Passes_____%

Strong Runs_____%

Weak Runs_____%

Strong Passes_____%

Weak Passes_____%

Going In (+20 to +10)

Runs_____%

Passes_____%

Strong Runs_____%

Weak Runs_____%

Strong Passes_____%

Weak Passes_____%

Coming Out (–10 to –20)

Runs_____%

Passes_____%

Strong Runs_____%

Weak Runs_____%

Strong Passes_____%

Weak Passes_____%

Goal Line (+10 to G)

Runs_____%

Passes_____%

Strong Runs_____%

Weak Runs_____%

Strong Passes_____%

Weak Passes_____%

Free Wheel (–20 to +20)

Runs_____%

Passes_____%

Strong Runs_____%

Weak Runs_____%

Strong Passes_____%

Weak Passes_____%

Two-Minute Offense

Run Chart

Pass Chart

Step #4: Film Breakdown on Opponent's Personnel

Center Checklist

- Strength
- Mobility
- Athleticism
- Initial quickness
- Can he handle being covered?
- Can he block level two (work in space)?
- Is he able to block one-on-one
- Can he pull?
- Shotgun snapping ability
- Pass-protection ability (does he need help)

Guard Checklist

- Strength
- Mobility
- Athleticism
- Initial quickness
- Can he handle being covered?
- Can he block level two (work in space)?
- Is he able to block one-on-one?
- Can he pull?
- Pass-protection ability
- Can he be collapsed (bull rush)?
- Can he pick up twists and lane exchanges?
- Overextender
- Can he pull on screens?

Tackle Checklist

- Strength
- Mobility
- Athleticism
- Initial quickness
- Girth
- Footwork
- Long/short arms
- Can he get to the second level?
- Pass-protection ability
- Can he be bull rushed?
- Can he be beaten inside?
- Can he pick up twists and lane exchanges?
- Overextender
- Can he pull on screens?

Fullback Checklist

- Speed
- Runner/blocker
- Blocker/runner
- Effective in space
- Effective blocker (dominant lead blocker)
- Running style: high/low
- Gains yards after contact
- Effective in short-yardage situations
- Durability
- Inside running ability
  - ✓ Moves piles/falls forwards
  - ✓ Cutback ability
  - ✓ Explosiveness

- Outside running ability
  - ✓ Speed
  - ✓ Acceleration
  - ✓ Can he turn the corner?
- Pass game
  - ✓ Effective receiver
  - ✓ What routes does he run?
  - ✓ Best routes
  - ✓ Can he gain a mismatch?
  - ✓ Blitz pick-up ability
  - ✓ Does he sell play-action?

Tailback Checklist

- Speed
- Vision
- Effective blocker
- Running style: high/low
- Gains yards after contact
- Effective in short-yardage situations
- Durability
- Inside running ability
  - ✓ Moves piles/falls forward
  - ✓ Cutback ability
  - ✓ Explosiveness
- Outside running ability
  - ✓ Speed
  - ✓ Acceleration
  - ✓ Can he turn the corner?
  - ✓ Home-run threat
- Pass Game
  - ✓ Effective receiver

- ✓ What routes does he run?
- ✓ Best routes
- ✓ Can he gain a mismatch?
- ✓ Blitz pick-up ability
- ✓ Does he sell play-action?

Receiver Checklist

- Size
- Weight
- Speed (home-run/elite speed)
- Stance (different for run-pass)
- Splits (ball in middle/hash)
- Pre-snap habits
- Alignments (does he show run-pass)
- How competitive is the receiver?
- Durability (can he be intimidated)
- Hands
  - ✓ Go-to receiver (game breaker) or possession receiver
  - ✓ Catches ball well on the run
  - ✓ Has over-the-shoulder catching ability
  - ✓ Catches the ball away from his body
  - ✓ Effective catching the ball outside the body frame
  - ✓ Leaping ability (downfield or red-zone threat)
- Routes
  - ✓ Most effective routes (in/out, short/medium/deep)
  - ✓ Over the middle receiver or sideline preference
  - ✓ Type of stem used on various routes
  - ✓ Cut tip-offs on routes
  - ✓ Does he lose speed on cuts?
  - ✓ Effective in traffic
  - ✓ Effective versus zone (can he find holes or seams)

- ✓ Effective versus man-to-man coverage
- ✓ Tips off screens
- Run after catch
  - ✓ First move after catch
  - ✓ Tackle breaker
  - ✓ Makes tacklers miss
  - ✓ Across-the-grain runner
- Release
  - ✓ Can he beat press coverage?
  - ✓ Escape moves—rip/swim/size/quickness
  - ✓ How quickly does he reach top speed?
  - ✓ Can he separate?
- Blocking ability
  - ✓ Motivated to be a blocker
  - ✓ Block technique (position/aggressive)
  - ✓ Tip-off cracks (eyes/split/release)

Tight End Checklist

- Size
- Weight
- Blocker/receiver
- Receiver/blocker
- Does it all
- Split tip-offs
- Stance tip-offs
- Can he handle a 7 technique?
- Can he be held up?
- Favorite route
- Does he tip off routes by his release?
- Does he have speed to get deep?
- What is his first move after the catch?

- Can a linebacker or safety cover him one-on-one?
- Running ability after the catch
- How well does he pass protect?

Quarterback Checklist

- Height
- Weight
- How does he scan pre-snap?
- Conservative/risk-taker
- Rhythmic/non-rhythmic cadence
- Check off ability
- Stare down/eyes move defense
- Arm strength
- Release
- Contain/pressure
- Foot placement pre-snap
- What moves first (quarterback's feet, hands, butt—serves as tip-off on snap)?
- Does he set the defense?
- Hand mechanics
- Pocket presence (stays in there, or pulls down the ball and runs)
- Carries out fakes
- Pocket passer/scrambler
- Take him away on options/make him keep on options
- Need spy on him
- Leader or caretaker
- Toughness

Step #5: Practice Plan

Practice Plan

Runs (Prioritize Runs):

#1. _____

#2. _____

#3. _____

#4. _____

#5. _____

#6. _____

#7. _____

#8. _____

#9. _____

#10. _____

Passes (Prioritize Passes):

#1. _____

#2. _____

#3. _____

#4. _____

#5. _____

#6. _____

#7. _____

#8. _____

#9. _____

#10. _____

Top Five Runs:

Top Five Passes:

Fronts to Use:

Coverages to Use:

Stunts to Use:

About the Author

Kenny Ratledge is the defensive coordinator at Sevier County High School (5A) in Sevierville, Tennessee. Ratledge has published numerous articles about football in national publications, as well as three books, *Attacking Football's Wing T*, *Football's Attacking 46 Bear Defense*, and *Coaching Football's Special Teams*.

Ratledge previously coached at Doyle High School in Knoxville, TN, and Lenoir City (TN) High School. A defensive coordinator for 28 years, Ratledge has coached defensive line, inside linebackers, outside linebackers, secondary, and offensive line. During his career, he has also coached baseball and basketball. His defense led the state in scoring defense in 1997, as Sevier County went to the state semi-finals. Sevier County won the State 5A Championship in 1999, setting a state record with five interceptions in the championship game. From 1995 to 2000, Sevier County finished first or second in defense in the Big East Conference, which has four former state champions (one of those teams leads the state in all-time wins). In the last five years, Sevier County's defense has forced 114 turnovers—60 of those during the last two years. Sevier County gave up an average of nine points per game in 2005 and 12 points per game in 2006, when they finished first in rush defense.

A graduate of the University of Tennessee (B.S., M.S.), Ratledge earned an Ed.S. degree from Lincoln Memorial University, and has attained a professional teaching rating of Career Ladder III (highest level). Ratledge also played baseball at Hiwassee College, and was named the AFLAC National Assistant Coach of the Year in 2002.